HERE WE GO AGAIN

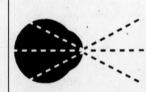

This Large Print Book carries the
Seal of Approval of N.A.V.H.

HERE WE GO AGAIN

MY LIFE IN TELEVISION

BETTY WHITE

THORNDIKE PRESS

A part of Gale, Cengage Learning

Detroit • New York • San Francisco • New Haven, Conn • Waterville, Maine • London

GALE
CENGAGE Learning™

Copyright © 1995 by Betty White.

Insert photograph credits appear on page 485.

Thorndike Press, a part of Gale, Cengage Learning.

ALL RIGHTS RESERVED

Thorndike Press® Large Print Biography.

The text of this Large Print edition is unabridged.

Other aspects of the book may vary from the original edition.

Set in 16 pt. Plantin.

LIBRARY OF CONGRESS CATALOGING-IN-PUBLICATION DATA

White, Betty, 1922–
    Here we go again : my life in television / by Betty White.
        p. cm. — (Thorndike Press large print biography)
    ISBN-13: 978-1-4104-3259-9 (hardcover)
    ISBN-10: 1-4104-3259-9 (hardcover)
    1. White, Betty, 1922– 2. Television actors and actresses —
United States — Biography. 3. Large type books. I. Title.
PN2287.W4577A3 2010
791.45′028′092—dc22
[B]
                                                                    2010040825

Published in 2010 by arrangement with Scribner, a division of Simon & Schuster, Inc.

Printed in Mexico
3 4 5 6 7 14 13 12 11

To Al and Don and Jack and Mark —
and to so many others who continue to
make the journey such fun.

ACKNOWLEDGMENTS

Thanks are in order to several people whose interest (and good manners) helped provide the best support system possible. They include:

Loretta Barrett — three books ago she was my editor, then went on to become my literary agent as well as a treasured friend. Her light but necessary pressure is undetectable.

Lisa Drew — any writer's dream of an editor. Her approval and enthusiasm mask her expertise, but keep you striving to make it better.

Rudy Behlmer — for his infallible memory regarding the early days at KLAC-TV.

Bob Stewart — for inventing the television games that so influenced my life, and for his patience and encouragement in reading these pages in progress.

Thanks must also go to David Schwartz, Steve Ryan, and Fred Wostbrock whose *En-*

cyclopedia of TV Game Shows was invaluable in keeping the chronology and personnel of those many early games in order.

And my gratitude, as always, to my secretary and right arm, Gail Clark, for keeping my real life on track so that I could be free to play author.

INTRODUCTION
TO THIS EDITION

When I wrote this book in 1995 the original idea was to revisit those earliest days of television while I could still remember them. I figured I would soon be forced to pack in my career — not by choice but because I had been around so long. Who could have dreamed at the time that, fifteen years later, I would still be hanging in there, busier than ever before. How lucky can an old broad be?

The title, *Here We Go Again,* was in reference to the burgeoning role something called "computers" were beginning to play even in uninformed circles — like mine. I had lived through the explosion of something called "television" early on and had seen it totally revise life as the world knew it. I began to sense another major change in the wind. I can't help but believe that even the most informed experts at the time could not quite foresee what an unprecedented, life-altering world we were moving into.

Take the above "we" with a grain of salt. I am still a total computer ignoramus. As the saying goes, "I have people in to do that." Nevertheless, my life — and everyone else's — has been totally affected by these little monsters.

On a more personal note, let me bring you up to date from where this book originally closed. It ended just as the pilot for the Marie Osmond series *Maybe This Time* was picked up by ABC. We did make it to air but for only one season. However, in the process I gained some very good friends — including Marie.

Also in the cast was a young man newly arrived from Scotland, where he had been a major comedy star — one Craig Ferguson. He wasn't given much of anything to do on our show and he felt frustrated. We struck up a friendship that I still treasure. Craig went on to carve out a great career for himself over here and today he is the very popular host of *The Late Late Show* on CBS. Every few weeks I visit the show and we do a silly fake interview together and laugh a lot. He is a joy.

Work continues for me and I continue to enjoy it. I visit *The Tonight Show* often and Jay Leno came up with a silly running gag:

Can we make Betty blink? I stand behind a big sheet of Plexiglas on stage as various projectiles are thrown against the glass at my face to try to make me blink. One night they shot an arrow at me, another night they threw a raw egg at me — whatever. The capper was when they sent a dwarf down a steep slide into the glass. Meanwhile, Jay calls on a member of the audience who bets on whether or not I'll blink. Not the classiest bits in the world but Jay and I have fun.

The work goes on. I keep busy with guest shots, talk shows, and even a few movies, which I never expected: *Bringing Down the House* with the incomparable Steve Martin and a lovely time with Sandra Bullock and Ryan Reynolds in *The Proposal*. There was also *Lake Placid* for David E. Kelley, in which my dialogue would have fit a longshoreman. The most recent movie just came out, *You Again,* with Kristen Bell, Jamie Lee Curtis, and Sigourney Weaver.

Along with the laughs, some hurtful changes have taken place. Losing our Golden Girls — first Estelle Getty, then Bea Arthur, and, just recently, my beloved Rue McClanahan — has been very hard to take. When you work so closely together, for so long, and are blessed with such success, you wind up locked at the heart.

The year 2010 turned into the wildest one yet. It started with a Snickers commercial that landed during the Superbowl and then came a gig hosting *Saturday Night Live,* which seemed to turn everything on.

Somewhere in here I agreed to do a guest stint on a pilot for a new series starring Valerie Bertinelli, Wendie Malick, and Jane Leeves called *Hot in Cleveland.* Because of my packed schedule, I said yes provided it would be only a one-shot deal and I would not be involved should it go to series. Three weeks later, the show got picked up for ten episodes — unbelievable, as you often have a long wait before learning your fate. The producers asked me to do more shows and I reminded them of the proviso. I had had a great time, the girls were so dear, the whole experience so enjoyable, but not another series. Strong character that I am I wound up doing all ten. Pushover. As a topper, TV Land has just picked us up for twenty more episodes and guess who's doing all twenty? I must be making all this up!

So that catches us up from where the book left off. Now I can only hope you will read the book and see what went before.

Thank you with all my heart.

BETTY WHITE

INTRODUCTION

"And now, here is Betty White — a woman who has been on television *forever!*"

That is always a safe bet whenever I am introduced, and I've heard it often enough through the years. My husband, Allen Ludden, loved to say, "Meet my wife — one of the pioneers in silent television." He'd get his laugh, but it was practically true.

Television was a fledgling, barely out of the nest, when I began taking my first stumbling professional steps. Since we were both beginners, we started hanging out together, and we have, more or less, stuck with each other ever since. The fledgling, of course, grew into a far bigger bird than anyone possibly could have foreseen and continues to burgeon. Somehow, it still manages to be kind to an old friend; as of this writing, television and I have been having at each other for the past forty-six years. Now that may not mean much to anyone else, but it boggles my mind that in such a transitory field of endeavor, I am still allowed to hang in there.

Experimental television had been in the works as early as 1928, and by 1939, at the New York World's Fair, NBC presented the first television demonstration to the American public. After a few years of finding its footing, by 1947 programs were being telecast regularly from Chicago and from New York. It was soon obvious that the new kid on the block was here to stay, and by 1948, certain names began to rise above the rest.

The long-running *Howdy Doody* was among the earliest shows presented.

Meet the Press, a first of its kind, debuted in 1947.

William Boyd, an actor who enjoyed only fair success in the movies, became one of TV's first superstars as Hopalong Cassidy on NBC. He would one day sell the rights to the series for $70 million.

Milton Berle, with his *Texaco Star Theater,* soon became a household staple and was dubbed "Mr. Television." So many people watched him on Tuesday nights, legend has it, that water usage showed a marked increase during his commercial breaks, when everyone headed for the john.

Many established performers from other venues found the new medium made to order. Like radio, it offered a chance to go *to* the audience, instead of the other way around. Ironically, the more people stayed home, the larger the audience became. What's more, on television one could be *seen* as well as heard, which made it well nigh irresistible.

In the beginning it was generally assumed that, once television crawled to its feet and could walk without staggering, we "pioneers" would be out the back door, and the big-time varsity players would move in. So it is understandable that I am perpetually surprised, as well as eternally grateful, to find myself not only still here, but "working steady." They haven't caught on to me yet!

I suppose it was inevitable that, sooner or later, I would get the urge to write about those beginning days of television, in contrast to the giant octopus the industry has become today. Surprisingly, I often see parallels between then and now, as though we continue to reinvent the wheel. Tempting as it was, however, I kept pushing the writing project to the back burner in favor of more immediate pursuits. For one thing, my memory, capricious at best, can be diabolically selective the rest of the time, with an agenda all its own. Now and then, gaps show up in the circuitry that make the Nixon tapes pale by comparison. Trivial details stand out in startling relief, while important events, even people, are blurred, if not missing altogether. I can't blame it on age, because it has been that way all my life. I have even been accused, on occasion, of only remembering what I wish to remember. If only that were true.

Ingrid Bergman called it right when she said, "Happiness is good health and a bad memory."

Then along came an experience that put things in a whole new perspective for me.

Recently, I attended an all-day seminar on the UCLA campus presented by the Academy of Television Arts and Sciences, regarding the revolutionary technological developments in television that are looming on the horizon. Current buzzwords like "Information Superhighway" and "Interactive Television" are heard so often they have already become clichés, but I had yet to hear them clearly explained. When I read about the seminar, I purchased a ticket out of curiosity to see where my old buddy Television might be headed now.

In attendance were some eighteen hundred of the top executives and CEOs in the telecommunications industry. Make that seventeen hundred and ninety-nine, because I had absolutely no official business there at all. Had the proverbial bomb been dropped on the assemblage that day, I don't think there would have been anyone in the telecommunications business left to mind the store.

For twelve hours, from 7:00 in the morning, there was a series of panel discussions among all the heavy hitters. The panels were moderated by the likes of Dick Cavett, Pat Harvey, Paul Saffo, Lynn Sherr, and Bernard Shaw, all endowed with enough gray matter of their own not to be intimidated. Vice President Al Gore had also flown out to address the group midmorning.

Under discussion was what this Superhighway, with its claims of up to five hundred channels and interactive diversity, is all about. What will we be seeing? What new hardware and software needs will arise? Most of all, what influence will all this have on the future? My pal TV seems to be getting pretty carried away.

At the end of the day, host Rich Frank, president of The Walt Disney Studios as well as president of the television academy, summed things up:

"Each of the individuals we have heard from today is betting billions of his corporate dollars on how this Superhighway will evolve and what impact it will have on the future of the industry. As we have seen, they do not agree, which means there will be some winners and there will be some losers. But one thing is certain — *everyone* is betting."

Much of what was discussed that day was technologically beyond my ken, but enough got through to make the experience totally fascinating. What grew more apparent as the day went on was that, although we are on the threshold of another "milestone technological breakthrough," even the powers that be are guessing at what the long-range effect will be.

Well, here we go again! This sounds like where I came in!

Fifty years ago, when television made its entrance, no one possibly could have foreseen what impact it would have. For broadcasters at that moment, the preoccupying gamble was whether or not to commit big bucks for innovative equipment on the chance that the public would latch on. Would there be enough homes with television receivers to make producing shows worthwhile? Conversely, those at home had to decide if they could justify investing in an expensive major appliance to receive what few telecasts were currently available. At that time, buying a television could set one back several hundred dollars.

Obviously, the situation today is vastly more complex. The stakes have increased by geometric progression, as has the number of players, but the fact remains that a new technological monster is coming onstage and no one has any clear idea of what part it will play. Will broadcasters, once again, have to retool to accommodate those who opt for the new toy? Will the numbers balance out?

Guess who will be deciding the ultimate route of this Superhighway into the future? We will — the viewing public. We may not know how it *works,* but how it *evolves* will depend on how many of us buy in. And this time around, over the long haul, we have changed as an audience; we are no longer enchanted by everything that comes through that magic box in the corner. Today, we already have a supply of alternative choices, and our tastes have become jaded. Instead of paying rapt attention, we are more likely to surf through the channels, remote control in hand. Perhaps we *are* ready to take a more interactive role in what we watch. As Rich said, there are a lot of people who are willing to bet on it.

A few nights ago on the news, a group of nine- and ten-year-olds were asked their preference between watching television and using computers. The unanimous, vociferous vote was "computers!" A direct quote from one youngster was interesting: "TV you watch. Computers you make it — with a click of the mouse."

If that can be taken as an indication, we'd better get used to the term "Superhighway." It looks like traffic is coming through, and our only choice will be to get on or get out of the way.

The foregoing is a prime example of oversimplification. Just because I have been around the business awhile is no guarantee that I know what I'm talking about, but it is a great excuse for joining the free-for-all game of opinionating. And it has made me realize one thing: that before I start trying to figure out where we are going, I had better take a look at where I have been, if only for the sake of comparison. I have no idea what I am going to dredge up — or forget to include. I shall try and keep personal digression to a minimum. So let's have a go at it, and leave chronology to the historians.

BETTY WHITE
CARMEL, CALIFORNIA

My dad, Horace White.

My mom, Tess White. Neither one could disown me.

BEFOREWORD

As an only child, I lucked into the best parents ever invented. They adored each other, and perhaps I should have let them enjoy that a little longer, but, through no fault of my own, I showed up eleven months to the day after Tess and Horace White were married. They didn't seem to hold it against me, because they made me very welcome and dealt me in on everything from the very beginning.

So often, "only child" conjures up the image of either a spoiled brat or a lonely only. For the record, I never had a chance to be one or the other. If being spoiled equates with being dearly loved, I was, but appreciation was the name of the game. And there were rules. The word "no" was not used lightly, and it didn't mean "perhaps," or "I don't think so" — those were negotiable. When the answer was "No," that was it, and you might as well move on to something else. Nor was I ever lonely, in the forlorn sense of the word. I had lots of friends, but I could send them all home and keep the two I liked best — Tess and Horace.

They were directly responsible for my passion for nature in general and animals in particular. Every year I pointed for summer vacation, when the three of us would pack into the High Sierras or drive to Yellowstone National Park and camp out. I'll bet I was the only kid on the block whose *parents* would come home with a dog and say, "Betty, he followed us home. Please, can we keep him?"

It wasn't all sweetness and light. There were some stormy times between my mother and father, but they would eventually clear, making the good stuff seem even better.

My big ambition was to be a writer, until I wrote myself into the lead in our graduation play at Horace Mann Grammar School. It was then that I contracted showbiz fever, for which there is no known cure.

The first time anybody paid me to show up on television was in the summer of 1949 — forty-six years ago as of now. However, for my initial performance on the tube, I have to go back some ten years earlier. It took place about two months before NBC did its first regular broadcast of the new medium at the New York World's Fair. It also happened to be about one month after I graduated from Beverly Hills High School in January of 1939, although that didn't make the papers.

My big thrill at graduation was being chosen to sing at the ceremony. I had been studying singing diligently, and my mind and heart were set on an operatic career. Unfortunately, my voice had no such plans. This didn't deter me one iota: I was sure that if I worked hard enough, I could whip my voice into submission.

Wrong.

Blissfully, I didn't know that at the time, so I was thrilled and proud to accept the invitation to sing at graduation. Who chose the song I sang, I don't recall. It was probably my very serious singing teacher, Howard Hughes's uncle, Felix Hughes; or perhaps some itinerant muse with a sense of humor. The song was "Spirit Flower" and it was what might be called a heavy number.

It began:

My heart was frozen
Even as the earth
That covered thee forever from
*   my si-i-ight.*

The music was lovely, if a tad lugubrious, and while the song finally wound up celebrating a flower that grew and bloomed on a lover's grave, it was perhaps an odd choice for a just-turned-seventeen-year-old to sing for high school graduation. The surprising result: it led to my television debut.

Shortly after we graduated, our senior class president, Harry Bennett, and I were invited to take part in an experimental television transmission taking place at the old Packard Building in downtown Los Angeles. It was to be a capsule version of Franz Lehár's durable operetta *The Merry Widow,* which delighted me because my idol, Jeanette MacDonald, had once starred in the role on the screen. Admittedly, my interpretation may have lost a little something in the translation, but then, she had been paid for her performance.

I wore my graduation dress, a fluffy white tulle number held up by a sapphire blue velvet ribbon halter, which I fervently hoped would be enchanting as we waltzed and sang. The "studio" was a converted office on the sixth floor of the building, which was as high as that edifice went. The lights were, if not efficient, at least excruciatingly hot; both Harry and I had to wear deep tan makeup and dark, *dark* brown lipstick "so

Betty around the time of The Merry Widow *adventure.*

we wouldn't wash out," we were told. The beads of perspiration served to give us luster.

To view this epic, the audience, consisting of our parents and a small handful of interested parties, had to stand around the automobile showroom downstairs and watch a vintage monitor, since our telecast only carried from the sixth to the ground floor, unfortunately. Or perhaps not. The show may have been less than enchanting, but for this young "Merry Widow" it was totally exciting.

Ten years elapsed before my next foray into television, but the decade was hardly uneventful, either personally or globally. By this time reality had set in regarding any chance of an operatic career, but I was still very interested in show business. Eager to get started, I opted not to go to college, and while I'm sure my dad was disappointed, he supported me in my decision, as did my mother — typical behavior for both of these good friends.

The world, meanwhile, was going through a little altercation known as World War II, and though I was aware of it, even concerned, it all seemed very remote. However, once America became directly involved in 1941, my priorities did an immediate about-face and dreams of showbiz dissolved into the war effort.

For the next four years I worked with the AWVS — American Women's Voluntary

Working for American Women's Voluntary Services during World War II.

Services. I had had my driver's license for about twenty minutes; nonetheless, I drove a PX truck, carrying toothpaste, soap, candy, etc., to the various gun emplacement outfits that had been set up in the hills of Hollywood and Santa Monica. I also attended the "rec halls" regularly in the evening, where we would dance or play games or simply talk with the young men who were so far from home. Ever hear of the age of innocence? Believe me, that was it. How many films have there been dealing with that particular moment in time? They are countless, some good, some awful, and looking back on that period is almost like watching one more old movie: it is all so totally unrelated to the rules — or lack thereof — by which we play today.

Naturally, during the course of those social evenings, I met some very nice boys, and I corresponded with several after they were shipped out. It was all on a strictly platonic basis, however, for I belonged heart and soul (two out of three!) to a young man whose ring I had accepted before he went overseas in November 1942. Every single night I wrote him a V-mail letter, and he did the same, from somewhere in North Africa or Italy or who knew where. I would receive stacks of letters from him in intermittent batches as the mail got through. The really important man in my life during that time was the mailman.

Sad to say, true-life love stories don't always work out as neatly as movie scenarios. After two whole years of V-mail, I chickened out and wrote the proverbial Dear John letter — in this case, Dear Paul. I sent the ring back to his mother to keep for him. Paul later married a girl he met in Italy; they are still together. I met and married a P-38 pilot; it lasted six months. Talk about getting your just deserts.

In 1945 the war ended at long last, and a few months later my brief marriage was also over. It hurts to fail at something so important, and telling yourself it's all part of the learning process doesn't help one damned bit at the time.

Now that my life was back in my own hands, what was I going to do with it? My emotional fuel tank was very low, but the time had come to concentrate on what I must do for a living. Show business of some sort was my objective; even then it never crossed my mind to seek my fortune in any other field.

There was a little-theater operation on Robertson Boulevard just outside of Beverly Hills — or just outside the high-rent district, if you will. The Bliss-Hayden Little Theater was run by two busy film character actors, Lela Bliss and Harry Hayden, husband and wife. (If you watch old films on American Movie Classics, you would recognize their faces immediately.)

Lela and Harry didn't pretend to run an acting school per se, they simply gave aspiring performers what they needed most — a place to perform in front of an audience — and they presented a play every four weeks. By paying a "tuition" of fifty dollars a month, one could try out for the next production and land either a part in the play or the privilege of working on the backstage crew. It sounded like the big time to me, since I hadn't been on a stage since high school — except, of course, for my triumph on the sixth floor in *The Merry Widow*.

So, clutching my fifty dollars in my hot little fist, I went in to see Harry and Lela. I'm not at all sure that anyone with fifty in cash was ever let out of the building without signing up, but as luck would have it, I landed the ingenue lead in their next production, a Philip Wylie play, *Spring Dance*. It was just what I needed, and I realized that this was what I must do for the rest of my life.

A play at the Bliss-Hayden ran something like eight performances, and then the next one was put into rehearsal. In this case it was to be the comedy *Dear Ruth,* fresh from Broadway. Just before closing night of *Spring Dance,* Lela and Harry called me into their office. Now, despite being a prototypical WASP, I was born with a major built-in guilt complex, so, naturally, I assumed they were going to point out something I was screwing up on stage. On the contrary, they had some wonderful news — they wanted me to play Ruth in the next production. And, as if that weren't enough, I wouldn't have to pay another fifty dollars! It all seemed too good to be true. I was going to be able to stay around these nice people for another month; I had the lead in a marvelous play; best of all, I was going to get to work for *free!*

For me, *Dear Ruth* was a delight in more ways than one. On opening night, a young agent from National Concert Artists Corporation stopped by to check out the play. This was just routine. Many of the talent agencies sent out scouts as a matter of course, to see what new faces might be showing up around town. Lela came backstage after the final curtain with this nice young man in tow, whom she introduced as "agent Lane Allan from NCAC." Undeniably, my heart jumped a little, but I wasn't sure if it was the word "agent" or the fact that he was frightfully good-looking. We exchanged a few words, he complimented me on the performance, and that was that.

The show ran its course, and closing night rolled around. I made my first-act entrance and nearly blew my opening line, for there *he* was, smiling, in the first row. My concentration — the actor's safety net — was, needless to say, shot to hell.

By the time the curtain came down, there he was, backstage.

"I'm here with a couple of friends, and I was wondering, since it's closing night, if I could ask you to join us for a drink?"

"Well — uh — I guess — yes — I think that would be okay."

Those may not have been my exact words, but whatever I said was equally witty. It didn't seem to matter. I had met someone nice, as opposed to smooth. Handsome, not pretty. Someone who was — I seemed to have forgotten all about the fact that he was an agent. I don't think he was thinking about that, either.

Lane Allan truly was all the good things I thought I had seen. I learned that he was an actor turned agent, and that his real name was Albert Wooten; he had changed it for the stage when he played in *Brother Rat* on Broadway, in the role that Ronald Reagan played later in the movie version. He had come to realize that being an agent on a full-time basis offered a little more security than being an actor once in a while. It didn't take us long to fall very much in love.

My husband — Lane Allan was his stage name — actually he was Albert Wooten.

Unlike Lane, I had been burned once, and the idea of marrying again panicked me. I spent the next few months running scared, while I continued my efforts to get my embryonic career off the ground.

Far from getting a foot in the door, I was so green that I didn't even know on which doors to knock. It was Lane who suggested I try the various radio shows that were so current and choice at the time. Most of them had a regular casting day once a week, so, diligently, I began making the rounds of the different offices. I would give my name. They would say, "Nothing today." I would say, "Thank you," and leave. Each week I would go through the same ritual in the hope that I might begin to look familiar; they might think they had hired me before and maybe use me again. Even vain hope springs eternal.

Sure enough, the day came when I was actually ushered in past the front desk to meet a real live producer! It was at a large advertising agency, Needham, Louis, and Brorby, the people responsible for putting on the very popular radio comedy *The Great Gildersleeve,* starring Hal Peary. The nice producer, Fran Van Hartesveldt by name, took it upon himself to point out, as kindly as he could, the one insurmountable hurdle standing in my way: before you could be hired by anyone, it was mandatory that you be a member of the union, the American Federation of Radio Artists. Oh, and the real catch-22: In order to join the union, you had to have a specific job! I was not just disappointed, I was flat out discouraged.

It was lunchtime as I left his office, and everyone was heading for the elevators. The offices were on the fifth floor of the Taft Building at Hollywood and Vine — high-rises were nonexistent in those days in earthquake-conscious Los Angeles — and I was just starting to think about walking down the five flights when an empty elevator finally showed up. As the doors began to close, someone stuck his hand out and caught them in time to enter. You guessed it — producer Van Hartesveldt. The elevator seemed agonizingly slow, and after smiling weakly at each other, there was nothing to do but wait in awkward silence as the floors crawled by. When we finally landed, I couldn't wait to be on my way.

Just as I stepped out, my fellow passenger spoke up.

"Listen, I know the spot you're in. It would help you one hell of a lot to get that union card, so here's what I'll do. I'll take a chance and give you one word to say in the commercial on this week's *Gildersleeve*. You won't break even, but it will get you your card. Think you can say 'Parkay' without lousing it up?" (Parkay margarine was the program's sponsor, which in those radio days ranked just next to God.)

My chin had dropped so far I was having trouble even responding. He added, "Come back to our offices after lunch and the girl will send you over to the union," and off he went.

That kind of altruistic above-and-beyond gesture doesn't happen often, but once it does, you must always remember to pass it on if you ever get the chance.

At that time, network radio programs still did two broadcasts of each show — one early for the eastern time zones, then the same show again three hours later for West Coast consumption. I was to say "Parkay!" once on each broadcast, for which I would receive a total of $37.50. It cost $69.00 to join the union. I called my dad and asked if he would loan me the difference, and, bless him, he was almost as excited as I was.

"Sure, honey. If you don't work too often, we can almost afford it."

Daddy lucked out. Today, that initiation fee is $800.

There were a couple of virtually sleepless

nights to live through before the broadcast, during which I fantasized all sorts of disasters, including saying "parfait" instead of "Parkay," but when the big day came, I actually made it through okay. Not too surprising, since I had the script in my hand.

I was in show business!

1

Once I was a legitimate, card-carrying AFRA member, I worked *The Great Gildersleeve* several times, sometimes with a line or two, sometimes just to furnish "crowd noise." There is a happy tag to this tale: Years later, when we were doing my second series, *Date with the Angels,* we had occasion to hire two additional writers — one Bill Kelsay, and the other none other than my benefactor, Fran Van Hartesveldt. He was a dear, silly, talented man, and whenever he'd hear me telling anyone how much I owed him, he'd say, "The moral of the story, boys and girls, is never walk — always take the elevator!"

By my next radio commercial, I had graduated from just one word — this time I got to sing. It was for American Airlines, and the song was lilting, to say the least:

Why not fly to Meheeco Ceety
You weel like the treep, ee's so preety.

41

Perfect casting. Today, that would elicit a protest demonstration on ethnic grounds. Deservedly so.

Lane and I were still seeing each other, although we had reached something of an impasse on the marriage subject, and I was becoming increasingly aware that the situation couldn't go on as it was indefinitely. Around this time, an opportunity came along out of the blue for a part in a movie being made for Ansco Film. Primarily, it was designed to demonstrate their new color film process, and would entail six weeks on location in the High Sierras. Timing is everything. Seizing the chance to run for the hills, in every sense of the word, painfully I told Lane it was over between us, and took the job. I knew that if I didn't have a reason to get out of town, I would never be able to make it stick.

The ensuing six weeks was a mixed bag. It was certainly another learning experience, but then so is a trip to Devil's Island. There were several good things, not the least of which was simply being in that glorious high country. When my mother and dad and I used to pack in and camp at about ten thousand feet, we wouldn't see another soul until, after two weeks of fishing, we rode out again. Trust me, *that's* the way to do it —

not with a movie company in tow.

Another plus was the fact that the leading lady, a beautiful girl named Sally Feeney, proved to be a delightful friend, even under very difficult circumstances.

The plot of this opus, entitled *The Daring Miss Jones,* involved a gorgeous young thing (Sally) becoming lost in the woods. She joins up with two orphaned bear cubs, also lost. In the course of their adventures, the three of them get into all sorts of jeopardy, or whatever would serve to show off the new Ansco color film to best advantage. If I remember correctly, it showed off some of Sally, too: early on her dress had somehow caught on a branch, and she spent most of the trek in her surprisingly discreet undies. Meanwhile, her best friend (me) is fretting back home until she can stand the anxiety no longer, and eventually flies a plane (!) in to the rescue. Of course, there was also a villain in pursuit as well as the obligatory handsome hero to ensure a happy ending, the later played by Ted Jordan, who went on to marry exotic dancer Lili St. Cyr. How do you like them apples?

After we got on location, Allan Dwan, the producer/director/ cameraman, asked me if, since there were a lot of scenes I wasn't in, I would mind acting as script girl, keeping

The Daring Miss Jones. *Betty as best friend to Sally Forrest.*

track of shots, footage, continuity, etc. — as a favor, that is? Sure — what the heck, I'd rather be busy than waiting around; besides, it would keep me close to the two tiny, adorable bear cubs, with whom I got along famously. It was fortunate that I did, because after a very few days it became abundantly clear that the hired "trainer" was far more dedicated to his bottle than to his bear cubs. Once again, Allan Dwan asked me if, since I seemed to get along so well with the cubs, I would mind handling them on the set — as a favor, that is? Sure — what the heck, bear wrangler, script girl, sometime actress, I'd rather be busy than etc., etc. Hey, this was show business!

Now, at that tender age bear cubs grow like weeds, and as the weeks went by they nearly doubled in size; to the extent that the script girl had trouble rationalizing the different-sized bears in what were supposed to be matching shots, while the bear wrangler was having more and more of a challenge controlling her charges, and the supporting actress was having one hell of a time trying to cover her scratches with makeup.

We all lived through it, and ultimately *The Daring Miss Jones* was actually released to the public. Or perhaps it escaped. Years later I even managed to find a copy of it on tape for my collection. The lovely Sally Feeney changed her name and became the successful young star Sally Forrest. It never occurred to me until this minute to wonder if she got the idea for her new name from the woods we spent so much time in with the cubs. She could have become Sally Bear. No.

To say I was glad to get home is an understatement. Even with the various added jobs, I had still found lots of time to miss Lane terribly, so when I got back and found a package from him waiting for me, I couldn't open it fast enough. It was a Carl Ravazza record of *our song* — "I Love You for Sentimental Reasons." To an incurable romantic, home at last from a difficult adventure and still very much in love, that was all it took.

Two months later, we were married.

The Daring Miss Jones. *Betty as bear wrangler.*

2

Not long after our wedding, National Concert Artists Corporation closed its doors, and the new bridegroom was unemployed. Lane finally found a job in the furniture department at The May Company, and he would take time off now and then if he was lucky enough to pick up a day or two in a movie. He was on commission at the store, and every night when he got home, the game was to see if he had sold more or less that day than the day before. Sale of a couch was cause for celebration. Something like today's preoccupation with watching one's television ratings rise and fall, it was more than a game — let's face it, in both cases, numbers equate with livelihood!

The bottom line was, finances were spare, to say the least. Once in a great while, as a special treat, we would stop for a hot dog and a Delaware Punch at the then famous Tail O' The Pup — a tiny stand at the corner of La Cienega and Beverly Boulevards, built in the shape of a hot dog on a bun. No hot dog since (and there have been many, dog lover that I am) has ever measured up to theirs, but our limit was one apiece because we couldn't spare the twenty-five cents for a second one. I also remember one day returning some Coke bottles for the deposit in order to scrounge up the fifty cents to get my dress out of the cleaners so I could go on my appointed rounds of the radio casting offices.

On one of those casting day circuits, instead of the customary "Nothing today," it came as something of a shock when I was asked if I would care to speak to a producer who was putting on a *television* show! I was ushered in to meet a friendly young man, Joe Landis.

"Can you sing?" he asked.

"Oh yes!" I said.

You see, the cardinal rule in our line of work, as any budding young hopeful can tell you, is that you *can do* whatever the part calls for. Time enough to worry about *how* later, should you land the part.

"Can you juggle? Standing on your head? On a horse?"

"Oh yes!"

The subject of union membership never

came up, which was understandable once Mr. Landis carefully explained that a guest appearance like this didn't involve any fee. It was an opportunity to be *seen* — on *television* — a wonderful showcase! Now, at that moment in history, there were only two or three TV stations in town — KTLA-TV, Channel 5; KLAC-TV, Channel 13; and possibly KHJ-TV, Channel 9 — some of which didn't sign on till late in the day. Probably fourteen people in the entire city of Los Angeles owned a television set, and most of those were busy having the neighbors over to watch wrestling. (Okay, fourteen is an understatement, but not by much. The actual number of sets in the area at the time was somewhere just under a thousand.) It sounded great to me.

Recognizing this new medium's possible potential, a few local radio performers were becoming curious to try it out. Joe Landis explained that the show he was putting together was a special for Dick Haynes, a popular KLAC-Radio disc jockey, not to be confused with the singing movie star Dick Haymes.

By now I was impressed. *Haynes at the Reins* was one of the staple morning radio programs in L.A., and here I was being offered a chance to sing on Dick Haynes's first television special! Well, since working for nothing was one of my best things, what was there to say but "Oh yes!"

The union card wasn't all that was left out of the conversation. Joe also didn't ask me to sing — he simply took it for granted that I could. How's that for living dangerously? All he said was to choose two songs and show up at the studio — in wardrobe — in time to go over the numbers with the small combo they had hired. "Thank you. We'll see you Tuesday."

Choose two songs. That was a heavy decision, requiring much soul-searching and consultation — with my husband, with my folks, with *his* folks, with the dogs. Since Joe had mentioned he wanted something bright, I finally settled on "Somebody Loves Me" and "I'd Like to Get You on a Slow Boat to China," neither of which was too challenging. (I could have done "Spirit Flower" up tempo, but it didn't occur to me.)

As per instructions, I showed up at the studio with a black taffeta skirt and a white blouse that had some sequin flowers over one shoulder. It could not have been more wrong. The taffeta skirt rustled louder than I sang, and without special lighting and modern cameras, white and sequins are discouraged even today. White flares and reflects

51

against the face, making it look like you need a shave, and sequins kick light back into the camera. That day, however, everyone was scrambling and had no time to worry about what I was wearing.

I ran the songs a couple of times with the musicians, and the leader, Roc Hillman, was most patient and helpful with the rank amateur. Who knew we would work together again one day, and stay friends for decades? Fortunately, I never had to look at the performance that night, since it was live, with no postmortems.

It was all very scary but exciting for all concerned. Dick Haynes was in totally unfamiliar territory himself, but he couldn't have been nicer — to me, and to everyone else, as far as I could tell. Nerves can often bring out the worst in people, but not in this case, for sure.

Dick's generosity didn't end with the show. Shortly afterward, he recommended me for a new fifteen-minute comedy program that was about to start, also on KLAC, called *Tom, Dick* (not Haynes) *and Harry.* Lo and behold, I had a regular weekly job — for a few weeks.

Tom, Dick, and Harry were three outrageous vaudeville comedians. The premise of the show — highly original — was that they were supposedly running a hotel, and the whole show took place behind the hotel desk. That was lucky, because that was all the set we had — just a hotel desk in front of a painted flat. Obviously, money was no object. I served as their foil and fall guy (we didn't even think about gender semantics in those days), and I never knew what to expect. The show always opened with all four of us hiding down behind the desk. As the show started, the boys would pop up, one at a time, singing, "It's Tom — Dick — and Ha-a-ree!" in harmony. Then, as the music faded, I'd pop up, dusting madly with a feather duster, and the show began, usually in disarray. One good piece of advice: try never to get caught behind a desk with three comics and a feather duster! The format was unstructured. No — *loose* is what it was. Whether or not the viewers laughed I cannot guarantee, but we sure did. A lot.

That was probably my first taste of what I find so remarkable about the business I'm in. No matter what major concerns may be going on in your life on the outside, you have to leave them at the door when you come to work, because you will be forced to concentrate on something other than yourself to get the job done. And somehow there is often an inordinate amount of laughter in the process for anyone who thrives on that sort of thing, which serves to replenish the strength you need to pick up your problems again as you leave. That isn't as frivolous as it sounds. It works.

After a few short weeks, Tom, Dick, and Harry took their feather duster and went out to find other worlds to conquer. Luckily, I segued into another job at the station. This time it was on a new game show they were putting together called *Grab Your Phone*. Or, as my father insisted on calling it, *Grab Your What*?

The emcee was a man named Wes Battersea, and there were four of us girls seated on the panel, each with a telephone in front of her. Wes would ask a question of the audience and we would "grab" our phones as people called in their answers. It must have looked like a tiny telethon, but we weren't taking pledges — we were giving out five whole dollars for each correct response! Before we went on the air with the first show, the producer took me aside.

"Betty," he said very confidentially, "I must ask you *not* to mention salary to the others. We are going to pay you twenty dollars a week because you sit on the end and ad-lib with Wes, but they are only getting ten a week."

At those prices, my lips were sealed. Then again, maybe he was paying the other girls twenty-five and they didn't want *me* to find out.

Grab Your Phone was certainly not the first game show on television. Mike Stokey, for one, had been using celebrities for his *Pantomime Quiz* since 1948. However, it was my first and served as the precursor to the countless TV games I would be playing through the years. You name it, I've played it. Not just because I was hired to do so, but because it was such fun. Still is.

Mom and Dad and I had always played games since as far back as I can remember. Some we made up as we went along — at the table, in the car, wherever — so playing on TV was a bonus. Where else can you spend a couple of hours playing games with nice people and get paid for it? My dad's response to that was always, "Just think of all you gave away before they started paying you." Dad had a way with words.

As with everything else, television programs are cyclical, and game shows are a classic example. Through the years, they have had intense periods when they were all over the dial, then relatively quiet spells, only to resurface in greater numbers than ever.

Games have been at a comparatively low ebb of late, with a few obvious exceptions: *Jeopardy!* and *Wheel of Fortune* in syndication, and *The Price Is Right* and *Family Feud* on the CBS network. However, the tide is beginning to roll in once again: The Game Channel, a cable channel devoted exclusively to games, has just gone on the air. All the old Goodson-Todman and Mark Goodson Productions shows are being shown, plus many others. Good news for us game nuts.

It was during the run of *Grab Your Phone* that another phone rang — this time at home — and I answered a call that literally changed my life.

I recognized the voice immediately, for I had been listening to Al Jarvis on the radio for as long as I could remember. He was the top disc jockey in the greater Los Angeles area, and his *Make-Believe Ballroom* had been going strong for many years. When Martin Block started a *Make-Believe Ballroom* of his own in New York, he had to pay Al a continuing royalty for the use of the name. Why in the world would Al Jarvis be calling me? Yet, there was no mistaking that voice.

Al introduced himself, unnecessarily, then went on to explain that he was in the process of putting together a daytime TV show, to be called *Hollywood on Television*. He said he

56

had seen me on *Grab Your Phone* and was calling to offer me a job as his Girl Friday on the new program.

My initial private reaction was, "Wow! *Two* weekly shows! Dare I hope for another twenty dollars?" How fast big money corrupts. What had become of the little girl who had been so thrilled to work for nothing?

Before I could recover enough to respond, Al continued, saying that not only would I be his Girl Friday, but I'd be his Girl Monday, Tuesday, Wednesday, and Thursday as well. He intended to put his daily record-playing radio program on camera and wanted a girl on the show with him.

"I like the way you kid with Wes Battersea, and since we are going to be on the air for five hours every day, I thought that might come in handy. The job pays fifty dollars a week. What do you say?" Television was not yet covered by any union — there was no such thing as "scale." Salaries were determined at the discretion of the employer.

My mind suddenly went into slow motion. My answer was mostly gasping for breath. Had this been an audition, I would have flunked ad-libbing. There was a sense of total unreality. Five hours a *day? Fifty dollars* a week? *Every week?*

How I finally responded, or how the rest

of the conversation went, I have no idea. I guess, eventually, it must have percolated through my thick skull that this wasn't some practical joke — it was all really true.

I had no way of knowing that my lifelong love affair with television had just begun.

Al Jarvis, my benevolent boss. (Courtesy DeMirjian)

3

It was October 1949.

In the months since my first foray into TV on the *Dick Haynes Show,* the new medium had begun to open some exciting doors. Not only for us beginners, but all over the country, television itself had taken root, sprouted, and begun to grow — fast.

Even in such a rapidly expanding universe, the concept of a live five-hour daily show was unique. This new adventure, *Hollywood on Television, H.O.T.* to its friends, was to emanate from what had become my alma mater, KLAC-TV. Al soon began calling it "KLACtive — where things are active." It didn't take much to hit us funny.

On that red-letter day of the phone call from Al Jarvis, I couldn't wait to break the big news, first to Lane, then to our families; there was, naturally, great excitement. If Lane's initial reaction seemed a trifle measured, that could have been chalked up to surprise. He was thrilled with the fifty dollars part, of course, but almost immediately he began to fret about how much time would be involved. I should have heard the first faint warning bell; could it be that my taking a job when I could get one was okay, but an actual career for me was not high on his list of long-range plans?

Early on in our relationship, Lane and I had spent countless hours on that very subject, discussing the inherent problems in a two-career family. We had even stopped seeing each other over it, as you already know, because I didn't believe it was possible to try and have a successful career as well as a married/family life, and expect to do justice to either one. There are some outstanding examples to the contrary, so let me clarify by saying I just don't feel it's feasible to *start* them at the same time and still expect to give full attention to both. The fact that I'm compulsive explains a lot.

At least I had been honest with Lane. But the man was a great salesman; whether selling furniture or a future, Lane was tough to resist. He had struck down all my arguments, while offering reassurance, total understanding, and nothing but supportive encouragement for my work. Well, of course, I wanted to believe it, so I did. As for that exciting day of Al's call, the warning bell was so faint it could only be heard in retrospect, so I found Lane's enthusiasm for the project totally convincing.

Considering the length and depth of the pool of airtime Al and I were about to dive into, I now realize, looking back, that there was a surprising minimum of preparation before we were to debut on the air. In present-day television *nothing* is simple; to do a straightforward thirty-second commercial takes, literally, an army of people and weeks of cogitation. All we had, as I remember, were a couple of meetings, attended by everyone who would be connected with the show, during which Al and the sales department did most of the talking. Rightly so, because between them they were the ones who would have to make the program pay for itself, or it wouldn't fly.

Al Jarvis was no stranger to multihour broadcasting. After eighteen years of being a highly successful fish in the pond of Los Angeles radio, it was understandable that he wielded considerable clout at KLAC. The audience would buy anything from him — and did — making him a hero with the sales department. When he added five hours a day of selling time, you can imagine their euphoria.

Physically, Al was a chunky man of medium height, pushing forty — from one side or the other — with bright red hair and alive brown eyes that saw everything. They twinkled much of the time; they filled with tears when he laughed hard; they could also shoot sparks when his redheaded temper was triggered. He had four sons and was married to his fourth wife, Marilyn. Theirs was something of a volatile sunshine/stormy relationship, which often affected Al's mood for the day.

Regarding the part I was to play on the new show, the extent of Al's instruction to me was, "All you have to do is respond when I talk to you. Just follow where I lead." In today's climate, that undoubtedly sounds grossly chauvinistic and possibly cause for a grievance call, but with no ulterior motive, Al was simply giving me shorthand for exactly how the show was to be done. And it kept me paying attention.

There would be no script, no writers. Al would simply wing it from the floor. Just as he first described it, this was to be his radio show, except done in front of a live camera, with a more-or-less live girl sitting next to him. Thank goodness the records he would be playing would fill up most of the time.

■ ■ ■ ■

They erected a simple set for us, directly underneath the tall radio tower of what had been station KMTR before the call letters were changed.

We were located in the heart of old Hollywood, on Cahuenga Boulevard just south of Santa Monica Boulevard. Two blocks to the north, straight up Cahuenga, at the corner of Fountain Avenue, there is a tiny white house, still standing today, surrounded by tall cypress trees. I celebrated my sixth birthday in that house; my father planted those cypress trees as seedlings. Dad was in the lighting business and sold the floodlights to illuminate the KMTR station. I have a vivid memory of standing with my mother when those lights were being installed and being terrified watching Daddy climb to the top of that tall, skinny, *swaying* tower to focus the lights. Almost two decades later, Dad got a kick out of watching his daughter broadcast from under that same tower.

One block *south* of KLAC, down Cahuenga, was a studio complex which would be bought by Desi Arnaz and Lucille Ball and become the Desilu Studios, where we would eventually rent space to do my second series, *Date with the Angels* (more on that later). Desilu would ultimately dissolve and become Ren-Mar Studios, where we would spend eight happy years, from 1985 to 1993, taping *The Golden Girls* and *The Golden Palace*. It seems I have been personally involved with a small six-block area of early Hollywood for the past sixty-odd years. Some *very* odd.

Hollywood on Television went on the air in early November of 1949. It was within a day or so of Lane's and my second wedding anniversary.

The format of our show was primitively simple. Al sat behind a small desk with me on one side of him and his turntable on the other. Al opened the show each day by addressing a few remarks into the camera, to our viewing audience; he'd introduce me, then spin his first record. Between records we would chat briefly, then on with the music.

While the records played, the home audience could see us moving around the small set. (Believe me, we couldn't go far.) Al and I could talk to each other, but the viewers could only hear the music. There was also a large tank of tropical fish, which the cameraman would dolly in on now and then to perk things up. That's right — cameraman,

In front of the house at Fountain and Cahuenga. My sixth birthday.

singular. One camera, one man, five hours.

We managed to get through our whole first week; as each day went by, Al became more comfortable and would talk a little longer between records. By week's end, the mail and the phone calls began to come in, giving us a reading on the audience reaction. It was almost unanimous. The consensus was that they were interested in hearing us talk, but it drove them crazy to see us speaking to one another during the records and not know what we were saying!

The result? By the following Monday, the start of our second week on the air, Al eliminated *all* record playing, got rid of the turntable (the fish stayed), and we now had five full hours of live airtime to fill. Dear God!

Because of Al's radio show, which was still thriving, we didn't go on the air until 12:30. This was an ideal work schedule for me, since it meant I could get my household chores done in the morning and still make it to the studio by eleven. That gave me time to dab on a little makeup (we did our own in the beginning, such as it was) and to go over any last-minute ideas Al may have come up with. That constituted our "rehearsal." We would sign on at 12:30 and never come up for air until we signed off at 5:30. This allowed me to get home in time to get dinner under way before Lane came in.

I even managed time for dog walks.

We were living in an apartment in Park La Brea, where Lane had lived since before we met. Pets were strictly taboo, but that didn't stop Lane from surprising me with a six-week-old Pekingese puppy as a wedding present. His black mask made naming him easy — Bandit.

Little Bandy was as good as gold, and once he graduated from the newspaper, he immediately caught on to the fact that he would be walked at certain specific times and arranged his schedule accordingly. I would smuggle him out, draped over my arm under a coat, so that the security people, making their regular rounds, wouldn't get wise. We would go across the street into the park that contained the famous La Brea Tar Pits and have a glorious walk among the prehistoric animal statues; then we would go into our smuggling act again to get back home. It didn't occur to us that perhaps Security was simply choosing to look the other way, until one day I met a guard on my way out with my customary coat over my arm. Without even slowing up as he passed, he muttered, "Mrs. Allan, your tail is wagging." I looked back and, sure enough, sticking out from under the coat, Bandit's feathery plume was greeting the world! The guard just grinned and continued on his way.

Hollywood on Television began to take off immediately. Even with five hours to fill, we never seemed to have enough time; always running late, 5:30 would arrive before we knew it.

We received a lot of feedback from our viewers, which kept us very much in touch with what prompted audience response. Al would pick a topic of current interest and, if it struck a chord with him, he would expound on it in depth. This was always a real mail-puller. We would share some of the opinions expressed in the letters with those watching at home, which, in turn, elicited more mail. One subject might run for several days. Ironically, one of the first subjects I can remember Al taking off on was sex offenders and the increasing havoc they were wreaking on our streets. Al and our viewers were calling for more stringent punishment for offenders. Sound familiar? Just this past week a lead story in the national news reported the debates over some proposed new legislation designed to put more teeth into the penalties for those very crimes. Sadly, the more things change, the more they stay the same — trite but true.

Those campaigns of Al's were merely one element of the show — we certainly weren't always that dour. Al would invite his friends to drop in from time to time, and since he had some very famous friends, especially in the music business, this was a major plus. With his radio disc jockey identity, Al Jarvis was high on every song plugger's list, but the only way he would allow them on the show was if they brought a well-known performer along.

We also had guests who were not so famous.

Part of our set incorporated the patio wall, including a wooden gate which opened directly onto Cahuenga Boulevard. On impulse, and with no warning, Al would occasionally open that gate, and chance passersby would find themselves on camera; we would bring them in and interview them. It worked well for us at the time, but it might not be such a good idea now, since that neighborhood has changed drastically over the years. Today, we might be more tempted to put a dead bolt on the gate. Or perhaps seal up the wall entirely.

The positive reaction to our show was thrilling, but let's keep in mind there were only a couple of channel choices at the time, and, in the beginning, KTLA didn't sign on

69

until later in the day. It was us or the test pattern. By now, my folks had bought a little ten-inch Hoffman TV so they could watch their daughter — my loyal mom kept it on Channel 13 for the whole five hours every day — but Lane and I still hadn't made that rather substantial investment.

H.O.T. had been on the air for three weeks when suddenly it was Thanksgiving. This, of course, made no difference in our schedule — Thanksgiving, Christmas, New Year's — we worked them all as per usual.

After we signed off on that particular Thursday — Turkey Day — Al asked me if he could speak to me for a few minutes in his office. My heart sank. All this had been too good to be true — I should have known it all along.

I entered the office and sat down, realizing how much more official and intimidating Al looked sitting behind his own desk, than as the rather chubby redhead with the twinkle in his eye beside whom I had been working every day. I was determined that no matter what he had to tell me, I was *not* going to cry.

Al began by saying he was sorry — for delaying me, that is; he realized we both had holiday dinners to attend, but he wanted to share some news: the station manager, Don Fedderson, and the sales department were so pleased with the impact of our show that they were getting behind it with an all-out promotional push, life's blood to any program. In fact, they were so carried away that they had decided to add a half hour to our airtime every weekday, plus another five and a half hours on Saturday as well!

Before I had a chance to let that sink in, Al added the clincher: "As of next Monday, I am increasing your salary from fifty to three hundred dollars a week."

I just sat there staring at him. The devilish twinkle came back in the brown eyes, and he looked more like Al. He began to laugh, while I did what any red-blooded American girl would do under the circumstances. I dissolved.

Many years have gone by since that brief meeting, filled with more good fortune than any human could possibly hope for in my uncertain chosen profession, but not once in all that time has anything work-connected — award, prize, contract renewal, increased income, you name it — *ever* meant as much to me as Al's unsolicited gesture of approval that night.

Not even the Pilgrims ever had a better Thanksgiving.

Hollywood on Television was now on the air thirty-three hours a week — live. The show's acceptance grew. For that matter, the television audience in general was increasing every day, as more and more families were buying sets and including TV in their way of life. We were all too close to the day-to-day operation, and much too busy, even to speculate on the immeasurable influence this new medium was already beginning to exert on the American public.

Young television continued to grow like a weed, and soon everything was too small. Typical kid. Inevitably, our station had to be remodeled and expanded. New offices were being built, which caused us to lose our cozy nest under the tower. Extensive renovations were going on at the other end of the lot as well, one of which was to be a new studio for us, but that would take awhile. In the meantime, a huge tent was erected over the patio around which the station had originally been built, in the middle of which was a very large fish pond. They drained the pool, moved in our simple set, and that became our home for the next few months. Our business went on as briskly as usual, but it was not the most glamorous place for greeting visiting VIPs.

Professionally, I couldn't have asked for more. *H.O.T.* had hit its stride and was an ongoing and growing pleasure to do. Al and I had fallen into the comfortable groove of reading each other that is so vital when people have to work together — especially on an ad-lib basis — *especially* on live television. With no script to fall back on, it was like walking along the edge of a cliff in a high wind — there was nothing to hang on to but your mental editor. Al and I had to trust each other.

In real life, everything was on a fairly even keel. The three hundred dollars a week seemed to have quelled any qualms Lane may have felt about the added work schedule. To be sure, things were just okay at home — I didn't want to dig too deeply in that department.

4

Thrilled as we were with the warm reception of our show, the fact remained that spending thirty-three hours a week on camera, without a net, was not the most relaxed way of making a living. Whenever the subject comes up in an interview — usually in response to that cliché of clichés, "How did you get your start in show business?" — the next logical question is, "Wasn't that schedule exhausting?"

In all honesty, I have to admit — no. It wasn't at all.

For whatever reason, be it workaholism, lack of good sense, emulating a father who loved working above all else, the truth of the matter is, it was plain, flat-out *interesting*. It wasn't simply the novelty in the beginning, or the fact that I was in showbiz at last, because that same feeling of excitement and enjoyment has lasted for forty-six years and shows no signs of abating. Sure, I get physically tired sometimes — really bushed — but only after the show is over and the makeup and the shoes come off. Soon, the battery recharges and I'm ready to have at it again. Could be I'm hooked on adrenaline.

Some shows, of course, are more enjoyable than others, and *H.O.T.* still ranks pretty high on the list. However, even with all the rose-colored retrovision, there is no getting around the fact that there was all that time to fill each day, fifty-two weeks a year. How did we *do* it? From this perspective, I'm damned if I know. I can remember doing some of everything, but in what order I can't begin to tell you.

The Girl Monday-through-Friday — and now Saturday — idea caught on, and Al always addressed me by the appropriate day. What he didn't know was that my silly mother, as a gag, had given me a set of silk panties embroidered with the days of the week, and, of course, I had to wear them in proper order or it was bad luck. It was our nutty private joke. Today, I'm sure, they would have been shown on camera, at the very least — perhaps modeled.

Recently, when I went for my routine annual mammogram, the ladies at the desk were comparing notes as to when they had first seen me on television. They were digging back pretty far, but finally, one gal over in the corner looked up from her computer with a smug smile.

"Want to know the first time *I* saw her?" — pregnant pause — "When she was Monday-Tuesday-Wednesday on that old daytime show!" It goes without saying, she won.

Well, what *did* we do for all those hours? Al led, and I would do my best to follow. Now and then, he would suddenly throw a question at me out of left field, and I could tell by the gleam in his eye that he didn't expect, or want, a straight answer. Rather than flub around trying to come up with something clever, I would say the first thing that popped into my mind (a most dangerous game) and we would improvise from there. This became a small challenge that was fun for both of us, since we hadn't the foggiest where we were going. Once in a while, Al would bang out a couple of sentences on the typewriter just before we went on and hand them to me at the last minute. I can still see the yellow legal tablet paper and his abysmal typing. We'd make up characters out of whole cloth, and sometimes Al would suddenly ask for a report on one or another of them, with no warning whatsoever. Even a rattlesnake will at least clue you in before he strikes! If a person happened to have a bawdy sense of humor, a person had to keep a death grip on a person's aforementioned mental editor.

One of our favorite made-up "people" became a running character — not every day but only when the mood struck Al. She was my alleged drama teacher, Madame Fahgel Bahgelmahcher. As it developed, that was the name she had taken for the theater — her real name was Madam Fagel Bagelmaker. The Madam, as we called her, had one real advantage: her lessons, which she gave in the living room of her rather seedy apartment, were dirt cheap. She had a parrot, as I recall, and there was a beaded curtain that hung in the doorway to her private quarters. On some days, I would report to Al that the Madam hadn't felt well enough to teach and had sent me to the corner to get her "medicine," which, miraculously, always seemed to make her so much happier. There was one day when all Al typed on the yellow paper was "carriage lesson." I have no idea of what he may have intended, but somehow we got into five minutes of the Madam teaching me the proper, and the improper, way to get in and out of a carriage. She felt that was something every serious young actress *must* know how to do.

The Madam was very near and dear to my

heart. I have always suspected that somewhere, in whatever place she landed, she is being played by Bea Lillie.

The steady parade of celebrities continued; if they came to town, you could bank on it, they did our show.

Sarah Vaughan was a promising young talent, as was Peggy Lee. The latter came on dressed to the nines the first time she was on the show, and my dad was really taken by her. He always referred to her as "that girl in the green suit." There were major stars of the day — Herb Jeffries, Billy Eckstine, Tony Martin, even Nat King Cole.

Robert Clary had *just* arrived from France as a highly touted new singer, and he spoke French almost exclusively. He learned with lightning speed, and by his next visit he was telling funny anecdotes in fractured English. This was long before he became one of *Hogan's Heroes,* or developed into a magnificent painter in oils.

Johnny Mercer and Hoagy Carmichael, two of the best — and the nicest — songwriters, came by whenever they had something to plug, which was often.

And the list went on. Perhaps it reveals a character flaw, but, even at this late date, I still get a big kick out of meeting famous people. Those who are noted outside the show business community even get double points in my rating book. At least I'm admitting it and not trying to play it cool. I also find amazing, and will never take for granted, the fact that I've had the privilege of counting a few legends among my personal friends: Fred Astaire, his wonderful sister, Adele, John Steinbeck, Helen Hayes, George Burns, Lucille Ball, Bob Hope, Jimmy Stewart, Carol Channing (we've been buddies for over thirty years). It's best if I stop naming names or I'm sure to leave some people out and get in real trouble if they think I don't consider them legends.

Speaking of legends, there was Buster Keaton. One of the truly classic silent film comedians, Buster had a syndicated half-hour show of his own in 1950. One afternoon he stopped by *H.O.T.* to chat with Al. True to form, we were running a little behind schedule, so Al momentarily interrupted his interview with Buster to throw it to me to do a Thrifty Drug Store commercial.

Thrifty was an important sponsor, since they were on with us twice every day, but it was never my favorite spot to do. It always involved a clumsy board, set up on an easel, containing what must have been every item they ever sold, and they wanted them

Buster Keaton — for him, this was a big smile! (© AMERICAN BROAD-
CASTING COMPANIES, INC.)

all mentioned. I was hurrying through as
fast as I could when Buster ambled over to
"help." Without saying a word, he became
fascinated with every item on the board, ex-
amining them minutely and demonstrating
their purpose where possible — all with that
woebegone deadpan of his. The spot must
have run ten minutes. If *only* tape had been

invented at the time. I'd sell my soul to see it today.

As really funny as Buster was, I was a little anxious, hoping that Thrifty would think so too and not be upset, or, heaven forbid, cancel the account! To their credit, Thrifty loved it (not always the case). They loved it a lot more than some of the other sponsors whose spots simply didn't get on that day.

One more celebrity story I have to share, although he never actually appeared on the show. Remember the movie *The Day the Earth Stood Still,* with Patricia Neal, in which Michael Rennie played the role of a man from another galaxy? Well, when I went to see it, sure enough, the earth stood still for me. Michael Rennie absolutely did me in. I went to see it again — and again — and yet again. Al caught on quickly and began to tease me about him, until it became a good-natured running gag.

One day on the show, Al turned to me and, without preamble, said, "You can take the afternoon off — you're excused, see you tomorrow."

Having no idea where he was going with this bit, I tried to go along with it, staying where I was.

Al was insistent. "Get out of here. He's waiting!"

I looked over, and there, standing offstage, was *Michael Rennie* — smiling, and looking even craggier than on screen!

Al literally pushed me off the set, and I had no choice but to go, all the while praying that God would strike me dead — *now*.

To his dying day, Al swore it was Michael's idea to come tell me how much he enjoyed our little game about him on the show. Michael, too, insisted that was the case, and, of course, I never believed either one of them. I had seen Al's devious mind at work before.

Whatever the reason, there he was. Michael was charm itself, and he swept me off to a fine lunch at Frascati's, a chic Beverly Hills restaurant of the day. As for me, I stayed beet red, which must have looked great with the icky chartreuse wool dress I happened to be wearing. ("Why *this* dress *today?*") I guess I gradually relaxed a little as Michael persisted in putting me at ease. Don't ask me what we talked about — I haven't a clue. I don't think I spilled anything, but who knows? After lunch, he brought me back to the studio, and I knew I had enjoyed a delightful joke.

What thoroughly confused the whole picture was that three days later he was back. This time I had only a half hour before the show, so we went down to the corner and had a quick sandwich at this genuinely awful little greasy spoon. I remember how it cracked me up when, with a perfectly straight face and in his ravishing British accent, Michael asked me if he could make reservations there for New Year's Eve.

And that *was* the end of my Michael Rennie adventure. I never saw him again. Well, except on screen. I determined that from then on I would try to watch my mouth when it came to whom I admired, but for me that is a lost cause, unfortunately. Besides, it's great to have an ongoing fantasy person in your life, and it's especially handy when responding to silly questions on talk shows. These days I find myself talking about Robert Redford — I am not chumming, I swear.

No, he has never shown up.

With the delightful exception of Buster Keaton, the "entertainment" (a euphemism) portion of the program — the guests and the games and the giddiness — all had to take place between and around the inviolate core of our show, the commercials. As our audience multiplied, our commercial load increased proportionately, and if an interview ran a little long or Al happened to get carried away on a subject, or if we began having a little too much fun, we knew we would have to pay for it. Once we slipped behind, we'd face having to do three or four spots in a row to catch up. Invariably, by the last half hour

Al and Betty. Our daily commercial load was a heavy one.
(Courtesy Leo Kanter, KLAC)

every day things would become somewhat chaotic, to make sure none of our paying customers got short-changed.

When people hear of all those commercials in a bunch and shudder at the idea, they seem to forget that today we get the same thing at every station break. Ours *were* longer, I will admit. But check out the increasing number of "infomercials" on the air at present, wherein almost any pretense at entertainment has been dropped and they spend thirty full minutes aiming straight for your wallet.

Keep in mind, too, that early on there was no such thing as film or taped messages. They were all done l-i-v-e in the studio. Al would do some of them, particularly if they were sponsors from his radio show; à la Arthur Godfrey, he might run three or four minutes extolling the virtues of a given product. Other spots would fall to me to do. After a hasty briefing from the sales department or a quick look at a fact sheet, often sent over during the show with the ink still wet, I would valiantly try to remember enough of the information to impart to the audience. Neither Al nor I would ever be caught dead *reading* anything; we considered that cheating. As a result, to this day I cannot use cue cards — I have to memorize everything. Now, of course, it's because I can't *see* them, and I'm not about to put on my glasses.

As soon as a couple of other stations began daytime telecasting, there came into being a growing procession of pitchmen, carrying their products and shuttling between stations to hawk their wares. Sometimes they would come back two or three times in the same day to catch a different set of viewers. No one but my mother lasted through the whole five and a half hours every day.

As relaxed as Al was in his own commercial approach, he would get a tad testy with some of these salesmen if they began to stretch a little over their allotted *two minutes*. (Infomercials aside, can you imagine if every commercial were two minutes long today?) When the sales department found Al getting somewhat high-handed with any of the pitchmen who had paid for their commercial time on the program, one of my functions was to act as a buffer. We would set up the spots without Al having to deal directly with some of the people he didn't like. Diplomacy was not Al's long suit.

There was a wide variance, beyond our control, in the quality of our commercials, and sometimes in their integrity. Tell you what: Stay up very late some night and take a look at the "miracle buys" being offered now, and you will get the flavor of some of our early pitchmen at that time.

There was Martin Gilbert, who would schlep in his portable sewing machine, offered at the "unbelievable low cost of $19.95!" It *was* unbelievable, as there wasn't a chance in hell anyone could buy the machine he showed — the customer would invariably be drawn/pushed to a more expensive model. Does the term "bait and switch" ring a bell?

Phil Green and his vacuum cleaner offered the same type of dubious deal, except Phil's presentation was a little more colorful. He would race in, throw some dirt on a piece of carpet, then make the dirt disappear before your very eyes! The pitch was done at the top of his voice over the roar of the vacuum.

There was Lou Slicer, who called himself by the name of the product he sold — a handy dandy little cutting machine that could slice *anything,* including many of our viewers' fingers. We discovered that when the mail started coming in.

And Charlie Stahl — a giant of a man who pitched his sofas by jumping up and down on them to demonstrate their durability.

Ted Lenz used to bring his little dog, Gypsy, along as his partner (shill?). I was always so carried away with Gypsy that I can't for the life of me remember what Ted was selling.

Some of our spots were classier; eventually we even had a few institutional commercials for national products. My problem in doing the spots assigned to me was that I had no sales resistance whatsoever. I pitched the O'Keefe & Merritt gas range — we bought an O'Keefe & Merritt gas range. The Exercycle I demonstrated, I absolutely had to have. Once I got it home, there was no time to use it, so after a couple of years of gathering dust, it was finally given away. I really shouldn't have listened to myself; I even fell for those paste-on permanent manicures. "Simply choose your shade of polish in this already shaped fingernail, peel off the backing, and stick the permanent polish on your own nail. No chipping. No smearing. To change polish, just peel off and apply a new set."

Unfortunately, in my enthusiasm, I was unaware that the whole top layer of your nail came off as well. It took me a year to get my nails back in shape. Chalk that one up to inadvertent consumer research. I have seen something similar being advertised today. I assume — at least I pray — that some of the glitches have been ironed out in the interim.

I was worse than any classic pigeon — I was buying from *myself!* No discounts, mind you, full price!

Considering the glut of commercials and the law of averages, there were some inevitable disasters. We sold Dr. Ross Dog Food daily, which always ended with a little jingle played from the control booth:

Give him Dr. Ross Dog Food
Do him a favor
It's got more meat
And it's got more flavor
It's got more meat to make him feel the way
  he sho-ould
Dr. Ross Dog Food is doggone good.

Another regular sponsor was Kermit's Frozen Meat Pies, and every day Mr. Kermit's daughter came by to extol the qualities of her father's delectable meat pies. One afternoon, we were running behind, as usual; Miss Kermit finished her spiel with a big smile and — you've got it:

Give him Dr. Ross Dog Food etc., etc.

For some still unexplained reason, our engineer didn't catch it in the booth, and it just played on — and on — the whole jingle! Did Miss Kermit turn green? (Sorry.) No, but she didn't laugh, either. We never saw Miss Kermit again.

The commercials continued to multiply. Our all-time record for a single day eventually stood at fifty-eight live commercial spots in one five-and-a-half-hour program. With that kind of indoctrination it's no wonder that to this day, when I pick up a package or a can, even at home, I automatically turn the label out as I would to camera.

As our show expanded, so did our cast of two. One by one, a group of regulars and semiregulars began to form. Mary Sampley was the first one to come aboard.

One of our local sponsors, the Kelly Kar Kompany (Kute?), came up with the idea of dressing a gal in a bright Kelly green uniform, complete with the comp — excuse me, Kompany logo. Each hour throughout the afternoon, when the KLAC sports director, Sam Balter, stopped by to give a sports update, Mary would follow his spot by holding up a tote board containing the latest race results from whichever local track was running. It wasn't long before every bar in town was glued to *Hollywood on Television* all afternoon. The great serendipity was that Mary fitted in like a glove and added a wonderful off-beat, down-home sense of humor.

Mary and I both had very low thresholds when it came to breaking up. Much as I love all the laughter that goes with the territory, there are times when it can be a serious hazard. Also, it isn't something you outgrow over time. It still doesn't take much to set me off and, of course, it does not help when your coworkers go out of their way to take advantage of your problem. At that time, whenever Mary Sampley would get the giggles, they could at least dolly in on her tote board. Wonder what some of the bar patrons thought, seeing the race results suddenly shaking out of control? It could be a little unsettling — especially after a couple of drinks.

Personally, my darkest moment in the breakup department came when, after a quick glance at some copy just handed me, I enthusiastically began explaining a new product that sounded like a great idea. It was an attachment for your kitchen sink. "You put the soap in here, then press this little button, and — and soapy water comes out of your — of your —" Well, I was so carried away with this wonderful contraption, I momentarily blanked on the word "faucet"

— it just wasn't there. I finally finished off lamely with "and soapy water comes out of your gizmo." Now, I might expect Mary to go on that, but Al *and* our cameraman, Bill Niebling, were the worst. Not only were tears shooting from Al's eyes, but I could see the drops flying from behind the trembling camera, which, it figures, was all it took for me to fall apart. For the next three minutes there was no one to mind the store. Because it was genuine and totally unplanned, the audience forgave us — in fact, they loved it when anything like that happened; but the client took a somewhat dimmer view. That was another product that never returned. Maybe they went somewhere else and had Miss Kermit make the pitch. It seems only fair.

So, while we weren't the only ones who got a little flaky from time to time, Mary and I usually got the blame. Small wonder that people sometimes got our names mixed up, calling her Betty and me Mary. A few years later, Mary added to the confusion by marrying a man named Art White, and thus becoming, legally, Mary White.

About this time, there was a very special addition to our group. The station manager of KLAC, Don Fedderson, had a good friend, Dr. Ernest Wilson, who was a Unity

92

minister. Mr. Fedderson prevailed upon him to stop by our show one afternoon, just before closing, to give a Thought for the Day. Right after the last race results.

Dr. Wilson proved to be one of the best ideas ever, and he immediately became a daily feature on the last five minutes of the show. There was no booming rhetoric, no denominational oversell. Everyone fell in love with him, with his gentle stories and delicious sense of humor. For his part, Ernest always said he loved doing the show because it was the only way he knew to be heard in every bar in town. We remained close, loving friends for the rest of his long life.

James McNamara joined Sam Balter for sports updates.

Music was added when Ronnie Kemper brought his piano and joined us.

Somewhat later, Al brought in a beautiful fifteen-year-old Irish girl whom he had heard sing. With the face of an angel and a voice to match, Erin O'Brien eventually moved on to become a promising young movie star, but in the meantime she joined our little family. I use the term "little" advisedly, as we were pikers compared to Erin's own family. She was one of thirteen children when we met her, and her mother gave birth to number fourteen while Erin was with our show! And speaking of birthdays, an odd coincidence came to light the following January when my birthday rolled around on the seventeenth. We discovered it was also Erin's birthday. *And* Mary Sampley's! What are the odds against that long shot, do you suppose?

With all due respect to Madam Fagel Bagelmaker, she couldn't hold a candle to Al Jarvis as a teacher. He set a pace and precedent that holds me in good stead to this day.

Going from obscurity to high-profile local success is heady wine. We've all seen sad cases of what happens when young people begin believing their own publicity and assuming that their good luck will be a permanent way of life. Between my folks and Al Jarvis, I was steered away from that trap. Often, I'm sure, I was probably a royal pain in the derrière, but they were benevolent dictators, and never was I allowed to be "boss." I was always too busy just trying to keep up.

I think about that sometimes.

Who is my watchdog today? My folks are gone, as is Al; my husband, Allen, always my benign critic, is gone; friends mean well but aren't reliably objective, and they have a tendency, I suspect, only to tell me what

Cast of Hollywood on Television. (Courtesy H. S. "Dusty" Rhoades)

I want to hear. The fact that I have lived a long time doesn't mean that I'm any better at self-appraisal than anyone else. As time goes by and I find my acceptance has increased, I realize, and it's a chilling thought, that there is no governor on the accelerator and my ego is at the wheel. I try to keep that very much in mind at all times.

We didn't have an audience in the studio; we reached our viewers only through the camera lens. Al's basic credo was always to think in terms of the people watching at home:

Never to talk down to them — nor, for that matter, over their heads.

Without ever claiming such was the case, to give the viewers the comfortable feeling that you could have come to work on the bus.

Never to have any fun in the studio that the audience wasn't in on. Even in our most devastating breakups, there were never any private jokes tolerated; the reason for our laughter was always explained. Of course, in the case of soapy water coming out of your gizmo, any explanation would have been somewhat superfluous.

Plunging necklines and tight sweaters were off limits. (For *me,* that is — Al loved it when a guest would come on with everything in the store window.)

All in all, things were fine in our happy little Camp *H.O.T.*

At home, things were deteriorating fast. The faint warning bell I spoke of had grown consistently louder and had finally sounded a death knell for the marriage.

Lane at last had to admit that he simply couldn't handle having a wife with a career. In spite of all his earlier denials, I'm sure he had a more conventional family picture in mind. And — in all honesty — I knew

I couldn't promise to change and make it stick. It's a familiar story, and oh, such a painful one.

We separated, but the divorce didn't happen for quite a while. Neither of us could handle anything that final right away.

Lane, bless him, didn't learn by his mistake; a few years later, he married a very successful young actress, Randy Stuart, but that marriage didn't make it, either.

Eventually, the third time was the charm — for both of us.

5

It was 1950. Harry Truman was in the middle of his term as President. Eleven percent of homes by now had television, and the upstart was moving at warp speed, trying to provide enough programming to satisfy the voracious appetite of an ever-increasing audience.

Aren't those almost the same words we hear these days in regard to the five hundred or so channels possible in the near future? Except now they refer to it as software. However, that percentage figure has changed dramatically. Today, with 200 million sets in use, around 70 percent of U.S. homes have two — or more — TV sets. Interestingly enough, a recent survey found more people would prefer a VCR over a second TV. *Seventy-seven* percent of homes have at least one VCR. Is it beginning to sound more and more like we are approaching an on-ramp to the Superhighway?

■ ■ ■ ■

In 1950, the big national shows still emanated from New York or Chicago, and as a result, fuzzy kinescopes were the order of the day for four-fifths of the country watching those programs. *Lux Video Theatre,* which went on the air that October and was performed live, chose to spend extra money to also shoot their shows on film, for improved quality and to have on record, but not too many others went that route.

It didn't take long for the American Federation of Radio Artists to catch on to the fact that television was here to stay, and it was time to get in on the action. So AFRA reached out to include TV and became AFTRA — the American Federation of *Television* and Radio Artists. Already, television got top billing. Because of the varying lengths and types of shows, setting pay scales was something of a challenge; much the same problem the Academy of Television Arts and Sciences faces today when it tries to simplify the Emmy Awards system.

When it came to figuring out the local salary structure in Los Angeles, AFTRA suddenly found their problems compounded. Each time they would arrive at what seemed a fair pay formula based on ten-, fifteen-, thirty-, and sixty-minute shows, they would run into this thirty-three-hour-a-week monster called *Hollywood on Television,* and all their figures would be blown out of the water. They had to regroup, or our show would have been prohibitive in talent fees. Back to the drawing board.

Finally, they put us in a separate category of our own; a freak, so to speak. As a result, my salary went up to $400 a week, and I signed a seven-year contract (my first) with increments of $50 a year. If I managed to survive for seven years, I would be making $750 a week! I was in hog heaven.

When I hear figures quoted today for one-hour daytime shows (we won't even *discuss* prime time), my head reels. Case in point: It was announced not long ago that Oprah Winfrey has signed a new contract with King World that takes her to the turn of the century — at a reported $500 million. That multitalented lady is the best of the best at anything she turns her hand to and worth whatever the traffic will bear. I only question the powers that be who made the offer. Doesn't half a billion sound a bit like the national deficit? According to the corporate spokespeople, the numbers are based on the returns Oprah brings into the company. Can't knock that.

Okay, so her show is better; but ours was longer! So there, tee hee.

We ended 1950 on a high note, and proceeded to ring in the new year — in the most literal sense.

January first was always an atypical day for us. The commercial load would be predictably light because our regular audience was scattered among other New Year diversions. Even our guests were not as readily available, since most people had more sense than to work on a holiday. As a result, we would have more feature spots booked in than we normally had time for, some of which were just names on our rundown, and we didn't always know what to expect.

Bear in mind that on this day much of the audience we did have was probably lazing around, trying to recover from the previous night's festivities. Hungover is perhaps the technical term I'm seeking. We were aware of this and always tried to be as considerately soft pedal as possible.

Consequently, Al and I were somewhat surprised when one of the feature spots turned out to be a troupe of Swiss bell ringers. We introduced them, and on came four bouncy, *happy* folk, two men and two women, wheeling in a table containing more bells than you would expect to see in a lifetime. They proceeded to play a medley of songs, long and loud — kind of a good-natured Heavy Metal. There was an immediate segue into a second "comedy" number, with much raucous laughter, and a *lot* of footstomping, as I recall. Before these ecstatic folk could launch into a third offering, Al was out of his chair like a shot to shake their hands warmly, never letting go until he had ushered them offstage.

As unexpected as these bell ringers were to us, perhaps they were an appropriate way, after all, to usher in a new year that would hold so many surprises. The winds of change had begun to blow.

6

By 1951, there were now seven channels in Los Angeles from which to choose. At ten cents a copy, the magazine *TV-Radio Life* (formerly *Radio-TV Life* — the inversion of the title was itself a sign of the times) would report that "three out of ten families now have television in their homes, and more [sets] on the way!" They got that right.

H.O.T. was still on for the endurance hours, but KLAC had put in an afternoon movie, which gave us a little breathing room. Not a heck of a lot, at that, for we would still break in frequently — repeat, frequently — to squeeze in as many commercials as possible.

To the casual observer, it might seem that our weekly on-camera time would be almost sufficient for any normal person, but let's face it, no one of sound mind would be doing that sort of thing in the first place. So, when it was suggested that I do a little show on Sunday evening in addition, I thought it was a swell idea.

The Betty White Show was anything but original. I would read letters sent in by viewers and respond to their questions regarding romance. Wasn't I just the person to be handing out advice? I would also sing a couple of songs, although what that had to do with anything, don't ask. A nice young man and a great musician, George Tibbles, was brought in as my accompanist. While I wheezed away with the letters, George sat at the piano — I guess so that he'd be sure to be ready whenever I felt a song coming on.

Just for luck, on the first show I brought Bandit on and introduced him, and then he was supposed to leave. Instead, the little ham lay at my feet under the coffee table and stared into the camera for the whole half hour. Naturally, he became a permanent member of the cast — he would have it no other way.

This show went on for a few weeks, and while I enjoyed it, Al soon had an even better idea. We would do an evening show together, in addition to the daytime marathon, for one hour on Saturday nights. Al had been wanting to do nighttime for a long while, and he figured out a way to tie it into

Betty and the Bandit. That's Captain on the wall behind us. Cappy was no longer with us.

the daytime show without just doing more of the same thing. How about an hour *amateur* show!? There may have been those of the opinion that that was what we had been doing all along. Be that as it may, it sounded a lot more exciting than my letter-reading — besides, it was a whole hour. Overexposure? We thought that just meant you stayed out in the sun too long.

The idea on the evening show was to showcase new talent, and then the winner would appear every day for a week as a paid guest performer on *H.O.T.* I can't quite remember what the night show was called — something like *The Al Jarvis Hour,* I think — but wouldn't *Star Search* have been a great name?

Some of the winners were very good, and the best of them all was a young lady whose voice was like wine. After a successful week on *Hollywood on Television,* she decided it was time to take a professional name, and she chose — Gogi Grant. Gogi went on to a wonderful career as a recording star and is still singing beautifully these days.

Had we overextended our energies? Did we find ourselves exhausted after yet another hour on the tube? Not in the least. I can't speak for the audience, but we were fine.

The show was great fun to do, and little did I dream it would also prove to be a prophetic step on the road into the future.

During the course of the hour, I, too, would sing a couple of numbers. So that the audience could distinguish me from the rest of the amateurs, we would always lead into my number with some short, silly sketch. As a payoff to whatever joke we were going for, I'd go into the song.

George Tibbles was brought along to do this show, too (Bandit didn't make the cut), and we all got a real surprise, George most of all. We had all thought of George as a fine piano player, period. George thought he was a piano player, too. He had toured the country as accompanist with Eddie Cantor, and then had been playing for some years at Billy Gray's Band Box — a well-known nightspot on Fairfax Avenue that was a precursor of today's crop of comedy clubs. George had also written many popular songs, including the inescapable "Woody Woodpecker Song." That little gem proved to be an annuity.

Just for the hell of it, George took a shot at writing a couple of lead-in sketches for our show, and they worked — above and beyond anyone's expectations. As a result, he got up from the piano bench, another good piano man, Cliff Whitcomb, sat in, and George was in the writing business — permanently.

For the next several years, George wrote everything I did (on camera, at least). He grew into one of TV's top comedy writer/

Cliff Whitcomb was better at the piano. (COURTESY H. S. "DUSTY" RHOADES)

producers — *Life with Elizabeth, Date with the Angels, My Three Sons, Family Affair,* et cetera — as well as a prolific playwright. Many of his plays are still being performed around the country. Best of all the Tibbles family — George, his wife, Mildred, and their four children — have remained among my dearest friends. We lost George to cancer in 1987.

Those early lead-in sketches were absolutely ridiculous, which made them such fun — for us, anyway. I am willing to make book that our motivation was identical to that of Johnny Carson so many years later, with his Mighty Carson Art Players. It was kids playing dress up!

We actually worked backward on our nonsense. George and I would go to Western Costume Company, and when I found a costume I liked, we'd pick an appropriate song. Then George would write the sketch to fit the outfit.

"Oh, you like that gypsy thing? Okay — say we have a campfire — we get a funny fiddler — you tell a funny fortune, then go into 'Golden Earrings.'"

Well, that took care of half of next week's show, right there. George had to go home and write it, of course. A minor detail.

The other sketch always involved the same

regular characters. Al Jarvis and I would play husband and wife, Alvin and Elizabeth, in some domestic situation or other, and after a couple of pages of dialogue, I'd burst into song as a get-out. We had the guts of a burglar. Meanwhile, we didn't give up our day job.

In spite of a schedule that precluded very much outside observation, we were still somewhat aware of the many things that were happening elsewhere in our business. More and more new shows were surfacing, among them, a half-hour situation comedy starring a real-life husband and wife team. *I Love Lucy* premiered in October of 1951. Since we were doing both of our shows live, most of our off-camera time was spent preparing for on-camera time and we weren't able to watch their shows. I have had ample opportunity since.

Down the road, Lucy and I became dear friends, as did our two dynamite mothers, DeDe Ball and Tess White. After Lucy lost her mom, she sent my mother violets every year on DeDe's birthday. Some kind of lady.

In light of today's "political correctness," it is interesting to note that there was real resistance on the part of the network and the sponsor to using Desi as Lucy's vis-à-vis, for fear his strong Latin flavor might alienate the audience! Lucy really had to go to bat for him. Two years later, when Little Ricky was born, it was a national scoop — including the cover of *TV Guide*. The word "pregnant," however, was strictly taboo. As of today, pregnancy is standard grist for the television comedy mill, and we are dealt in on every painful graphic detail — before, during, and after.

I Love Lucy was not the only one. *The Red Skelton Show,* featuring another redhead, first saw the light of day — or night — in 1951. Dinah Shore blew us a kiss and won our hearts on her first fifteen-minute musical program. Other big shows had surfaced earlier.

In 1950, Sid Caesar debuted *Your Show of Shows*.

Jackie Gleason's *Cavalcade of Stars* introduced some of the great running characters Jackie created, including Ralph Kramden. I was surprised to realize that *The Honeymooners,* with Jackie, Art Carney, Audrey Meadows, and Joyce Randolph, was only on for one season, later on, as a series of its own. The thirty-nine episodes were not successful when they began in 1955 and were canceled. Today, *The Honeymooners* is still getting laughs in reruns every night, some forty-plus years later.

The panel game *What's My Line* was one of the early winners from the Goodson-Todman stable and finished our week off in style every Sunday night.

Arthur Godfrey's television show began in 1949.

One of my personal favorites, *Kukla, Fran & Ollie,* began locally in Chicago in 1947; it appeared as a network show in the Midwest in 1948, added the East Coast in 1949, but we didn't get it on the West Coast until 1951.

But who had any idea, in the beginning, which of these shows would become classics? *Every* show starts out with the highest expectations, but only over time do the giants emerge. Countless offerings die aborning, year in and year out. It's like a songwriter deliberately sitting down to write a standard; it can't be done. It takes a lot of distilling, a lot of time, to make the determination as to how it will hold up. I try to keep that in mind in regard to television when I find myself railing against the bad shows "they" foist off on us. I must remember that there is also a collective "we." By the numbers, "we" decide the fate of all shows.

That all makes a great deal of sense to me,

until a show that I absolutely hate becomes a raging hit, and then the argument doesn't hold water.

I think it was Larry Eisenberg who said, "For peace of mind, resign as general manager of the universe." Well, I abdicate my role as judge; I'm just not ready for the responsibility.

You do it.

7

Those were vintage years in early television, and as we headed into another new year, the trend continued.

Now, this is where my memory drives me up the wall. The recollection of those silly New Year's bells is crystal clear. Yet when I try and picture the day Al told me he was leaving the show, I can't for the life of me bring it into focus. It's diffused and blurry around the edges. Perhaps because the news was so shattering.

Al was not only leaving the show, he was leaving the station altogether and moving to KABC to do a dancetime show for young people. His wife, Marilyn, would be the co-host.

Marilyn Jarvis had visited *H.O.T.* from time to time, to sing a song or join us in some comedy schtick, and she couldn't have been sweeter to us all. On a few occasions, however, Al had indicated that inviting his wife to guest on the show was the best way — and sometimes the only way — to keep the peace at home. In rare moments of confidence, he had allowed as how Marilyn really wanted to be on television. He would underline the *really wanted*. He even hinted that she might be secretly sticking pins in little Betty White or Mary Sampley or Erin O'Brien dolls. Whether Al was using Marilyn's ambition as a cop-out for jumping ship I will never know, but the dismal fact remained — he was leaving. I couldn't begin to imagine what would happen to our little show without Al.

I didn't have long to wonder. What transpired in the front office I have no idea, but the day soon came when the transition was made, as smoothly as anyone could wish. The prominent young movie actor Eddie Albert, no less, was brought in as the new host.

Change is, and always has been, difficult for me; however, Eddie was such a charmer that in no time at all he had won over not only his coworkers but the audience as well. *Hollywood on Television* was still in business.

Eddie was far too smart to make any drastic changes immediately, other than choosing to sing a few bars of "Just Around the Corner" at the beginning and end of each show as a theme song. We had a small musical group by this time, under the direction of the same Roc Hillman who had been so kind to this neophyte back on that first Dick Haynes special. How I loved singing duets with Eddie. *We* thought we were simply smashing in our rendition of "Farewell

With Eddie Albert on Hollywood on Television.

My Tani" and would sing it at the drop of a hat.

Coming from the leisurely pace of movies, Eddie Albert was entering a whole new bailiwick, especially on a marathon such as ours, and he had to get used to the constant time constraints. One of our regular sponsors was Laura Scudder's Potato Chips, which took great pride in the freshness of its product. One day, after getting repeated firm speed-ups from the stage manager, Eddie launched into the potato chip commercial with great urgency, painting a picture of the Scudder trucks *hurtling* through the streets of Los Angeles to bring their chips to you at the peak of their freshness! It picked up the pace all right, and even the Laura Scudder folks enjoyed it enough so that it became part of the commercial from then on. I still have to smile whenever I see a potato chip truck on the street, definitely not hurtling.

Eddie and his wife, Margo, and I became warm friends socially as well as on television. Margo was a fine actress in her own right, both on Broadway and in films. She was unforgettable as the girl who aged before our eyes in *Lost Horizon,* with Ronald Colman and Jane Wyatt.

We would spend long evenings together, into the wee small hours, at their house or mine. Eddie would play his guitar and sing sea chanties, or he and Margo, whose voices blended like velvet, would harmonize on Mexican folk songs. They did their best to teach me to pour wine into my mouth from a goatskin held high, but I never did get the hang of it. I'm sure my dry cleaner appreciated how hard I tried to learn.

The first time I went to the Alberts' home, their Christmas tree was still standing in the living room, which was a little surprising, since it was mid-April. The ornaments couldn't camouflage the fact that the few remaining needles were brown and the branches were sagging, but Margo and Eddie said they just couldn't bear to part with it.

Their son, a brand-new baby at the time, looked so solemn lying in his crib that Eddie dubbed him "The Counselor," a name that stuck. Years later, in 1971, I was doing a series called *The Pet Set* and had invited Eddie to bring his dogs and be my guest. He had accepted, with the proviso that he could also bring his son, who by now was a handsome young man with acting aspirations; this would afford a good chance to get some film footage on him. As it happened, it didn't take The Counselor long to become the successful young film star Edward Albert.

Edward and Eddie Albert. "The Counselor" has grown! (1971)

Eddie stayed with *Hollywood on Television* for six months, and I think he had a good time. I know we did. Then, as happens in this business, an offer came along that understandably he couldn't refuse: to star with Gregory Peck in *Roman Holiday,* which was to be the first American film for a beautiful girl named Audrey Hepburn. Eddie was off to Italy, and who could blame him?

Many years would slip by before Eddie and I worked together again — in 1993, when he did a lovely guest shot with us in an episode of *The Golden Palace.* It was such a strange coincidence that on the first morning we met for rehearsal, the news report came in that Audrey Hepburn had passed away.

Eddie's departure from *H.O.T.* meant that the host's chair was empty once again. This time around, based, no doubt, on longevity and convenience, I inherited the job. By now the show had a life of its own and really only needed someone to steer the ship who knew where the rocks were.

Certainly, I was very flattered, and told myself I could handle it in spite of one slight complication, which had come up shortly after Al left the station. It might just take a bit of doing, that's all. Of course, *not* doing it was out of the question.

Obviously, when Al left it had meant the automatic demise of our Saturday-night show. Too bad, but certainly understandable. A very few weeks had gone by when one ordinary morning a surprising summons came down from that inner sanctum sanctorum, The Front Office. George Tibbles, who was still working on the lot, got the same message — that the station manager, Don Fedderson, would like to have a talk with us; could we please meet him for lunch at the Wilshire Country Club at twelve noon?

Off the lot? George and I were both mystified, but since it came from the man in

Forty years later — Eddie and Betty together again on the set of The Golden Palace, *1993.*

charge, there was no such thing as "could we?" I was at least dressed for camera (we now signed on at 2:00 P.M.), but George was in rehearsal clothes and had to borrow a jacket from someone to go to the beautiful Wilshire Country Club dining room.

This time my memory hasn't let me down. It was one of those special milestone days that is etched in your mind for keeps. There were just the three of us. We sat down to lunch with "Mr. Fedderson." A little over an hour later, "Don," George, and I got up and left the club to go back to work, having formed a three-way partnership that lasted for years and a friendship that lasted for life.

What Don had to say was very uncomplicated. It seems there had been some positive reaction to the Alvin and Elizabeth sketches we had been doing on the night show. Would we be interested in a half hour a week based on those characters, with another actor playing Alvin? Did George feel up to writing it? Could I handle it, along with *Hollywood on Television*?

Yes! Yes! Yes!

We would be equal partners and go from there — the details to be worked out later.

By the wildest stretch of the imagination, can you picture a meeting like that today?

No team of lawyers, agents, managers, representatives, or spouses — just three people saying, "Let's go for it." George and I were not quite as terminally naive as it may sound. It was the man with whom we were dealing who made such an agreement possible. Don Fedderson's reputation for integrity was well known, and we were neither the first, nor were we the last, with whom he settled a preliminary deal on his word alone.

It was thanks to Don that a brilliant young pianist, Liberace, was already on his way to stardom. It was Don who put the *Lawrence Welk Show* on television and kept it there for decades. And Don would be the one to produce Johnny Carson's first network show, *Who Do You Trust?* We were in very good company.

George never got over the fact that he had to borrow a jacket for the most important meeting of his life.

We formed our own little company and called it Bandy Productions. We couldn't very well call it Bandit Productions or it would sound like we stole all our material. So, we were in business, with a new half hour of comedy to do. Piece of cake. But where do you start?

For openers, Don came up with the title, *Life with Elizabeth*. Oddly enough, I had been

CBS President Bob Wood with Betty and her other business partner, Don Fedderson.

christened Betty; my mother wanted to preclude nicknames, but then she proceeded to call me Bets from the beginning. I kind of like nicknames.

We found the perfect Alvin in a young

comic actor, Del Moore, whom George had known from a revue he had done called *Going Around*. Del caught the flavor immediately; he *was* Alvin. Both Alvin and Elizabeth had a tendency to be a little flaky and they may have had almost one good brain between them, but they suited each other just fine. Maybe the reason I felt so comfortable with Delsy right off the bat was that both he and I *were* a little flaky.

For the format, we opted to go for three separate situations, on the premise that when you or your friends tell a funny anecdote about something that happened, the stories last no more than five or six minutes — eight, max. My contention was that if you try to stretch that anecdote into a half hour, the joke wears thin. History has proven just how smart I was — a half-hour situation comedy would *never* work. Never mind the fact that they were springing up all around us. CBS was smart like that in 1984 when they announced flatly and publicly that situation comedy was over — finished — history. That was at the beginning of the same season that saw *The Cosby Show* start on NBC and change the face of television.

In any event, we were happy with our three-situation format. We hired Jack Narz as the announcer and offstage voice, which

George Tibbles, Jack Narz, and "Elizabeth." (Courtesy H. S. "Dusty" Rhoades)

only Elizabeth could hear. Jack would lead into each segment: "Incident number one in life with Elizabeth took place one summer evening when Elizabeth was trying to keep Alvin from noticing her black eye," or whatever the subject may have been. Since the "incidents" were totally unrelated, we could skip around in time, even going back to their first date/first kiss on one occasion.

The opening situation always ended the same way: Alvin, thoroughly confused and exasperated by his wife, would pick up whatever was left of his dignity, say, "I shall leave you at this point, Elizabeth!" and stalk off. Jack's voice, off camera, would cut in with, "Elizabeth! Aren't you ashamed?" whereby

Elizabeth, with a fiendish grin into camera, would shake her head emphatically NO! To this day, strangers occasionally stop me with "Elizabeth! Aren't you ashamed?" and it tickles me. Not so much because of the show, but that at their age they can remember. Anything.

Life with Elizabeth went on the air at 8:30, live every Saturday night from the stage of the Music Hall Theatre in Beverly Hills. We were on locally for the first year, so we didn't have to worry about time zones. After the

We were in business! The Music Hall Theatre is still on Wilshire Boulevard in Beverly Hills. (COURTESY GREEN & TILLISCH PHOTOGRAPHY)

show each week, Del and I would schmooze with the audience and sing a couple of songs. One night George wasn't at the piano — he had just learned that their fourth baby, daughter Chris, had been born. Mil always bragged that it hadn't been easy to arrange for that to happen *during* the show.

Our director was one of the few women directors at the time, Betty Turbiville. She had been assigned to our show, not because of gender, but because she was so good.

Scheduling was a challenge. Because I was doing *H.O.T.* every day, we had to rehearse *Elizabeth* on Friday evening, do run-through after work on Saturday, then shoot the show that night.

George would drive me to rehearsal each week, which gave us a chance to dredge up silly happenings in our own experiences, or in those of others we knew. He would take them home, work his magic, and somehow hand us a script on Friday morning, week after week after week. As a result, Del and I were never too solid on lines. If, as so often happened, either of us got lost, we at least knew the idea of the sketch well enough to bail each other out.

Murphy's Law — it had to happen. One night we both went sky high at the same time, and when we looked into each other's eyes we knew there was nobody home. In this particular incident, we were seated in a restaurant booth. This was a live show, and this was happening in real time, on camera. Something had to be done *now*. Well, Del politely excused himself with something like "I have to powder my nose," got up from the booth, and casually walked offstage where he could run frantically for a look at the script.

Good for him; but I was left out there alone with a trusting audience. I began fiddling with the salt and pepper shakers, making them dance, then started building a wall with the sugar cubes. I got so involved with my mindless little demonstration that I was mildly surprised when, after an eternity, Delsy slid back in beside me, delivering a line that would get us back on track.

Del saved us that time, but there were others when he almost did us in — on purpose. He took a diabolical delight in trying to break me up and never passed up a chance. Whenever the script might call for me to open a box or use a compact or remove a lid from a pot, I could bank on it that somehow he had managed to get there first; there would be something outrageous either written or pasted inside. It would take all I had to stay in character. Finally, the time came on one show when I had to pick up a hand mirror from a dressing table while delivering a line. I could just feel Del's gleeful anticipation, and I steeled myself. I turned the mirror over and — nothing. There was *nothing on it!* Of course, with that, I lost it completely. That monster knew me so well, he got the exact reaction he had counted on.

Del's wife, Gayle, and their two lovely little girls, Laura and Leslie, were also part of our extended family, and we were a very close gang. In spite of publicity layouts with the Moore family, as Elizabeth grew in popularity there were inevitably those who thought Del and I were actually married to each other. The Moores would go for a weekend in Las Vegas once in a while, and Gayle said it always cracked her up, as they were checking in, to see the number of dirty looks she got from people who thought Del was cheating on Betty.

Delsy was a member of Alcoholics Anonymous and had been for a number of years. He and Gayle didn't make a thing about birthdays (except the girls') or their wedding anniversary, but they always celebrated the day of his joining AA. I remember one day on the set when an enormous cake was wheeled in as a surprise to Del from his wife. It was beautifully decorated, and on the top was a miniature water wagon pulled by six pink elephants. It was spectacular.

Launching *Elizabeth* was exciting, but there was still that day job, and I had to pay attention.

I worked with a series of male sidekicks: Wally Imes (his real name was spelled Ijams), a nice man from a station in Arizona; singer David Street; and our erstwhile pitchman, Ted Lenz, this time without his little dog, Gypsy. Ted had a darling baby daughter by

H.O.T. *followed* Mike Roy's Kitchen. *Here is Chef Mike with the White family — Horace, Tess, and Betty.* (COURTESY H. S. "DUSTY" RHOADES)

now, who would grow up to be movie actress Kay Lenz.

Things were busy, to say the least, and details are a bit hazy, but some highlights stand out.

Buster Keaton came back to play with us again. We set up an old-fashioned toy store on one side of the stage, which we told him about, but he didn't get to look at it before the show. During our interview I led him over to the area and left him to improvise. A whole scenario unreeled as he discovered each new toy — all off the top of his head, and without saying a word. Watching him was like taking a course in comedy.

Singer-songwriter-friend Matt Dennis stopped by often. One day he came in and said, "I wrote a song for Frank Sinatra last night — I haven't played it for anybody yet — would you like to hear it?" The song was "Angel Eyes." Frank used it as a sign-off in several of his farewell appearances, before he gave those up and went back to working steadily.

We had a feature we called "Pixie Parade," wherein I would conduct a very serious one-on-one interview with a four-year-old. (Someone on my intellectual level, you say?) We discovered that four was the magic number; any younger they could clam up on you, and any older they could get self-conscious and overly precocious, but at four, you could usually find one subject our little guest would take off on — more than I can say for one or two of my taller visitors. Some of the kids were incredible without being aware of it in the least.

Another feature involved dogs. *Quelle surprise!* The premise was that while a lot of people might recognize a full-grown Afghan, let's say, or a Pekingese, they may never have seen what they looked like as tiny puppies. Flimsy, maybe, but it was my excuse for bringing lots of dogs and puppies on, and according to the mail, it seemed to work.

One day we had a beautiful Saint Bernard mother with her *five-week-old* baby. I fell even harder than usual for this little guy, and it was tough handing him back to the breeders, Marge and Bob Peterson, but it had to be done.

It was two or three weeks later when, in the middle of the show one day, our producer, C. G. "Tiny" Renier, sent the Petersons onto the set to surprise me. They were carrying this same enchanting puppy, this time with not a keg of brandy but a can of Dr. Ross Dog Food tied under his chin with a big red bow. They presented him to me as a gift! Well, of course, the show went to hell

With my new baby, Stormy. (Courtesy H. S. "Dusty" Rhoades)

in a handbasket. I remember holding him up to camera and saying, "Mom?" My mother, not much stronger in this department than her daughter, reported later that she turned to our housekeeper, Claudia Johnson, and said, "What will he do when he grows up?" Dear, wise Claudie said, "He'll walk around like the rest of us!" And perfect Stormy did just that for the next eleven years.

Del Moore went crazy over the puppy, and when he found that Stormy had a litter brother, he had to have him. Stormy was a rough-coated Saint, while his brother — Del named him Wellington — was a smooth coat, and they were a pair to draw to. They were such characters that George wrote them into a *Life with Elizabeth* script, wherein Alvin and Elizabeth surprise each other with — you guessed it — Saint Bernard puppies. A couple of times Storm came on my day show, too, when the part was right. One time we rented enormous oversize furniture, fit for a giant. I was dressed as a little kid and sang "Young at Heart" to this huge, overstuffed live puppy.

Through the years there have been other four-legged gifts offered, and I have to steel myself to resist, in fairness to my resident animal family, but, oh, it's never easy.

We still had no fancy graphics department,

Betty and Del with Stormy and Wellington.

so when phone numbers or addresses were needed, they were printed on cards and set on an easel where the camera could shoot them. If more than one card was needed, you'd see the hand of one of our stage crew pulling the card. Sometimes we would have to remind our card puller to clean his fingernails. The stagehand, working his way through film school, was Sam Peckinpah. Sam went on to become one of the milestone directors in the film industry.

Somewhere during this time I was elected Honorary Mayor of Hollywood! Some red-hot promoter got the idea to hold a charity election, with all the TV performers from all the channels in town as candidates. At ten cents a vote, the public could vote as many times as they wished. I won, but at a dime a throw, it was anything but a free election.

Something I did feel good about was being honored with a star on the Hollywood Walk of Fame. Unlike today, it didn't cost any money in those days; it was just the honor of being selected, and I was delighted to be among the charter members. Today it costs $3,000. Thirty-five years later, when Ralph Edwards ambushed me for *This Is Your Life,* I was in shock for the whole show, but the best of all the wonderful surprises that were lined up that night was their sponsorship of

Honorary Mayor. Lots of luck! (COURTESY H. S. "DUSTY" RHOADES)

a star for my beloved Allen Ludden. A few days later, it was placed right next to mine on Hollywood Boulevard at McCadden, in front of the Pickwick Book Store. Allen would really have been thrilled. Johnny Grant and Bill Welch, who have been with the Walk of Fame since its inception, presided at the actual placement ceremony for Allen's star, just as they had at mine so long ago.

The work schedule was admittedly jammed, with both *H.O.T.* and *Elizabeth,* but as always happens, we eventually settled into something of a routine. Familiarity ironed out the rough edges, and it became almost comfortable. We became aware of the fact that we

Receiving Allen's Walk of Fame star on This Is Your Life. *Left to right: Johnny Grant, Grant Tinker, Ralph Edwards, Valerie*

were not the only Elizabeth, as Elizabeth II was crowned queen of England.

At KLAC-TV, if we thought we had been through changes in '51 and '52, we hadn't seen anything yet. Once again the calm waters began to churn, but this time the wind was a most favorable one.

Harper, BW, Jack Paar, Cloris Leachman, Robert Whitten, Mark Goodson, Ed Asner. (COURTESY RALPH EDWARDS)

8

The killer schedule didn't leave a lot of time for socializing. This suited me fine, for the moment, because it gave me a built-in excuse to avoid most of those inevitable "functions" that even now seem to go with the territory.

"For the moment" meant it was okay for a little while, but before long I began to be aware of someone I kept running into (not literally) almost every day on the lot. He was the television director of several shows at KLAC, though not connected to either *H.O.T.* or *Life with Elizabeth*. We would exchange greetings in passing, or even a silly one-liner or two. One day, to my surprise, he asked if he could take me to dinner some night when he wasn't working, after I got off the air. We finally found a mutually available evening, and I apologized for having to go in my television makeup. We had a wonderful time, discovering how many interests we had in common as well as the number of things that struck us both funny.

The next day I received some beautiful roses with a card that said, "For a lovely girl — with or without makeup." My heart began to come back to life, and before long, our schedules didn't seem nearly so restrictive and we found time to see each other as much as possible.

Ultimately, we didn't ride off into the sunset together, but in the long run, perhaps things turned out even better. After some inevitable rough spots and separations, our love changed character and mellowed into another treasured lifelong friendship. Today, Rudy Behlmer is one of the foremost film historians, and the author of several books — among them *Memo from David O. Selznick, Behind the Scenes: The Making of . . . , Inside Warner Bros., Memo from Darryl F. Zanuck,* and others — most of which are still in print, which is a neat trick in itself. Rudy's wife, Stacey, is also my dear friend and, best of all, I am godmother to Elsa, their golden retriever.

Back in early 1953, it was Rudy who took me to one of those must-do functions. This time I didn't complain about having to go, and I do remember the evening very well. It was a dinner at which the Emmy Awards for the previous year were going to be announced. I had actually been nominated, which made it all seem very glamorous. Zsa Zsa Gabor was also up for her show, *Bachelor's Haven,* and was an odds-on favorite to win. The fact that she was a shoo-in didn't spoil my fun at all. I was thrilled just to be "a contendah."

Dinner over, the awards began. As they got to our category at last, my heart was pounding with the sheer excitement of it all. I remember glancing over and seeing Zsa Zsa retouching her lipstick and powdering her nose as the nominees were announced. She looked gorgeous, of course, and I envied her her poise. As the announcer got to the punch line, "and the winner is . . ." Zsa Zsa set her evening bag down and put her napkin on the table, but she didn't get up. It's hard to say which of us was more surprised to realize it was my name that had been called!

There is no point in trying to be coy about it. Admittedly, it's a first-class ego trip, but having been chosen by one's peers to receive that lovely little statuette is a genuine thrill that never completely goes away. I had to wait twenty-two years for my next one.

On another occasion, somewhere back in that same general era, there was a formal gathering of some sort that Don felt it important to attend, and he arranged for

With Liberace. (COURTESY KLAC)

Liberace to be my escort. Lee was not only talented; he was also a warm, funny, and generous man. I liked him very much, as well as his mother and brother George, so I'm sure we had a delightful evening, even though I can't remember it. What I do recall is something that tickled me even at the time. It was a breezy California evening, and as the car stopped to drop us off, Lee got out first. Oh, where was the Madam when I needed her lessons on getting in and out of a carriage? I was left to climb out the best I could by myself, full skirt, petticoats and all, since Lee was holding his hair in place with both hands.

Bless him, Lee's generosity was legendary and has never stopped. Currently, even though Lee is gone, the Liberace Foundation provides funding to fifty-nine colleges and universities in thirty-three states.

George and I were both happy with the success of *Life with Elizabeth* in the Los Angeles area, and I was thoroughly enjoying the daytime show. Human nature being what it is, however, we both kept dreaming about what it would be like to be seen all over the country. "Going national" was our favorite fantasy. But for Don Fedderson, thinking about something wasn't enough. He went out and made it happen.

Syndication was a viable alternative to network by this time, and Don negotiated a deal with one Reub Kauffman, who headed up Guild Films, to put *Life with Elizabeth* on film and distribute it around the country. It was a straight-out distribution deal — we made the shows, Guild sold them to individual local markets. That same transaction has become bewilderingly complex through the years, what with barter deals and trade-offs and who knows what else, but in those days I almost understood it.

This expansion, wondrous as it was, meant that our cozy Saturday-night live shows in front of an audience were over. We moved into a studio to film our episodes on one camera. Our film director, Duke Goldstone, replaced television director Betty Turbiville, and he would work with the editor to cut the show together and bring it down to the prescribed time for airing.

Thrilled as we were to be (gasp) *national*, doing one-camera comedy is a far cry from performing it live. Each scene is shot in any of several different modes: first the master shot, then whatever is needed for editing — two-shot, over-the-shoulder angles, and close-ups. By the time they get what they want, the poor joke has been beaten to death. With any luck, it will be artificially resuscitated in the editing room. Once our show was put together in a rough-cut form, it was screened to an invited audience in a viewing room so that we could get a genuine laugh track to lay in under the film.

During the actual shooting, since there

Alvin and Elizabeth went into syndication — on film. (Courtesy KLAC)

was no audience, we would *try* very hard to leave room for the laugh that would, we hoped, accompany the joke. It was a little like doing comedy in a mortuary, and it threw our timing all off. Later, attending the audience screening, we would squirm to hear the people laugh in unexpected places and watch ourselves plow right on through without waiting, so that the punch line was drowned in the laugh.

Sometimes it was Delsy's weird sense of humor that helped make it bearable. During the filming he would do silly secret

146

things — switching his ring from one hand to the other, for instance — so that when we watched the film only he and I would notice the ring jump magically from one hand to the other. It was so unobtrusive that the director never got wise and the audience was unaware, but Del would be in quiet hysterics. It didn't take much with Del.

We filmed our first show September 25, 1953.

Although *we* didn't enjoy it as much, somehow it caught on; we were on all over the country, and twice every week in New York City, on the DuMont network. All in all, we wound up doing sixty-five half hours, which went into reruns several times over. That meant there were a hundred and ninety-five incidents. The show was eventually broken up and each incident was run separately, which, with commercials, wound up as a fifteen-minute show. These were played on the air as a five-a-week daytime strip. Even after the show finally faded away in this country, it ran for a long time in Australia, and I always had visions of Elizabeth winding up in the outback, still grinning and shaking her head but playing only to kangaroos.

I certainly can't complain — those filmed shows held us in very good stead, while all those happy live shows, of course, are gone without a trace.

I didn't have much time to worry about how much harder it was to do the show on film, for Don had yet another surprise up his sleeve.

Once again, a meeting was called, and it was Don's turn to break the news to us that he was leaving KLAC and taking Fred Henry, his assistant general manager and director of programs, with him to start his own production company. Before we could go into shock, he quickly went on to say that he wanted to take us with him! Bandy Productions would keep its identity, separate from Don Fedderson Productions, and would continue to include any other projects he, George, and I would do together in the future.

There were no soul-searching decisions to be made — *Elizabeth* would continue as usual; we brought *H.O.T.* to a timely close. The necessary loose ends were tied up. We were all moving on.

In short order, Don was in business. He set up a meeting with NBC, regarding my doing a daytime show for them. One of the first questions they asked was if I thought I could bear up under the strain of doing a half-hour show every day, five days a week. Well, after doing five and a half hours, *six* days a week, for four years, I wondered secretly what we would do with all that extra free time. The additional evening commitment with *Life with Elizabeth* didn't seem to cause any concern whatsoever, so the deal was made.

If ignorance is bliss, we were about as blissful as you can get. And it came to pass: *The Betty White Show* (the second BW show so far) would begin on the NBC network in January 1954. Live.

"Live," by now, meant that the rest of the country would see the show at the same time we performed it. However, with the time zone differences, the Pacific Coast would still have to be content with grainy kinescopes, since our show would be held to air in Los Angeles at twelve noon, the same as in New York.

Not to worry. We were (gasp) going *network!*

At last! We were going (gasp) network! (NBCU Photo Bank)

9

We were excited. We were scared. We were *busy* — once again putting a new show together from scratch.

This time, while the program would be five hours shorter every day than the one I had been doing, somehow it seemed more difficult. Some of that was due to the psychological tension of knowing we were jumping out of our cozy little local pond into deep water; in spite of all our best efforts, the realization was there. But also everything was so much more complicated, with so many more people involved. No longer could we just go out and do something: it called for a meeting. Of course, what seemed complex at that time was not even in the same league with preproduction today, which is comparable to planning World War III.

There were physical differences to get used to — everything was so much *bigger*. We were to do our first couple of weeks of shows from the old NBC studios at the corner of Sunset and Vine in Hollywood, and then move to the just-completed, paint-still-wet NBC facility in Burbank. It was gorgeous, and state-of-the-art then. Today, after so much expansion and building over the ensuing years, to me it is still the loveliest workplace of them all.

We were given Studio 1, which is right across the hall from where the *Tonight Show* still tapes, as we speak.

This was all very heady wine. I had a carpeted dressing room, my name on the door, and my own *bathroom* — with a shower! There was a makeup person, but also a *hair* person — and even a wardrobe lady to take care of my clothes! Surely, I had died and gone to heaven!

As usually happens, Don and George and I had been all caught up in the business and planning stages of our project, so, once all the loose ends were tied up, it came as something of a shock to realize that now we were actually going to have to *do* what we had just signed up to do. It was the moment of truth that comes with any venture, whether it's designing a television show, writing a book, or planning a wedding.

Okay. With four years of *H.O.T.* under the belt, we all decided that the best approach was to forget we were talking to so many more people all over the country, and to just relax and do the show.

Sure.

We had an audience in the studio for the broadcasts and I would talk to them before we went on the air or during commercials, but the show itself was played only to the viewer at home. I didn't want to lose the feeling of intimacy, which is the thing I love about this medium. *H.O.T.* had served as an invaluable grounding for dealing with the home audience: learning to think of the viewers as individuals, rather than a mass. The fact is, on TV you are playing to only one or two people at a time. If there are more than three in a room, they are talking to each other, not listening to you. Speaking to the camera lens becomes like having a one-on-one conversation, and sometimes, I swear, I can hear it talk back.

The format of the show was very simple: (Never *mind!*)

We would invite celebrity guests for brief interviews and try to find what interests they might have beyond their work. Sometimes this was easier said than done, depending on how outgoing the celebrity might be. In those days, there was no talent coordinator to do a preinterview and make up a list of questions for the host to ask. I would just get a short bio of each guest before the show and would wing it from there. Deliberately, I would wait to greet them until we were on the air because too often, out of enthusiasm or nervousness or both, a guest will tell you everything he or she has to say out in the hall. By the time you get to the actual interview, the bloom is off the rose. On some of today's predigested shows I can't help suspecting that many of the best interviews take place over the preinterviewer's telephone.

Some guests are just naturally more talkative than others, and once in a while I might have to try more than one opening gambit to get them rolling, but sooner or later they would open up. On only one occasion do I remember striking out completely, and that was with Guy Madison, a handsome young star, primarily in westerns. He must have been the prototype for "strong, silent," for he made our shyest guest seem positively loquacious by contrast. No matter *what* I tried, I would get first a long pause, then, if I was lucky, a "Nope" or a "Yup," and sometimes just a stare. I thought he was putting me on at first, but soon realized what I saw was what I was going to get, and desperation finally set in. That was a lot of years ago, but it still may hold the record for the longest five minutes I have ever lived through on camera.

Music was a big part of the show, and we were thrilled beyond words when Frank De Vol agreed to come aboard and put together our Little Band. Frank, one of the best music men in the business, had worked with all the top female singers of the day. It was intimidating, yes, but oh, such a pleasure. He and I had a running gag: Anytime the occasion arose for Frank to send me a note or a wire or a card or a memo, anything, it always started with "Dear Betty, not Dinah [Shore], not Doris [Day], not Margaret [Whiting], not Patti [Page], but Dear *Betty*" — then he'd finally get around to the message.

Frank put together a terrific group, musically *and* personally speaking: our old friend Roc Hillman on guitar; Cliff Whitcomb, piano; Dick Cathcart, trumpet; Bill Hamilton, saxophone and vocals; Eddie Robinson, bass and vocals; and Jerry Kaplan, you name the instrument, he played it. All under the great and funny leadership of Frank himself.

As fine and famous a music man as Frank is, he would pack it all in, I'm sure, for the chance to do comedy. Every once in a while, without tipping him off, I would call him away from the band to come join me, and we would talk a little before leading into a commercial. He had the face of a basset hound with the blues, and played everything dead straight, without a smile, so almost anything he said came out funny. He also had a library of toupees, and would change them without warning, depending on what mood he happened to be in that day. I never knew whether he would show up with wavy or straight hair, or a crew cut, or sometimes even au naturel — no rug at all. He was a priceless asset, as a member of the cast and as a friend. We also used him on *Life with Elizabeth* from time to time.

Arthur Duncan, the wonderful black song-and-dance man, had guested several times on *Hollywood on Television,* but on the new show he became a regular member of our little troupe. He did a number almost every day, and he could always count on knocking me out when he did "Jump Through the Ring." He also did *The Lawrence Welk Show* regularly.

It came as a frightfully ugly surprise, one day, when a few of the stations that carried our show through the South notified us that they would, "with deep regret, find it most difficult to broadcast the program unless

Cast of The Betty White Show *(II). Back row: Roc Hillman, Eddie Robinson, Dick Cathcart, Bill Hamilton, Jerry Kaplan. Front row: Cliff Whitcomb, Betty, Frank De Vol, Del Sharbutt (our announcer), and Arthur Duncan. Circa 1954.* (NBCU PHOTO BANK)

Mr. Arthur Duncan was removed from the cast." I was shocked, and it goes without saying that Arthur continued to perform on our show as often as possible. To its credit, the network backed us up. I was livid — this was *1954,* for heaven's sake! I wanted to tell them what to do with their stations, but wiser heads prevailed. To no one's surprise, that was the last we ever heard of the matter. They continued to carry us without another word on the subject.

Every day I would sing a couple of songs,

and also open and close the half hour with our theme song, written for us by George, the Multitalented:

It's time to say "Hello" again
And start our show again
And sing a song or two for
　all of you.

We'd do sixteen bars for openers, then at the sign-off it was:

It's time to say "Goodbye" again
Till we say "Hi" again
So-o-o long.

Maybe not a standard, but it got our adrenaline going.

On certain days we had regular features. What had been Pixie Parade on *H.O.T.* evolved into Wish Day. This time, however, it was more than a straight interview with a child. We worked with various organizations for underprivileged or orphaned children, and they would select a little one to be on our show. Much unobtrusive research went into those spots, and by the time a child came to visit we already knew a lot about what he or she was most interested in, the favorite pastime, favorite food, favorite celebrity, and biggest wish. We did our very best to fulfill as many of their hearts' desires as we could, even surprising them with their celebrity whenever possible. There were times, of course, when their biggest wish was beyond our power, and that was hard. Today, the Make-A-Wish and Starlight Foundations do a wonderful job of fulfilling dreams on a grand scale. Childhelp, another organization that continues to expand its reach to work wonders for abused children, wasn't around in 1954. It was founded years later by two dedicated ladies, Sara Meara and Yvonne Lime Fedderson — Don's wife.

Are you surprised that we also included animal features as often as I could come up with an excuse? One day we had a five-year-old on the show, but this time it wasn't a child — it was an endearing baby elephant I had fallen in love with when she appeared in *Life with Elizabeth*. While she was very young for an elephant, she was very *big* for a baby. I could just manage to put my arm over her back if I stood on tiptoe and she stooped a little. She charmed everyone. Her keeper told me he was thinking of selling her, and suddenly I had an inspiration! Wouldn't it be great if NBC had its own elephant? They could build special quarters for her on the back lot, and whenever they needed an elephant they would have one of their very own. It would also be a comfortable, safe home for the little/big girl, and sensational publicity for NBC — forget the peacock!

Even I can't believe this as I write it, but I actually went to John West, a very important NBC executive at that time, and tried to sell him on the idea! He should have called for the wagon immediately, but instead, John explained as gently as he could that he, too, loved elephants, but purchasing one didn't quite fit into the network's game plan, somehow.

It is an absolute fact that I should *not* be allowed out without a keeper of my own.

Yes, we were still doing *Life with Elizabeth*. Every week, after I got through work, I would leave Burbank around two in the afternoon and go over the hill to Filmcraft, a small studio on Melrose at La Cienega, where we would film *Elizabeth*. We'd rehearse one night and film the next, working on into the wee small hours. More than once we'd finish just in time for me to go back to NBC, shower, and get into makeup for the day show.

I was living at home with my folks in Brentwood. I was one of what are called boomerang kids today. After my marriage to Lane ended, Little Nell had come home again, this time with her four-legged baby, Bandy, in tow. By now Stormy had joined the family, and there was Dancer, my folks' little gray poodle. I knew a haven when I found one.

There was no freeway yet between Brentwood and Burbank, so it was a forty-five-minute drive to the studio. My makeup call was for 6:00 A.M., which was followed by a music rehearsal. I had to get up around 4:00 or 4:15 every morning to make it. My dad moved his alarm up a little from his usual early call and my mother would get up and fix breakfast, no matter how hard I tried to talk them both out of it. We'd eat together and Mom would see her two working stiffs off to the wars; then she and the dogs would race each other back to bed.

It always amazed me to see how many cars were on the road at that ungodly hour. Where were they all *going?* They couldn't all be doing television shows.

The typical day would start in the makeup room, with our two makeup men, Bill Morley and Paul Stanhope. No, it didn't take two of them to pull me together — at least not back then — but there were others in the cast! Bill was always there when I arrived, but sometimes 6:00 A.M. came a little early for Paul. Bill had a list of Paul's girlfriends' numbers, and he would start calling around until he got the answer he was seeking. "Paul? Oh, yes, he's on his way — he just left." He had always "just left." One morning, Bill got the same answer on two of the calls. Paul was a piece of work, but he was worth it for the laughs.

We'd go into the studio and do a run-through for camera moves, do the musical numbers one more time, and 9:00 A.M. would arrive before we knew it. Showtime! When we got off the air, we'd set the songs for tomorrow's show, then release the band and go into a meeting to plan for next week. At 12:00 we'd watch the show we had just done as it aired for the West Coast. A bite of lunch, another meeting or so, and it was usually out by around 2:00 P.M. I was having a *good* time.

The cliché excuse in those days for anyone who still didn't own a television set was "I'm waiting till color comes in." Color television had been the dream for quite some time — talked about, but not realized. At last, the first compatible color had been demonstrated the previous October in New York. By the spring of 1954 the dream seemed to be getting closer when one day at NBC we all received an invitation to attend an in-house demonstration of color television right on the lot in Burbank. And I must say, it was mind-boggling.

It began in the regular black-and-white mode we were accustomed to, and was a picture of bacon and eggs sizzling in a pan. Suddenly, it switched to color before our eyes, and the gasp that went up could be heard all over Burbank. The demo went on to show other examples, and we were all duly impressed. The fact that the studio engineers had the color adjusted to perfection didn't do any harm either, but, of course, they should have, since the color equipment was made exclusively by RCA, parent company to NBC. As excited as everyone was as they filed out for lunch (probably bacon and eggs), we would still have to wait awhile before color came in to stay. It wasn't until the late 1960s that NBC finally went all color, and then it was primarily so that RCA could sell a new generation of television sets.

Commercials had become a very lucrative sideline by now and were using quote celebrities unquote to pitch many of their products. I was always delighted when one came my way. Sometime that same year, I was approached to do something unheard of — I was offered a lot of money to do a TV commercial for Kotex sanitary napkins. They were going to test the idea to see if the public would accept it, and, according to them, they wanted to do it in a low-key, dignified fashion. I explained, as politely as I could, that there wasn't enough money in the world for me to do any such thing. Would you say times have changed somewhat since then? For TV, yes. For me, no. But it's all somewhat academic by now.

The Betty White Show was doing excellently in the ratings department and in spite of the early call, we were having the time of our lives. Oops — can't have that!

On NBC, every afternoon at 3:00, *The Kate Smith Hour* was broadcast, and the show's ratings had begun to slip noticeably. The time was ripe for the network to make one of those corporate decisions that can make grown men cry. Why not shake up the whole afternoon schedule, and then move their successful noon show up to 4:30? That should plug the leak. Never mind the fact that we had become something of a habit at the noon hour. Never mind that people had grown accustomed to having their lunch with us. Habit and the time slot were on our side at 12:00, but by 4:30 our audience had

164

other fish to fry; now we must start from ground zero and try to rebuild. In any event, we couldn't talk them out of moving us, and, predictably, we didn't work any better at 4:30 than Kate had been doing at 3:00.

Things haven't changed. The networks are all still playing their programs like chessmen, and many a successful program has been moved only to go down in flames. I'm sure it is a necessary evil from the network's standpoint, and once in a while it works or they wouldn't keep doing it. As I write this, the networks, ABC, CBS, NBC, and FOX, are all in the process of announcing their fall schedules, and they keep changing every twenty minutes as they attempt to outmaneuver each other. The screams of producers mark the autumn season as surely as the honking of migrating geese.

It didn't take too long for them to realize that the decision to move us might have been a bit hasty, so NBC shifted us back again. Oh — not to our old noon slot, but to 12:30. Close but no cigar. Now the audience was thoroughly confused, and so were we.

Toward the end of the year we could see the handwriting on the wall. Don and his right arm, Fred Henry, and I made a hasty trip to New York to meet with the powers that be and try to salvage the situation, but it was too late. Tennessee Ernie Ford would replace us after our last telecast on December 31.

It was my first trip to New York, and our bleak two days served as anything but an auspicious introduction to the city. I was convinced it was the end of the world for me. I would not only never work again, but any joy in life was over forever. It was my first brush with the classic showbiz rejection syndrome. It was certainly not my last.

At least we came out even — we were on for exactly one year, and we had had a marvelous time in the process. When the final show rolled around on New Year's Eve, I can remember fighting my way through that damned closing theme —

Till we say "Hi" again
So-o-o long.

It wasn't really a Greek tragedy. I only thought it was.

10

There wasn't time to indulge in feeling sorry for myself, since I had to be at work next morning bright and early. Early, anyway.

It was New Year's Day, and Bill Goodwin and I had been invited to do the Tournament of Roses Parade. The arrangements had been made weeks before, and I had been delighted, thinking what wonderful promotion it would be for our show. Now I was left with a parade but no show to promote. Hey! This was showbiz!

The Rose Parade actually takes place in Pasadena, down Colorado Boulevard, each New Year's morning as it has for the past ninety-some years, but that first broadcast we did from Burbank. A small set had been decorated with fresh flowers; Bill and I were seated next to each other, facing a couple of television monitors. We talked about what we saw on camera and added what extra information had been provided, which wasn't much. Our instructions had been bare bones — "Pretend you are actually there at the parade, describe what you see, and don't talk over each other." (The viewers could almost do that for themselves, couldn't they?)

One minor highlight that morning still stands out vividly in my memory. To get prepared for the telecast, we had to be at the studio before dawn. Paul Stanhope, my aforementioned friend from the late, lamented *Betty White Show,* had been assigned to do our makeup, and we have already discussed how Paul reacted to very early calls on occasion. However, on this particular morning he was bright-eyed and bushy-tailed — and just a trifle giggly. He had come to work directly from a New Year's Eve party where, evidently, he had had a *very* good time. I was a little gun-shy when he began to put on my eyeliner with a hand that could have been steadier, but we made it through all right.

Now, the parade lasts about three hours, so Paul had to stand by to powder us down from time to time or to refurbish lipstick. We had seen him become less and less exuberant as the morning wore on, until he had faded into silence. On the next commercial break, he climbed over the cables and around the cameras, powder puff in hand, to do a touch-up, but this time, as he raised his powder puff — *Timber-r-r* — he slowly collapsed at our feet, passed out cold. From that day on, poor Paul took such a ribbing; the story followed him through the years, probably with embellishments, but he accepted it with his usual good nature and sheepish grin.

There was no way of knowing at the time, but that 1955 parade would be the first of many in my future. As it turned out, I would spend every New Year's morning in Pasadena for the next twenty years — nineteen for NBC, and my last one for CBS; plus six Grand Floral Parades in Portland, Oregon,

With Roy Neal at the Pasadena Tournament of Roses. (NBCU PHOTO BANK)

and ten Macy's Thanksgiving Day Parades in New York. It got so that if I saw a line of cars waiting for a signal, I had to fight the urge to do a commentary.

The following year, after that first morning in Burbank, Roy Neal, a broadcaster for the space program, and I teamed up for the Rose Parade, and this time we actually went to Pasadena. Our NBC broadcast location was perched high atop the roof of the Elks Club building on Colorado Boulevard, and just getting up the ladder to it was a stunt in itself. To complicate matters, I can't remember ever being that cold in my life. We soon thawed out as the morning progressed, but when we first signed on our teeth literally were chattering.

The spectacular parade was going by below us, but we had to be careful to comment only on what was on camera, so that we wouldn't be talking about things the audience at home couldn't see. All hell could be breaking loose down on the street, but if it wasn't on camera, we must not mention it. We could have stayed in Burbank.

Roy and I worked together for several years, then there were other cohosts. After a couple of years they brought us down one floor from the roof to set us up on a balcony overlooking the street, and I can't say I was sorry to forgo the ladder act. Eventually, we moved to a small flower-decked room at the back of the Elks Club, away from the street altogether, and we worked from monitors sunk in the desk in front of us. It was warmer and quieter, but not nearly as exciting.

Just up the block from our location was the CBS setup, where for several years their commentator was Ronald Reagan. Bob Barker took over when Ronald went into another line of work.

We spent more and more time on preparation for the telecast each year. During the week after Christmas, we'd go out to the various locations where the floats were being constructed and watch them grow from their bare framework, until, on the morning of New Year's Eve, an army of high school students moved in to perform the gigantic job of pasting on the flowers, petal by petal, and the seeds and the ferns and whatever other growing things it took to make the magic happen. We'd talk to the various float builders and to the kids, and garner some personal stories, which gave us something to say beyond "Gee, three thousand chrysanthemums!"

One year, Arthur Godfrey came out from New York to cohost with me, and he made it abundantly clear that he would not do anything beforehand. "I've done a hundred parades — they're all alike. I'll show up New Year's morning and not before."

Well, the telecast was an adventure that year, to put it mildly. Evidently Mr. Godfrey hadn't expected the parade to be quite as huge as it is each year, for as soon as we signed on he started shaking his head and saying, "Jeez! Look at this thing! Jeez!"

He soon became fascinated with some kids who had climbed the trees across the street for a better vantage point.

"Jeez! Look at those kids up in those trees. What kind of trees are those?"

Unfortunately, the cameras were focused where they belonged — on the parade, which was moving on apace. Our standard broadcast equipment was a little earphone we wore in one ear so that the director could speak to us from the control truck — or, in this case, so he could *scream* at us, and with good reason. My heart sank when I looked over and saw that Arthur was holding his earpiece in his hand and ignoring the frantic stage manager as if the poor guy were invisible.

It was all downhill from there. The real low point came when a float came along carrying the University of Illinois football team, who would be playing in the Rose Bowl later that afternoon. The Illini (Ill-eye-nigh), as they were known, were touted as the hottest team in the country at the moment, and Arthur took off, describing, in great detail, the float carrying the "Illeeny." I tried to be subtle about correcting his pronunciation, but I must have overdone the subtlety, for Arthur continued to go on and on about "the Illeeny" this and "the Illeeny" that. The Illinois fans, who were legion, took a very dim view; the switchboard blew up and the mail poured in for days.

John Forsythe joined us for the next couple of years and was his usual delightful, classy self. One year there was busy Bill Cullen. Then came Lorne Greene, *Bonanza*'s Pa Cartwright, for several Rose Parades as well as those ten Macy's Parades every Thanksgiving. We felt like we were going steady. Michael Landon, Pa Cartwright's "son," Little Joe, followed in his "father's" footsteps for one year, and what can one say about Mike? He was simply one of the very special people who are so rare. He celebrated the positives in life without either being sanctimonious or feeling an apology was necessary for doing so.

We went from *Bonanza* to *Perry Mason* when Raymond Burr came aboard for two or three years, and he was a joy for both his

With Bill Cullen at the Rose Parade. (NBCU PHOTO BANK)

erudition and his sense of humor. Finally, I went over to CBS for my twentieth and last Tournament of Roses, with Bob Barker. I figured it was a nice round number and a good time to pack it in.

■ ■ ■ ■

With no daytime show to do following the cancellation of *The Betty White Show,* I was somewhat at loose ends. Come spring, when we received an Emmy nomination for it, the reaction was bittersweet. Of course, that was long before I'd learned how often that happens.

After years of tight schedules and hours at the studio, just doing guest shots and game shows didn't seem quite like an honest day's labor — all dessert and no entrée. Consequently, when Don and George began talking about putting together another series, I found myself becoming more and more interested.

At that point, half-hour situation comedies abounded, just as they do today. Some were more successful than others, but they were all quite similar in format, and the woods were full of them. In no chronological order, I remember there was *I Love Lucy,* naturally, with Lucy and Desi; *Ozzie and Harriet,* with the Nelson family, including Ricky and David; *My Favorite Husband,* with Joan Caulfield and Barry Nelson; *The Stu Erwin Show,* with Stu (Sr.) and wife, June Collyer; *I Married Joan,* with Joan Davis and Jim Backus; *The Life of Riley,* with William Ben-

Lorne Greene and I went steady for ten years at the Macy's Thanksgiving Day Parade in New York. Circa sixty-something.
(NBCU Photo Bank)

dix; *The Donna Reed Show; My Little Margie,* with Gale Storm and Charles Farrell; *Father Knows Best,* with Robert Young and Jane Wyatt; *Meet Millie,* with Elena Verdugo; *Private Secretary,* with Ann Sothern; *Our Miss*

Brooks, with Eve Arden — the list is endless, and I've probably missed twice that many. But — nothing ventured, et cetera — we made the decision to leap into the crowded pool.

There was an Elmer Rice play, *Dream Girl,* that had run on Broadway, which I felt could be great fun to play on a weekly basis. It was something of a distaff version of *The Secret Life of Walter Mitty,* wherein the leading lady would encounter a situation in which she didn't come off too well, so she would replay it in her imagination the way she would have liked it to happen. We finally obtained permission to use a similar premise by paying a royalty of $1,000 a week. We began to put our show together.

First of all, who were we? After much discussion, we decided to make our protagonists a young couple who had been married only a very few months and were virtually still honeymooners. While we were playing God, we also gave him a job in the insurance business, and she was — his wife.

Bandleader Skinnay Ennis and his orchestra had had a big record much earlier, "Got a Date with an Angel," and we thought it would be fun to give our characters the last name of Angel, and call our show *Date with the Angels.* (We may have been suffering from a sudden attack of adorableness.) This time we only had to pay a royalty for the use of the song as a theme.

We christened Mr. and Mrs. Angel Gus and Vickie, gave them a house to live in, another couple as best friends, a weird father and son as next-door neighbors, and a rich boss — pretty much formula, but current and choice.

We were now faced with a very painful decision. With George writing the new show, Don producing, and me playing the lead, we had to be ultra careful that it didn't look like a warmed-over version of *Life with Elizabeth*. So we bit the bullet and reluctantly decided to cast someone other than Del Moore as Gus Angel. We proceeded to interview an endless number of eligible young actors, but Del was a tough act to follow, so we kept looking.

Finding an announcer was a snap, as there was one ready-made right under our noses. Jack Narz had a younger brother, Jim, who was just starting out in the business and had worked on a few local shows. He would be a change from *Life with Elizabeth,* but it would still feel like family.

After office readings with what must have been every young actor in town, we finally signed Bill Williams, who had had his own western series, playing Kit Carson. Making a major casting decision is really tough, and you have to depend somewhat on blind faith. It's much like entering into a real-life marriage, but without some of the good stuff.

As I mentioned in the beginning of this opus, we hired two additional writers, one of whom was my guardian angel, Fran Van Hartesveldt, who had given me my very first job. The script for the pilot was coming along under George's fine Italian hand, and there were many more meetings.

Don was off doing what Don did best — selling. He came back to us with the news that he had hit a home run. The Plymouth Division of the Chrysler Corporation had put together a million-dollar deal for a firm year, with options thereafter, which was unheard of in television in those days. Plus the fact that we would air on the ABC network! Prime time, at last!

Plymouth was just introducing their breakthrough redesign for the new 1957 model and wanted to go all out to promote their really beautiful new baby. The slogan for the campaign was "Suddenly, it's 1960!" (Unfortunately, three years later, when 1960 *did* roll around, the 'sixty-model cars had lost something in the translation and weren't quite as innovative or attractive. Comics had a field day with "Suddenly, it's 1957!")

Part of our new deal was that they wanted me driving their product, naturally, so they gave me one of the beautiful 1957 Plymouths, tail fins and all, which meant I had to part with my beloved turquoise-and-white '55 Olds convertible, "Gorgeous." Somehow I get emotionally involved with my cars and it's hard to let go, but Gorgeous didn't stray far; Rudy Behlmer bought it and gave it a good home.

One thing I loved from the word "go" about the show we were building was that we would be using the new three-camera system. This meant shooting the show straight through, like a play, stopping only to change wardrobe; it was edited together later. This also meant we could play to a live audience in the studio to help us with our timing. In other words, the way most of today's sitcoms are done, only now they use four cameras — sometimes more.

Contrary to general belief (including mine until recently), Lucille Ball did not invent the three-camera system. In the 1947–1948 season, Jerry Fairbanks of the NBC film department had done a show called *Public Prosecutor,* and used three sixteen-millimeter Multicams. As I understand it, he introduced Ralph Edwards to the three-camera technique for Ralph's pilot of *Truth or Consequences* in 1950. *I Love Lucy* was the first *comedy* series shot that way. Whatever — I was just grateful that *somebody* had invented it, because it sure helped put the pleasure back into the funny business. At least for me.

Our pilot episode of *Date with the Angels,* which became our first show, turned out well, and we had a ball doing it. The premise was that Gus comes home from the office bearing great news. The Angels have been invited to a *very* fancy party at the home of his boss. Vickie is a bundle of nerves, isn't sure about the dress she bought or what she will say, borrows a miserable little fur piece from her mother-in-law (this was before the age of enlightenment about wearing fur), and off they go, with Gus hanging on tight to keep her from jumping ship.

The boss's house is a mansion, filled with beautiful people, beautifully dressed. A butler looks down his nose and directs Vickie up the wide, curving stairway to leave her "uh — wrap." Upstairs, Vickie lays the poor little dead thing on the bed, next to a sea of fur coats. As she turns to leave, two women enter and, in passing, point to it and laugh. "Remember those?"

Back downstairs, Vickie sees no sign of

Gus, who has been drawn away into a business conversation with his boss. After a couple of unfortunate encounters, Vickie finds an empty chair, out of sight behind some palms, and it is here that her imagination kicks in:

We see the same scene replayed, this time in Vickie's mind. Once again, the butler opens the door, and now Vickie sweeps in, with Gus trailing along behind. She is dressed in a to-die-for flowing chiffon gown, with a sable coat casually draped over her shoulders. There is sudden silence as all heads turn, then everyone clamors to greet this vision. Bidding Gus to wait "there!" she ascends the stairway, nonchalantly dragging the sable in her wake. Gus is almost lost among the crowd awaiting her return, but he stays where he was told. Vickie's reentrance at the top of the stairs prompts the pianist to launch into "her music," and she, of course, *must* favor them with a song as she floats down the stairway. Gus can't begin to get near her, and he himself falls victim to some getting-even misadventures his wife has dreamed up for him. Eventually, we snap back into the real world in time for the situation to be happily resolved — hardly a switch ending.

The only reason I bother to go into such

detail about this ancient history is that not having thought about it in a long time I was struck with how the exact same show would be perceived in today's climate — what a classic feminist statement of empowerment! In truth, all we were doing at the time was trying to be entertaining, with no hidden agenda whatsoever. Can you just see trying to convince some future student of television of that, as he or she is busy reinterpreting our motives according to current experience?

It would be like the story that director William Castle used to tell about an address he made to a group of film students. One young man brought up the creative special effects in the film *Strait-Jacket,* starring Joan Crawford, a movie Mr. Castle had directed. The student cited Crawford's spectacular first entrance in the movie, walking down the steps of a train. Suddenly, a burst of steam from the train rises up around her, enhancing the strangeness of the moment.

"How did you ever *think* of that, Mr. Castle?"

"I didn't. It was late in the day when the train let go, and we didn't have the time or the money to reshoot the damned thing."

Same with us. We had never heard of feminism or empowerment. Vickie was simply reacting as any red-blooded American wife would in the given circumstances.

Much as we enjoyed the concept of the dream sequences, Plymouth did not share our enthusiasm. Making the sweeping generalization that "fantasy never works with an audience," they gradually leaned on us to phase out the imagination segments in favor of at-home situations. (Ironically, it wouldn't be too long before Ray Walston would be charming us as *My Favorite Martian;* Julie Newmar would play a beautiful robot in *My Living Doll;* and on the dramatic side, Rod Serling would capture everyone's imagination with his timeless *Twilight Zone*. As they say, timing is everything.)

Without our dream sequences, our show flattened out and became just one more run-of-the-mill domestic comedy, but without Del Moore's impeccable comedic timing. Bill Williams was a lovely man, but he simply didn't think "funny." He also had no patience with, nor understanding of, either network or sponsor diplomacy. For some unknown reason, he considered them the enemy, even though they were paying the bills — and Bill's! This led to some awkward moments, as you can imagine.

I think I can honestly say that that was the only time I have ever wanted to get out of a show. We were plugging along and surviving — barely — but there was no longer any different spin on it, and as a result the fun was gone.

We still had thirteen weeks to go on our firm year's contract when we opted to do some major surgery on the remaining shows. We changed the format completely, and bid an amicable farewell to Vickie and Gus Angel and their friends and neighbors; we returned to the three-episode concept, which we still owned. The title had to go as well, so for the next thirteen weeks we were known as — guess! *The Betty White Show*! (Number three.)

Surprisingly, the parting of our professional ways was understood by all concerned and didn't affect our off-camera relationships. Bill and his wife, Barbara Hale, remained our good friends. Barbara you know not only from her early film career but from her years on TV with Raymond Burr, as *Perry Mason*'s secretary and right arm, Della Street. Their son now has a fine career of his own — as William Katt, which was Bill's real name also. Richard Deacon, who played one of the Angels' weird neighbors, continued to be a close and funny buddy. He went on to become Dick's boss on the classic *Dick Van Dyke Show* with Mary Tyler Moore.

The first thing we did, which should come

Del and Betty reunited on ABC. (© AMERICAN BROADCASTING COMPANIES, INC.)

as no surprise, was to bring Del Moore back into the fold. We put together a little stock company of semiregulars, including Reta Shaw, Frank De Vol, and Irene Ryan (the original Granny on *The Beverly Hillbillies*), and added two additional part-time writers — Seaman Jacobs and Sy Rose.

We had been filming on the Desilu lot in Hollywood, and we loved the atmosphere of that place. Lucy and Desi were doing their show just a couple of soundstages away, Eve Arden was being *Our Miss Brooks* across the street, and Hugh O'Brian, who had guested with us in the old *Life with Elizabeth* days, was shooting *Wyatt Earp* next door. With our change in format and the variety of sets it involved, we had to move down to the main ABC studios, farther downtown at Prospect and Talmadge. We were sorry to leave the Desilu lot. It would have been nice to have known that I'd be back there some-day, spending eight delightful years with *The Golden Girls* and *Golden Palace*.

This time around, the three episodes were unrelated, each being a sketch of its own with different characters. We reached out for some great guest stars to come and be silly with us. It's hard to imagine Boris Karloff or Basil Rathbone or Charles Coburn in such a setting, but they were wonderful and entered into our nonsense wholeheartedly, as did the rest — Buster Keaton, Jack Carson, Cornel Wilde, Sterling Holloway, Reginald Gardiner, Keenan Wynn, Billy DeWolfe, Marc Platt, Paul Dubov — what charmers.

If a character in a sketch worked, George and the boys would bring it back from time to time. One of those who turned up in several shows was Olga, a character I loved to play. Olga was a cleaning lady who worked late at night in office buildings. She wore a mob cap, a brown sweater full of holes, held together with a safety pin, a raggedy skirt, and army shoes. Plus, of course, her mop and bucket. We had great fun with her because,

After Date with the Angels *it's back to* The Betty White Show *(III). Reginald Gardiner, Irene Ryan, herself, Reta Shaw.* (© AMERICAN BROADCASTING COMPANIES, INC.)

With dear, gentle Boris Karloff (Betty is "acting"!). (© AMERICAN BROADCASTING COMPANIES, INC.)

while she was not right bright, she had an uncanny ear for the truth. One of our viewers sent me an Olga doll she had made by hand, complete to the last detail — pinned crooked sweater and all. Needless to say, I still have her. Several years later, I got a big kick out of it when Carol Burnett brought us her Mop Lady. She was like Olga's kissin' cousin whose time had finally come. She went a lot farther with Carol than Olga ever did with me.

Objectively, I have to admit *Date with the Angels* was a valuable learning experience, with a good share of enjoyment thrown into the bargain.

Del and his family and I continued to love each other dearly, but he and I wouldn't have another chance to play together. He went to work almost exclusively for Jerry Lewis, until a heart attack took Delsy at the end of the sixties.

Don Fedderson continued to be one of television's top producers. Lawrence Welk became a veritable institution in America, and Don also added some very successful series, *My Three Sons* with Fred MacMurray and *Family Affair* with Brian Keith among them. Early this past year, I had the privilege of presenting my cherished friend with a Lifetime Achievement Award. Last week, four days before Christmas, Don passed away.

George continued to work with Don as head writer and, soon, producer. George and I worked on one more series together when he joined the writing staff of *The Betty White Show* (IV). Mildred Tibbles is still the sister I never had.

For Jim Narz, *Angels* was a milestone. From the time he started out as Jack Narz's aspiring kid brother, he had always said that to avoid confusion, he would take a new professional name if he got a network show.

As "Olga" with doll sent in by fan. (© American Broadcasting Companies, Inc.)

Years later celebrating Don Fedderson's seventy-sixth birthday.

Well, ours was the show on which he turned into Tom Kennedy. (While he was choosing a name, he picked a good one!) Both Jack Narz and Tom Kennedy went on to great success in the game-show business.

Date with the Angels, the sitcom, ended after

that short half year of *The Betty White Show* in 1957, so you can imagine my surprise when, almost thirty years later, I walked into a video store one day and there we were — lined up on the shelf, with my picture on the tapes grinning back at me in glorious living color! I was amazed, and even more so when I discovered they were on video racks all over the country. Where they came from, I can't imagine. My representatives at the William Morris Agency sent them a letter to cease and desist, but it didn't have any effect. As far as I'm concerned, I get kind of a kick out of it after all these years, and I even bought a couple of them. (Back to working for nothing again — no, *paying* for it!) The clincher is that these tapes for sale contain only the domestic comedy episodes — none of the early dream sequence shows, nor any of the final thirteen featuring the guest stars. Goes to show how much I know.

There are also *Life with Elizabeth* tapes floating around, as I've seen them listed in various collector catalogs but not in stores. All I can surmise about the *Angels* package is that since electronic reproduction has improved over the years to the point that some pretty fair copies can be restored, those tapes must have come out of somebody's early collection, along with countless other old series. Never underestimate the zeal — or the enterprise — of a collector.

One year of working for Plymouth seemed disappointingly short to us, but compared to present standards, we had all the time in the world to sink or swim. Today, many shows are plowed under after only three or four airings — one was recently axed after being aired only once. Some are left with completed episodes in the can, never to see the light of nighttime. Finding an audience these days is like playing hide-and-seek. A certain promising prechosen few shows are nurtured in protected time slots next to established, high-rated programs, and through focused promotion, the audience is given a chance to say thumbs-up or thumbs-down. It's not an intentionally punishing system, just economically unavoidable. It is an overcrowded marketplace, astronomically priced, so some of the participants must inevitably be thrown to the lions.

I've given up even trying to speculate on what keeps us coming back for more.

What I didn't know in 1958 was that I was on the verge of a whole new chapter in my life. A lot of makeup would go over the dam before I was involved in another series.

11*

Once again I found myself without a steady job. Things weren't great, but I was okay financially, thank God. Never having been one to relax and enjoy a chance to play catch-up, I made up my mind that, this time, I would really give that a try. Above all, I was determined not to sink into those proverbial "I'll never work again" doldrums, which was at least a step in the right direction. But making busy work and actually working are two different breeds of cat to a workaholic. I soon ran out of drawers and closets to clean.

Don may have been aware of this, or perhaps it was simply his innate sense of timing, but it wasn't long before he found something for me to do besides going around kicking the furniture. He was sending Fred Henry back to New York for a month of meetings

*No pun intended. The chapters have just fallen that way by silly coincidence.

and decided it might be productive if I went back as well, along with Fred's wife, Mimi.

The network television business was headquartered in New York City, and it was only there that all the movers and shakers did any new business or decision making. It is much the same today, but not quite so exclusively; the business has become a little more bicoastal, so to speak.

So New York was the logical place to begin making new contacts for Bandy Productions. However, knowing Don, I recognized an ulterior motive when I saw one. He was determined to wash out that earlier dreary two-day first impression I'd had of the Big Apple and boost my morale with a better introduction to the city.

For openers, we checked into the Plaza Hotel, which was lovely. Along with the business of each day, we managed to really do the town, and I couldn't have asked for two better tour guides than Fred and Mimi: they loved New York, knew it well, and showed it off in great spirit and humor. However, after almost a month, I think we were all eager to get home. One of us was, I know that.

In between the eating and the socializing and theater and museums — and the eating — I did two television guest shots. Nothing out of the ordinary about that, except for the fact that both of them would prove to have a lasting effect on the rest of my life. One, I was invited to appear as a guest panelist on *What's My Line* and two, I was booked on *The Tonight Show* with Jack Paar.

What's My Line was a panel show from the top-of-the-line company, Goodson-Todman. Mark Goodson and Bill Todman built game shows into such a major industry that they became almost an art form. *What's My Line* had been on the air for about five years at that time, but even then it was virtually an institution, tucking America in every Sunday night, live at 10:30. Eventually, it became the longest-running network game show in television history, then went on in five-a-week syndication after that. It wound up with a seventeen-and-a-half-year record to its credit.

It was an awesome feeling, I remember, to walk into the makeup room that first night and find myself face-to-face with the people I had watched so faithfully — Arlene Francis, Dorothy Kilgallen, Bennett Cerf, and moderator John Daly. Above and beyond that, there was the man himself — Mark Goodson!

True New Yorkers of that day had a tendency to look upon those from the West

Coast as somewhat barbaric, but these people managed to be kind, especially Arlene. As for me, I was petrified — totally intimidated. I also knew that being the excellent players they were, they all took the game very seriously. Based on the old Twenty Questions, the object of the game was to guess a contestant's occupation by asking questions that could only be answered with a yes or a no. Donning blindfolds later in the program, the panel attempted to deduce the identity of a Mystery Guest, always a recognizable celebrity who had been asked to "Sign in, please!" It was a matter of record that if Dorothy Kilgallen went too long without guessing correctly, she had been known to wind up in tears. I was a rookie, and this was a major-league game.

How the show went that night or who the mystery guest was, I haven't a clue. I was just grateful to make it out alive. How surprised I would have been had I known then how many times I would be back in the future, both as a panelist and on several occasions, as a Mystery Guest.

The Jack Paar invitation was quite a coup: his show had captivated the audience in a big way. "Did you see Paar last night?" was a common opening gambit around the watercooler or at the luncheon table next day, all over the country.

Jack was warm and friendly that first evening — more than coolly kind — and I wanted to believe it when he said he had seen and liked our show. "Blow in my ear and I'll follow you anywhere." That was the first of some seventy appearances I would have the privilege of doing with Jack Paar, including hosting the show twice when Jack was out of town.

What separated Jack from other talk-show hosts, before and since, was his total involvement in the moment. With no preinterviews by talent coordinators letting him know what button to push to elicit a programmed response, when Jack asked a question he would actually listen to the answer. It often set him off in a whole new direction, leaving you no alternative but to go with him, and it made for an exciting ride. Even he didn't know where it would lead. At times, it was like an accident on its way to happen.

Each night, Jack and his great writer-producer, Paul Keyes, would agonize over the opening monologue, right up to the moment he stepped onstage — then it would roll out as if he was making it all up as he went along. Many times he was.

It was a celebrated and overreported fact that Jack's emotions lay very near the surface. It is true that he could be moved to tears on occasion, but that didn't mean the emotions were any less sincere or the tears less genuine; it was the same with whatever Jack was feeling — joy, irritation, apprehension, anger, or all of the above. That is what made him so unpredictable and so fascinating to watch. And to work with, I might add.

There was a coterie of people who returned often to the show — a Paar stable upon which he could draw. There was the incredibly articulate author Alexander King; comedy writer/author Jack Douglas with his Japanese wife, Reiko, who spoke virtually no English at all; outspoken French personality Genevieve, whose English was better than Reiko's, but not much; Peggy Cass, who, every time, would be in a panic in the makeup room because she didn't have any idea what she could possibly talk about — then she'd go out onstage and be wonderfully funny every time she opened her Irish mouth. I especially loved her story about the time she accompanied Jack and his wife, Miriam, on a trip to Germany. The first night there, when they were ordering drinks before dinner, Peggy asked for a dry martini. In due course, the waiter brought the order and proudly set three drinks in front of Ms.

Cass. *"Eins, zwei, drei* martinis!"

Another delightful Irish girl who returned often was redheaded Carmel Quinn. She not only sang well, but, in a rich brogue you could cut with a knife, she would pass out sage advice, such as, "Never even consider marrying a man until you've known him when he has a cold."

There was vague Dody Goodman, who marched to a different drummer altogether, and Pat Harrington, Jr., whose alter ego was the opinionated Italian golf pro, Guido Panzini; the oft-married Cliff Arquette, who had a wickedly funny slant on life, would come on as "Charlie Weaver" and read letters from his mama back in Mt. Idy.

The frequent appearances of this mixed bag of people lent a family flavor to the show, in contrast to the parade of megaguests who visited Jack. In return, the value of being seen often on the Paar show was like career insurance, for which I am sure everyone is eternally grateful.

I was more than thrilled to be dealt into this family, even though I lived in California. Jack issued an open invitation to come on the show whenever I could get to New York, and each time, they set a date for my next appearance. It was a long commute, but I found a way to work it out as often as needed, thanks as well to the various Goodson-Todman game shows. By combining the almost $400 for an appearance on *The Tonight Show* with a game show that paid $500 (eventually upped to $750), I could just about break even on a trip east. I would fly in, tape whatever game it was, stay over one night, do *The Tonight Show,* then head for the airport and take the red-eye back to L.A. Does that say something about what has happened to plane fares and hotel costs since then? It also says that once again, I was back working for nothing — or at least it wasn't costing me much. All this was before frequent-flyer miles were ever invented. Also, bear in mind, it was before jets, so it was close to an eight-hour flight one way.

It was worth it.

I didn't really appreciate the impact that the Jack Paar show had on the business until it was brought home to me loud and clear. By telling this story, I'm taking a chance on being put in a padded room somewhere, but bear with me.

At that time I was represented by the Ashley-Steiner Agency in New York. (This was prior to my going with William Morris, who have been my agents now for almost thirty years.) My agent of record, Herb Gottlieb, called me one day to say that NBC wanted a meeting to talk about something important; naturally, I went.

We were ushered into one of those paneled rooms where "important" things are discussed, and I learned that NBC was looking for a new girl on their *Today Show* and they would like to offer me the job. The schedule that went with the show was notorious — having to get there in the wee small hours each and every morning, et cetera. That part was of no concern, as I was well-acquainted with rough hours — but the show emanated from New York; there was just no way I could do that. Try explaining that to a roomful of New Yorkers.

The discussions went on for several days, lasting that long only because my agents wouldn't give up. They kept trying to tell me how much it would mean to my career, where it could lead, and on and on. NBC even offered to put me up at the St. Regis Hotel and to fly me home to California every weekend if I so desired. *That,* I must admit, was a momentary temptation, until I thought about it and realized that even with the energy level I had been blessed with, it would be unrealistic. The final answer was no. It's not easy to see a grown agent cry.

The poor network ultimately had to make

do with Barbara Walters. What she proceeded to build a "girl-on-the-show" job into is legend.

Not then, not since, have I regretted that decision for an instant. There is no way of explaining it to anyone, but where I live — not how, but *where* — has always been so important to me. I only relate this story because it has a bearing on some of my later decisions.

Being around those special people of Jack's was not only fascinating but was yet another great learning experience, especially so when you take into account that Hugh Downs was an important part of the equation. Hugh was to Jack what Ed McMahon was to Johnny Carson — the invaluable, trusted support system. I'm sure the only reason I made the cut on the show, aside from sheer blind luck, was that I'm a member of the If-I-don't-have-anything-to-say-I-say-it-anyway school. That is a viable credential in the talk-show business, but no doubt a liability to friends and family. I have honestly tried to curb it through the years. In vain, I'm sorry to say.

Paul Keyes and his wife, Miriam, were especially good to this out-of-towner, as were Hugh and Ruth Downs. To this day I find myself trying to live up to things I learned from Hugh in our brief encounters. Perhaps the most important was that you do better not to argue a point with someone who has a strong opposing view to your own. You don't have to agree, just listen. Hugh's reasoning was that you never learn a thing if you are talking, and all of the rhetoric rarely changes anyone's mind. I subscribe to that theory wholeheartedly — only sometimes I forget.

Prices aren't the only things that are different today. Talk-show dialogue also has, shall we say, changed. Whether for better or for worse is in the eye of the beholder. Small case in point: One night Jack and I were talking about finding homes for animals, and he said, "If anyone is looking for a dog or a cat, call Betty." I responded with something to the effect of, "Oh, please don't do that. I'm becoming a procurer in spite of myself!" Well, the shock waves were palpable, and the network folk even had to review the tape before releasing it to the West Coast three hours later. It was finally okayed, but with eyebrows raised. The *idea* that sweet little Betty had used such a word — and on *television!* She probably didn't know what she was saying. Of course, sweet little Betty had done her share of double entendres for years, but they never picked up on that. As of today, no situation comedy is worth its salt without frequent use of the word "slut" — used almost as a term of endearment, and proceeding onward and downward from there. *Mad About You* used "penis" recently. Now, on an ever-growing group of cable stations, nothing is out of bounds. What happens when the writers run out of body parts?

Jack himself was not immune to network reprimand, and encountered it inadvertently one night, with shattering results. He was telling a British story which involved the term "WC." Jack explained that, in England, "WC" means "water closet." Once again, the network watchdogs got nervous and bleeped out "water closet" before it could reach the West Coast. When Jack discovered this, he was so furious that he walked off the show. He kept going until he reached Hong Kong, and it wasn't until several weeks later, after a profound apology from NBC, that he finally returned. On that evening, along with many of his other friends, I made a special trip from Los Angeles just to be in the studio audience to welcome him home.

Only one other time did I see anger really get the best of him: Jack loved his family — his wife, Miriam, and his daughter, Randy, who was about fourteen at the time — above all else. Jack and Dorothy Kilgallen had had a real falling out about something, and it reached the boiling point when Dorothy took a shot in her daily newspaper column — not at Jack, but at Randy. Dorothy wrote that it was too bad that the child was overweight. Jack went ballistic. That night he had no difficulty putting the monologue together, and he came out loaded for bear. White with anger, he proceeded to tell Dorothy off, concluding with, "And let me say this, Miss Kilgallen — *you have no chin!*"

Jack had a different approach for each of his irregulars. The fact that I was single (happily so, but that cut no ice with him) gave him the perfect setup. My love life, or lack thereof, became his project, and he took on the job of frustrated matchmaker with a passion. With today's changed perspective, that would probably be considered politically incorrect, if not sexual harassment. All I know is, we had a great time with the subject through many a show.

One of Jack's good friends, and also a producer on his staff, was a dear man named Tom Cochran — still a cherished friend of all concerned. Tommy had a very famous brother, a celebrated and much-decorated flying ace from World War II. In fact, Low-

Jack Paar with Colonel Philip Cochran. (COURTESY TOM COCHRAN FILES)

ell Thomas wrote a book, *Back to Manda-lay,* about Colonel Philip Cochran and his heroism as a squadron leader serving with General Orde Wingate in the Burma-India campaign. For years, cartoonist Milt Caniff used Phil as the prototype for one of the main characters in Milt's classic "Terry and the Pirates" comic strip — Colonel Flip Corkin. Well, devious Jack started talking about what a great idea it would be to introduce Phil and Betty on the show some night. It became a running gag, and I took it for granted that it was all show talk — shades of Madam Fagel Bagelmaker.

Imagine my surprise when I answered the phone one day in California, to hear, "Betty, this is Tom Cochran's brother, Phil." He went on to say that he had been invited to do the Jack Paar show in about a week, the same night I was booked on as a guest. This nice man was checking to see if that was all right, as he didn't want to put me in an uncomfortable situation. In turn, I said I hoped Jack's teasing hadn't given *him* any problems, as we had been taking his name in vain for weeks. We both decided it would be interesting to see how much trouble Jack would get himself into under the circumstances.

It could easily have turned into one of life's more awkward moments when the night arrived, but Phil handled it so smoothly, and with such class, that he not only put me at ease, but even nervous Jack relaxed to a degree.

After we got off the air, the Paars invited a group of us out to dinner — Phil, Tommy, the Keyeses, crazy Shirley Wood, and me. Normally, I would have been heading for the airport as soon as the show was over, but, as luck would have it, I was staying over in order to leave very early the next morning for Ohio to do a summer theater engagement. So off we all went for a beautiful dinner at "21," no less. Typically, that kind of setup would turn out somewhere between uncomfortable, at best, or a total disaster, more likely. This proved to be a delicious exception.

After dinner, we all said our good-nights, but instead of taking me back to the hotel, Tommy and Phil had a couple of places they wanted me to see and musicians they wanted me to hear. When we finally wound up the evening, eating hamburgers at P. J. Clarke's, the sky was beginning to pale in the east. At last, they dropped Cinderella off at the Warwick Hotel, and she barely had time to change, throw her things together, and head for Ohio.

The ball was over, and Cinderella had to get her wits about her: she was on her way to do a challenging production for John Kenley at the Packard Music Hall in Warren, Ohio. This was another serendipity for which Mr. Paar was responsible. John Kenley had seen me on *The Tonight Show,* and invited me to his prestigious summer theater to do *The King and I.* At first, I had thought it was a joke. Asking me to play such a glorious role was like the game of funny casting — "How about Mae West as Mary Poppins?" "How about Bela Lugosi as Don Juan?" "How about Betty White as

The Phil I knew.

Anna Leonowens?" But it was a genuine offer, and because it was my favorite show of all, I was deadly serious about wanting to do a creditable job. I had been diligently rehearsing the music in California for weeks, as well as working hard with Christopher

Hewett to get rid of my Midwestern *r*'s in order to play the British schoolteacher. Staying out all night before the first rehearsal had hardly been in my game plan. Perhaps because I'd had such a good time, or because I was so thrilled to be doing *The King and I* — or maybe both — for whatever reason, I wasn't tired in the least. On the contrary, I felt mahvelous!

Phil Cochran lived in Erie, Pennsylvania, where he owned a large trucking firm and raised horses on his beautiful farm. Insisting that the drive from Erie to Warren was a cinch, he actually came to see our show on two occasions.

That was the first of eight productions of *The King and I* that I would have the privilege of playing in, but, somehow, that initial one was personally the most memorable. That silly matchmaking game and subsequent night on the town was the beginning of a deep and lovely love affair that lasted almost four years.

The Paars and I had exchanged Christmas greetings and run into each other occasionally at special television events over the years, but we hadn't spent any time together in a long while. A few months ago, Tommy Cochran found I would be in New York and invited Jack, Miriam, Randy, and me to lunch (at "21," ironically), and it was as though we had all been together last week. The one notable change was that beautiful Randy, still looking about sixteen, is now a corporate lawyer! The day before our luncheon she had won a case involving $6 million! Boy, turn your back on a kid, you don't know where she'll wind up.

There are very few total originals these days, and when you know one, you treasure him. Curious about everything under the sun, unpredictable, generous, volatile, vulnerable: Jack Paar.

12

Through the courtesy of Jack Paar and Mark Goodson, I was still in the television business.

Game shows became a mainstay for me, not only because I could use the work and the exposure but because they were just plain fun to do and kept me in touch with so many friends. Being in show business must be comparable to living in a small town, where everyone knows, or at least acknowledges, each other. In that analogy then, the group of habitual television game players must be neighbors living on the same street — we keep running into each other.

There have been peaks and valleys in game-show popularity ever since the genre first flickered on the screen. Styles in games have run the gamut as well, from panel show through intellectual quiz, physical contest, high-energy greed competition, big-money extravaganza, even some based solely on sex. But the game shows per se never disappear completely. In fact, they now have a cable channel all their own. The Game Show Channel is up and running. For the past several years, consistently, the number one and two syndicated shows have been games — *Wheel of Fortune* with Pat Sajak and Vanna White, and *Jeopardy!* with Alex Trebek. Both of these programs saw the light of day — or early evening — under the banner of Merv Griffin Productions.

Merv Griffin first entered the game-show scene back in 1958, as host for a show called *Play Your Hunch,* for — who else? — Goodson-Todman. Merv was a popular singer at the time, and Mark Goodson spotted this personable young man as good emcee material. I am sure even Mark, in his wisdom, could have had no inkling that Merv would eventually become the giant one-man conglomerate that he is today. As for Merv, the game bug must have burrowed deep in the Griffin until it ultimately surfaced in a big way with *Wheel of Fortune* and *Jeopardy!*

Wheel of Fortune, based on the old parlor game Hangman, went on the air daytime on NBC in 1975. Chuck Woolery was its first host; then Pat Sajak took over in 1981. When a nighttime first-run syndicated *Wheel* came on the air in 1983, the show went into orbit.

It has become the most profitable game show in the history of the medium. Interesting footnote: The theme song, "Changing Keys," was written by — Merv Griffin.

Jeopardy!, the number two syndicated show today, predates *Wheel* by over ten years. It started in 1964, with Art Fleming as host, and enjoyed a good run. Revived in 1984 with Alex Trebek, it has all the earmarks of being around for a long time to come. I love the story of how the show came about. Merv Griffin and his wife, Julann (now divorced), were on an airplane. Never one to waste a moment, Merv was fiddling around with a new game idea to pass the time. Julann casually put in her two cents with, "Why don't you switch it around? Give the answer and make them come up with the right question." The rest is game-show history. What about *Jeopardy*'s theme song, you ask? It's called "Take Ten" and was written by — Julann Griffin.

I got to know Merv when he brought his nighttime talk show on the air. It was one of the more enjoyable to do, because Merv kept everyone engaged in interesting conversation, even as each new guest was introduced. I was also understandably partial to the show because he let me bring on all sorts of animals from time to time. On two occasions he invited me to host the show when he was away.

Merv Griffin has grown into a veritable mogul before our eyes. For the record, that mogul has remained the same down-to-earth, funny, warm Merv that I first met.

The Price Is Right is another hardy game perennial on the all-time top-ten list. Bob Barker has emceed it for years, but when it started, back in November 1956, it was hosted by Bill Cullen, the most prolific of all game-show emcees. *Price* was conceived in the fertile brain of one Bob Stewart, a creative producer working at that time for — all together now — Goodson-Todman!

Bob recalls those early shows, before the advent of tape, with great fondness. "I loved doing live shows, because I always knew what time I'd get home!" The sarcasm was in reference to the fact that tape glitches can often cause frustrating delays — even now. Tape, however, changed the game-show business completely, allowing multiple shows to be produced in a day. On *The Price Is Right,* when Bob first told emcee Bill Cullen that they wanted to try two shows in one day, Bill was shocked.

"Are you crazy? I couldn't do that, I'd be exhausted!"

Before too long, Bill was doing five shows a day without giving it a second thought.

To Tell the Truth was another G-T game-show classic, created by that same Bob Stewart. I was surprised recently when Bob told me that the pilot for that show was emceed by Mike Wallace. At the time, Mike had been doing a hard-hitting talk show and appearing on various games. It was when that pilot sold that Mike made a major career decision. He made up his mind that the time had come to concentrate on what he most wanted to do — get into the news department — so he turned down the host job on *Truth*. It was a gutsy move: news was not an easy field to break into. Should there be any doubt as to it being the right decision, just check on Mike's news stature, and consider how many years *60 Minutes* has been in the top ten.

So *To Tell the Truth* went on the air with Bud Collyer, who hosted for several years until he passed away and Garry Moore took over.

The panel of four celebrities had to determine, through questioning, which of three people was the one telling the truth. "Will the real . . . please stand up!" The panel was drawn from a pool of regulars, among them Kitty Carlisle (on every week), Tom Poston,

Peggy Cass, Polly Bergen, Hy Gardner, and Hildy Parks.

At one point, Polly Bergen took a leave of absence, and I sat in every week for three months. Johnny Carson was also doing the show regularly at the time, and watching his mind work was a joy. I would fly in from Los Angeles on Wednesday, then back home on Thursday. This is what made those frequent trips to do *The Tonight Show* with Jack Paar — and to see Phil — possible. (I didn't care how many times I *went* to New York — I just had to know I had that return ticket in my hot little fist.)

Bob Stewart hit the jackpot yet again when he came up with one of the greatest games of all. This one he called *Password*. It debuted October 2, 1961, hosted by a rather attractive man by the name of Allen Ludden. We'll come back to that subject. You can bank on it.

After such a phenomenal record of hits, it was only natural that Bob would feel the urge to stretch his wings and go into business for himself. It also figures that Mark wouldn't be happy to lose such a valuable asset, and he did everything he could to change Bob's mind. Bob laughs when he remembers Mark taking him to lunch one day:

"Mark said to me, 'Bob, how can you do this? I made you a prince!' "

Bob's response was, "But, Mark — I want to be a king!"

Bob did indeed jump out into the deep water, and he swam very well. His first show was called, ironically, *Jackpot,* followed by *Personality.* Then, once again, he belted one out of the ballpark with another gigantic hit, *The $10,000 Pyramid,* which subsequently burgeoned into *The $20,000 Pyramid.* Prices rose in 1981 to $50,000, and ultimately in 1985 it became *The $100,000 Pyramid.* The $10,000 version started in March 1976, hosted by Dick Clark. There was later a syndicated version with Bill Cullen which ran simultaneously, and then John Davidson hosted for syndication only. One of the best, *Pyramid* is still running in some markets.

It was on *Password* that I first got to know Bob Stewart. He was the producer as well as the creator of the show. When he left Goodson-Todman, our paths took different directions for several years, but when they merged once more on the *Pyramid,* we determined never to lose track of each other again. Bob and Anne Marie Schmidt — one of the top producers in Bob's company for twenty-five years, as well as the love of his

Two talented and treasured friends: Anne Marie Schmidt and Bob Stewart.

life — and I have dinner regularly, which is great.

Even better than the dinners together are the most sacrosanct, unmovable dates on my entire social calendar — the meetings of our Pico Poker Club every four or five weeks. It started casually, but now eight of us make up the PPC — all having been connected in some way to the game-show business. The cast of characters (how aptly put) is Bob, Anne Marie, Ann Cullen (Bill's widow), Chester Feldman (still an executive producer with Mark Goodson Productions), Henry Polic II (an alum of Bob Stewart Productions, where he hosted *Celebrity Double-talk*), Tony Pandolfo (another Stewart alum; both Henry and Tony are now fine actors), Brenda Thomson, and yours truly. We vie fiercely for a trophy cup that Bob had made with all our names on it. The winner for the evening gets to take it home until the next game. Forgetting to bring the cup back carries a penalty of $2,000 or death, whichever is deemed more appropriate. It goes without saying that no one has so far failed to return the cup. There is also a bulletin board on which is posted an ongoing list of winners and amounts won, as well as pictures of each winner taking the cup from the loser, or from himself in the event of a repeat. As much as eight or ten dollars can change hands in a single evening of this Titan contest. We haven't, as yet, found a way to put a dollar amount on the ridiculous laughs we have.

One little postscript: I am always fascinated by the way different threads in our lives are woven into the tapestry. Back when I was doing *Life with Elizabeth* in California, I knew Bill Cullen only from seeing him on television from New York, and I didn't know Ann at all. However, I knew Ann's sister, Mary Lou, well, because she was married to our

Jack Narz. What is it they say about there being only six degrees of separation between everyone in the world?

Television game shows grew in number and diversity during the fifties and sixties. Along with the lighthearted games for fun and laughs, a new species began to emerge and attract a huge audience. This new breed eschewed the fun and laughs and went right for the money — *Big* money.

The $64,000 Question went on the air in prime time in June 1955, and a whole new era of game shows began.

Comedian Phil Baker had been hosting a successful radio show called *The $64 Question,* where the emphasis was more on comedy than game. For the television version, producers Joe Cates and Mert Koplin upped the ante to $64,000 and, still intending the show to have a comic flavor, hired comedian Hal March as host.

The show gave a contestant, well versed in a particular subject, the chance to double his winnings from $1 toward the potential $64,000. At those prices, comedy went out the window almost immediately. The audience was hooked. If a player achieved the $4,000 level of winning, he or she would be brought back for just one question each week, thus providing a tremendous cliff-hanger for the audience. One of the few to go the whole distance, psychologist Joyce Brothers, has built a lifetime career on the start she earned by answering increasingly difficult questions on boxing.

So successful was the show that the next year the producers mounted a successful spin-off, *The $64,000 Challenge,* hosted first by Sonny Fox, then by Ralph Story. Contestants on *Challenge* got a chance to compete against players on *Question* who had won at least $8,000. It was on *Challenge* that the biggest winner in the whole big-money quiz era took home the tidy sum of $252,000!

As the money grew, so did the number of viewers, inevitably spawning a whole slew of big-cash shows. One of these was *Dotto,* emceed by our old buddy Jack Narz. Another was *Twenty-One* hosted by Jack Barry and packaged by Jack Barry and Dan Enright.

Unfortunately, as audiences and competition both burgeoned, and the shows became really big business, the temptation to fudge the rules proved irresistible. When a promising and charismatic contestant would begin to entice the audience into following his or her progress each week, it was only too easy to leak answers surreptitiously to that player to ensure a return next week.

Finally, the inevitable happened — someone blew the whistle, and it hit the fan, triggering the notorious quiz-show scandals of 1958.

We had all watched anxiously as Charles Van Doren agonized and sweated over his responses each week, building his winnings to $129,000 on *Twenty-One,* and we were bitterly let down when he later admitted that he had been given the answers ahead of time. It was the first time, to our knowledge, that TV had lied to us. The age of innocence was over.

The movie, *Quiz Show,* directed by Robert Redford, dealt with the scandals brilliantly and was nominated for an Oscar last time around.

Fifteen years would elapse before Jack Barry was able to get an on-camera job on television again. Jack Narz fared somewhat better after *Dotto* was abruptly canceled for questionable conduct: he had been the emcee only and was not involved in the production of the show in any way. However, while he continued to work on various games, his career had taken a hit. The big-money quiz-show business had done itself in, and from then on, some stringent rules were put into effect and enforced in all game shows to preclude a repetition.

The Goodson-Todman shows made it through the storm with a clean record, and for one simple reason: there was no big payoff involved. Questions were worth perhaps fifty dollars, and totals might not make it to four figures.

The most successful of these was *Password*.

I told you we'd get back to the subject.

Betty in 1956.

Betty and Frank Sinatra on The Betty White Show, 1958.

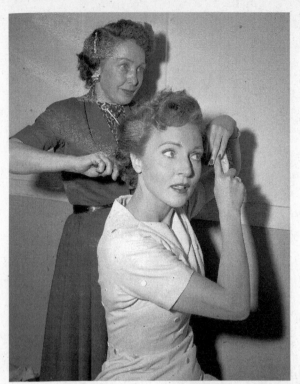

Betty getting ready for Date with the Angels.

A publicity shot for The Betty White Show.

With Steve Martin and Tim Conway on The Carol Burnett Show.

The Mary Tyler Moore Show *cast.*

The Golden Girls.

The Golden Girls *together again in 2004.*

On the set of The Bold and the Beautiful.

Shooting it up on Boston Legal.

Betty and Pontiac.

With Vanessa Williams on Ugly Betty.

Celebrating with the cast of The Mary Tyler Moore Show *at the Academy of Television Arts & Sciences in 2008.*

Challenging Jimmy Fallon on Late Night.

Receiving the Screen Actors Guild Life Achievement Award.

13

When Goodson-Todman went on the air
with yet another game show, it was hardly
news, because they had such a string of hits
already under their collective belt. *Password,* however, hit the ground running and
almost immediately became the hottest daytime show around. A very short time after
its debut, in October of '61, CBS ordered a
sixth show to run in prime time once a week.
After the notorious quiz-show scandals of
the fifties, big money payoffs were out, and
a high-quality game, above reproach, was a
hot property.

A couple of things set *Password* apart from
other games at the time. Until then, celebrities had been used primarily to make up a
panel that attempted to deduce information
about, or from, a contestant. The panel was
totally separate from the players in *What's My
Line, I've Got a Secret,* and *To Tell the Truth.*
For the first time, *Password* paired up a ce-

Password Plus — *Contestant, Peter Lawford, Allen, Burt Reynolds. Peter held the record for the fastest lightning round — twenty-seven seconds.* (COURTESY CBS)

lebrity *with* a contestant, and they worked together as a team, competing against a similar team on the opposing side. It worked like a charm. The celebrities became totally engrossed in the game itself and tended to forget they were in show business. Keeping order in the court was the man in the middle — the host, Allen Ludden. Allen was already known to the television audience as the emcee of the popular *G.E. College Bowl* every Sunday evening, which earned him something of an egghead image. It was a pleasant surprise to see the sense of humor that surfaced on *Password.*

I had seen Allen many times on *College*

Bowl, just as he had often seen me on *The Tonight Show,* but we had not met until I guested on *Password* the third week it was on the air. He was the perfect host in every sense of the word, off camera as well as on, making his guests feel welcome when they arrived, and never too busy to say a warm good-bye after the last show finished.

The game itself was such a good one that I was always delighted to be invited for a return visit. I actually made an effort to watch it at home whenever I could, which was unusual for me — as a rule, my television doesn't go on until the evening news. Even with the show on five days a week, I couldn't catch it very often. When nighttime

First nighttime Password *— Allen, Garry Moore, Carol Burnett.*
(CBS/Landov)

229

Password went on the air it helped me a lot, although CBS may not have done it solely for that reason. I remember Carol Burnett and Garry Moore were the guests on the premier evening show.

Sometime around the following March, my agent called with an offer for me to do a play in August — one week in Dennis, Massachusetts, on Cape Cod (Kennedy country, although I didn't realize it at the time), then on up to Skowhegan, Maine, for another week. The various summer theaters put their seasons together early in the year. It seemed that Allen Ludden had booked to do a production of *Critic's Choice* and they had asked if I would be available to play opposite him. Sounded fine: I hadn't booked my summer yet, and Maine was a part of the country I had not seen.

Early in May, I was surprised to receive a phone call from Allen, calling from New York to say that *Password* would be coming out to do a week of shows from Los Angeles. He discovered that *Critic's Choice,* with Ed Binns in the lead, was playing at a little theater in Hollywood. Didn't I think it would be helpful for us to see the show on its feet before we went into rehearsal?

Yes, that sounded like a wise idea to me,

too, and we made a date to go to dinner and the play with friends of Allen's, Mary Kay and Johnnie Stearns.

When the evening arrived, my folks got a kick out of meeting this nice man when he came to pick me up, as Tess and Horace had enjoyed watching him on both *College Bowl* and *Password*. Allen also met Dancer the poodle that night, and big old Stormy, but he only heard Bandit bark from my room. A tired little old man of fifteen plus by now, my beloved Bandy didn't feel it was worth the trip to come all the way out to see someone he didn't know. I have always been sorry those two never met.

In the car, on the way to meet Johnnie and Mary Kay, we made the usual small talk. I learned that Allen was born in Mineral Point, Wisconsin, then grew up in Corpus Christi, Texas. After doing a show or two at WTIC in Hartford, Connecticut, he had moved his wife and three children to New York, where he did *College Bowl*.

At one point in the conversation, Allen said something — damned if I can remember what it was — something about what he and his kids did. Anyway, my joking response was, "I'll bet your wife loves that!"

There was a long beat before he said simply, "I don't have a wife. She died last October."

There was no way to fix it. I felt like such a blithering idiot. Perhaps I should have known, but until that moment I hadn't given it a thought, merely taking it for granted that he had left his family at home because the trip was so short. I could only apologize.

No more small talk. Allen began to tell me what had happened. Margaret had lung cancer, and the week that *Password* started on the air things went from bad to worse. He left the hospital only long enough to do the shows, and after three weeks, he lost her. I didn't say it, but privately I was shocked to realize that was the same week I had done *Password* for the first time; I remembered the warm, smiling man I had met that day. Incredible how we can insulate ourselves for short periods when it is absolutely necessary to get the job done.

After eighteen years of a wonderful marriage, Allen admitted to being devastated without her, as were the children. David was fourteen, Martha would turn thirteen and Sarah ten come August. That was why he had responded to the idea of doing a play during his hiatus from *Password*. It would be the family's first summer alone, and he thought staying home — or worse, trying to plan some forced vacation trip without Margaret — would be tough to handle. When the play offer came along, it seemed a viable alternative, keeping them all together; and yet it would be something totally different for everyone. Then he had come up with an even better idea: there was a substantial part for a young boy in *Critic's Choice,* and Allen talked David into playing the role.

Certainly, on that first evening in California, we had no trouble making conversation. We joined Mary Kay and Johnnie for a lovely dinner, enjoyed the play, then stopped on the way home at La Cage Aux Folles, a local nightspot now long gone, to hear some of Eddie Cano's special piano. All the way home Allen kept apologizing for talking so much, which I found refreshing because that was usually my closing speech.

It was as if the floodgates had opened and he was able to say some of the things that had been bottled up. I said something to that effect to Phil on the phone next day, and somehow he didn't seem to find it as heartwarming as I did.

My frequent trips to New York continued. Phil would fly in from Erie — life went on, business as usual.

One day Allen called me in California and

invited me to dinner on my next trip east, saying he had something to discuss regarding the upcoming work situation on Cape Cod. Phil was all right with that part of it; he just had a little trouble understanding what going on to the theater to see Barbara Bel Geddes and Barry Nelson in *Mary, Mary* had to do with anything. I wasn't quite sure either, but I enjoyed the play immensely.

What Allen had to discuss concerned the fact that since his visit to California, he had bought two little poodle puppies for the kids, and he needed advice on what to do with them during the three weeks they would all be away doing the play. Naturally, he got the response from me he had been counting on: "Why, bring them along, of course!"

August rolled around, as it almost always does, and I arrived in Dennis, Massachusetts, to be met by an assorted group of Luddens.

The accommodations were beautiful. Overlooking the sea not far from the Cape Playhouse, the property had once belonged to Gertrude Lawrence and her husband, Richard Aldrich. The large main house was perfect for the Luddens, and a short distance away, over rolling green lawns, was a charming small cottage that had been Gertrude's retreat. I found it delightful, and much of the time, so did two giddy young chocolate poodle littermates, Willie and Emma.

Critic's Choice was a play Henry Fonda had done on Broadway. It was charming and not too demanding, and David did an exceptionally good job for his first time out. It was also his last, for he proved to be totally immune to the acting bug. You just can't count on some kids — instead of becoming an out-of-work actor, all he managed to do was graduate from Andover and then Yale, spend a year or so in India on his thesis, then wind up as a published author and tenured professor at the University of Pennsylvania. Go figure!

We all had a very good time together. We celebrated Sarah's tenth birthday, then Martha becoming a real live teenager at thirteen. We became great friends and played a lot during the day.

Phil, as always, came to see the show — this time on closing night on the Cape, so he could drive me up to Maine the next day. He met Allen and the kids briefly before showtime, and we arranged to all have dinner together after the performance.

Allen and I played husband and wife in the play. At the end of the third act there is an obligatory confrontation scene, where the loose ends get tied up, problems are solved,

Betty, Allen, and David in Critic's Choice. *Betty was falling in love and too dumb to know it.* (COURTESY GRANT MILLS)

Critic's Choice. *The last scene — just before the extended kiss!* (COURTESY GRANT MILLS)

and everything works out after all. There is a warm kiss of reconciliation before we head up the stairs. Curtain.

On this particular evening, Allen held the kiss longer — much longer — than usual. No one else may have noticed, but from the third row there was suddenly a loud and expressive clearing of Phil's throat. We laughed about it later at dinner. Some of us more than others.

Phil drove me to Skowhegan the next morning, then stayed one more day before he had to head back home. He mentioned at one point on the drive that it was obvious what pals we had all become, and then he allowed as how he didn't like Allen Ludden.

I wasn't being coy, I was genuinely surprised.

"*Everyone* likes Allen Ludden!"

"Not somebody who's in love with you."

"Phil Cochran! You have seen me play opposite other men so many times and you've never reacted this way."

"This time it's different. I don't know why, but it is."

Phil was way ahead of me. I was just too dumb to know it.

After Phil left, there was almost a week of days left to explore the beautiful countryside before doing the show in Maine each evening. The Lakewood Theater was a rustic little playhouse in the woods, on the edge of a spectacular lake, where loons called across the water all night, singing you to sleep. During the day we had the area almost to ourselves, so it always amazed us, come showtime every night, to find a full house of eleven hundred happy souls. Where did they come from — just materialize out of thin air?

Under such delightful circumstances, how could we fail to have a wonderful time? Allen and the kids even challenged this nonswimmer to swing out over the lake on a rope and drop into the water — screaming all the way.

Along with the fun and games, I remember that Allen was wrestling with an important decision. *Password* was on the CBS network, and *College Bowl* was on NBC. He had no difficulty doing both shows, but NBC suddenly shuffled the schedules, and *College Bowl* landed in the time slot immediately following *Password*. While it was on a different network, General Electric took a dim view of Allen following himself, and he had to decide which of the two shows he would give up. It was a tough call. *Password* was the more lucrative, and exciting in its own way, with the constant parade of celebrities. *College Bowl,* on the other hand, was his baby. He had made up the game in his backyard in Hartford, on one of his omnipresent yellow legal pads. Unfortunately, he didn't own any piece of the show, and, as popular as it was, participated only as moderator.

After some soul-searching and much Libra scale-balancing, Allen opted to give up *College Bowl* and stay with *Password.* The irony was that the schedule change only lasted for thirteen weeks before another reshuffling. Had G.E. not forced the issue, he could have remained with both shows.

NBC hired a new moderator for *College Bowl,* named Robert Earle — blond, about Allen's age and weight, same short haircut — and they took him to Allen's optometrist and ordered the same tortoiseshell frames that Allen wore at the time. I'll never forget, one night he and I were at Radio City Music Hall, and a lady rushed up to him saying, "Oh, Mr. Ludden! Who is this new man they've poured into your glasses?" A pretty clever line from a very perceptive viewer.

In the long run, Allen's choice turned out to be a good one; he would remain with *Password* — through all its versions — for the next twenty years.

Being together so much in Maine's beautiful environment, we formed some easy friendships. And some running jokes. Instead of "Hello" or "Good morning," Allen soon began to substitute, "Will you marry me?" The kids got into the game immediately; if they heard Allen or me say anything nice to each other, one of them would holler "Check!" and chalk up a point in their father's "campaign." Even the puppies caught the spirit, bouncing gaily back and forth between the Luddens' cottage and mine. All in fun.

This group nonsense was harmless, and not unusual among temporary professional families. Come closing night, there are always heartfelt good-byes and hopes that paths will cross again someday, then everyone heads back to real life. As a rule, the good intentions of keeping in touch are rarely realized.

That is how it is supposed to work, anyway, but our closing-night celebration rang a little hollow — we had all grown genuinely fond of one another. Besides, youngsters can't be expected to understand showbiz rules that can form great friendships, then turn around and put them on hold for long periods of time.

Next morning, I was driven to Bangor, where I boarded the plane for California.

■ ■ ■ ■

Phil was right. This time it *was* different. I missed the loons and the laughs and the kids and the puppies. And I missed their father. Allen called rather frequently — just friendly touch-base calls — and at one point I agreed to save an evening on my next trip east for a reunion dinner with the Luddens. This did not sit well with Phil, and who could blame him? I don't like to think of what my reaction would have been had the situation been reversed.

We had a long and serious talk, and I admitted that I needed a little slack to clear my head. Phil reluctantly agreed, on the condition that we continue to see each other, as friends, while I was sorting myself out. Great in theory, but I have never been able to see more than one person at a time that I cared about without becoming thoroughly confused. However, it seemed the only viable compromise at the moment.

My trips east, and my life, for that matter, became something of a challenge. Both Allen and Phil were fully aware of the situation and not overly fond of each other, shall we say? I continued to see them both, without getting heavily involved with either one. We were all being so "teddibly" civilized, it was almost funny.

Sometime during this period, I brought my mother back with me for a few days of exploring New York. She was always a great playmate and had a way of making everything more fun.

Phil and Allen both latched on to this as a golden opportunity to make some brownie points, and as a result, Tess never had it so good. If Allen got tickets for a show one night, Phil saw to it that *he* got *better* ones the next. The same with top restaurants or special day trips. I was just along for the ride — all this fence-walking was strictly for Tess's benefit. On her part, she really liked them both a lot — in every way but geographically — so she was no help at all. Forget the almost — now it *was* funny. Mom's description of the trip to Dad when we got home was a classic.

When Tess watched *Password* at home she would sometimes kiddingly greet Allen's entrance with "Hi, Doll!" I teased her about that when we were with Allen one night in New York. I should have known better. On every single show, from then on, as Allen was introduced, he would make his entrance and, under the applause, say a quiet "Hi, Doll" right into camera. For years I had to keep explaining to people that he was not saying it to me.

At one point while all this was going on, I was invited to Cleveland to cohost for a week on *The Mike Douglas Show*. This was before he moved his show to Philadelphia. Allen and I had been seen out together on occasion, and Mike thought it would be a good bit to fly him in to surprise me on the show. Fortunately, some cooler head thought it might be wise to clear the "surprise" with me first, and I was able to nip that idea quickly in the bud. I'd like to think Allen would have refused, but the way things were

Mike Douglas, my mother, and Louis Nye. Mike conned Mom into coming on the show. (P.S. She had the best legs in any town!)

going, I couldn't be sure of anything, and I didn't need another TV installment of my personal soap opera.

Doing the Macy's Parade telecast with Lorne Greene meant that I would be in New York for Thanksgiving. I accepted an invitation from Allen and all three children to join them for dinner at their home in Briarcliff Manor, up in Westchester County. That day starts very early, and the weather was what Lorne and I had come to expect on Macy day — gray and drizzly. After shivering through the parade in an icy broadcast booth, I finally made it to Briarcliff. The enthusiastic greeting from all the Luddens in their lovely, warm house seemed to personify what holidays are all about.

It was good to see David and Martha and Sarah again, and we picked right up from where we had left off. Their wonderful housekeeper, Lessie, outdid herself putting on a perfect Thanksgiving turkey dinner. It was a good day.

Lessie Clymer had been retired for some time, but when Margaret died, she came back to work for Allen, to supervise the Ludden household — an offer welcomed by one and all, as she was dearly loved. Lessie was older than time, but strong and oh, so capable, and she ran the family with a firm and loving hand. Her long experience "in service," as she put it proudly, instilled in her a passion for good manners and some of the finer points of protocol, which, I'm sure, rubbed off subliminally on all the children in her charge through the years.

Allen reported later that Lessie had given me a most favorable review. "Mr. Luttin, I think you gonna marry that woman. We gotta get us a silver tea service. She should have a silver tea service." I had to laugh, in spite of the forbidden "m" word. Bless Lessie, she never talked us into getting that silver tea service, but it was her dream.

The "m" word.

Phil asked me to marry him only once — long before I met Allen Ludden. Unlike Allen's persistence, Phil's proposal was quiet, purposeful, very firm, and there obviously had been a great deal of forethought. He laid out all the reasons why it should happen.

It came as a real surprise: I had been so sure of how completely comfortable he was in his role of the perennial bachelor. I responded as honestly and carefully as he had posed his question: he must know that he meant a great deal to me; however, there was absolutely no way that I could ever pull up stakes and move east, any more than he could envision himself moving to California. Once and for all, we covered the subject thoroughly, and he had to accept the fact that I meant everything I said. The subject was not brought up again.

Phil must have found the memory of that conversation, as truthful as it had been at the time, somewhat painful down the road.

We all made it through the Christmas holidays, which proved to be a peaceful respite without complications. I was with my folks in California, Phil with his four brothers and their families all congregated in Erie, and Allen at home with David and Martha and Sarah.

The tightrope act had about run its course. It was becoming increasingly impossible to pretend we were all just good friends. I loved Phil dearly; that would never change. But I could no longer kid myself — I had fallen very much *in* love with Allen Ludden. Perhaps the only one who wasn't surprised was Phil Cochran.

Early in January, I was in Cleveland for another week on *The Mike Douglas Show*. Phil flew in to take me to dinner — and to resolve the situation. It had to be done, but there is never any easy way.

Phil flew home to Erie. Before he left, he said, "You may change your mind one day.

You know where I am."

It was straight out of one of the old movies, as was the whole situation, which should have struck me funny. It didn't.

I boarded a plane for New York — my mind suddenly was clear of cobwebs.

When my plane landed at Kennedy Airport, Allen was at the gate. I had told him on the phone what had transpired, and now the look on his face said it all.

"I have two days all planned. Okay?"

"Okay." My answer wasn't the most eloquent, but it seemed to suit him just fine.

The sun was bright and the air was cold as we drove through the countryside, beautiful in its own wintry way. I had no idea where we were going, nor did I care. We stopped for a late lunch at an old converted mill, beside a waterfall that was frozen and sparkled in the sunshine. At least I think it did — the way we were feeling, everything sparkled.

Inside, the place was lined with handhewn logs, a fire was crackling in the big fireplace, and, except for a man who turned out to be the owner, "not another human in view." We ordered a warm drink and some lunch, and settled by the fire. For two hopeless romantics, what could be more perfect? For me, it was about to get even perfecter.

When the man brought the drinks, toddling at his heels was a tiny Maltese terrier puppy, which I scooped up immediately.

The man laughed. "You like him? Want to see the rest of the family?"

With that, he pushed open a door and three more Maltese came trooping in — mother, father, and another puppy. Everyone but the man joined us for lunch.

It was one of those unforgettable times — etched forever. Allen said he had been pretty proud of the mill and the waterfall, but the dogs were a bonus he wouldn't have thought to include.

When we returned to pick up our lives once again in the real world, all the problems had not magically evaporated. In love as I was, nonetheless marrying and moving east was still not in the equation. Allen, however, had eighteen years of a happy marriage behind him, not two divorces. He truly believed in what he was selling and kept the pressure on.

One night, at dinner in New York, Allen handed me a small package. I opened it to find a beautiful gold wedding ring with a circle of diamonds.

"You might as well keep it, because one of these days you'll put it on for keeps."

It was all closing in and I was scared. So — naturally — I took the logical approach.

I got mad. I told him to let me up or forget the whole thing. Without taking the ring out of the box, I gave it back to him.

Instead of biting back, Allen put the ring in his pocket and quietly waited for me to simmer down. Now, that can *really* make you mad!

The storm blew over quickly. It's hard to stay mad when you are the only one fighting. Allen taught me that valuable lesson over the years. I assumed he would return the ring to wherever it came from, and that would be that.

Not Allen Ludden. He put that damned ring on a chain around his neck, where I would be constantly aware of it; I watched it get full of sand and suntan oil. This went on for three months, but he never referred to it.

Why couldn't he just let well enough alone and leave things as they were? Well, of course he couldn't do that, and in my heart of hearts, I knew it. He had three great children, and they deserved more than a long-distance relationship for their father.

Easter came, and I was in California. A package arrived from Allen, and opening it, I found a beautiful soft-stuffed white bunny. Clipped to its ears was a pair of small flower earrings — petals of gold, with tiny diamonds, rubies, and sapphires. The note said, "These won't fit on a chain. Please say 'YES.'"

The choices were suddenly very clear and very narrow: stay in California and spend the rest of my life watching this man on television, knowing what I had lost, or . . . When the phone rang that evening I didn't say, "Hello." I said, "YES!"

Once our intentions became public, I kept running into people who would say, "I knew it from the first time I saw you two on *Password!*" They would actually stop us on the street to say, "I was the one who first said you two would get together!" It became a cliché. If everyone else was so sure, why had it taken me a whole year to get smart? The day would come when that precious year of indecision would haunt me.

A telegram arrived from Phil. One word — "Ouch."

We were married June 14, 1963.

Allen had used up all his time off from *Password,* so now all he had was a long weekend. To get a marriage license in California at that time required a blood test, meaning a three-day waiting period, which Allen didn't have. So, he flew to Los Angeles; then, along with my mom and dad, we flew over to Las

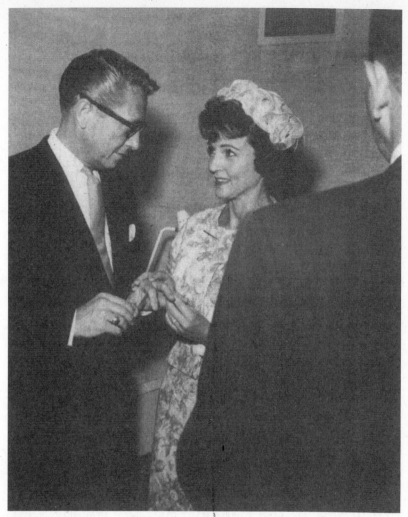

"With this ring . . ." *My ring, which he'd been wearing on a chain, is already on my finger.* (Courtesy Las Vegas News Bureau)

Vegas for the ceremony.

It was typical of this thoughtful man that at one point he drew my mother aside to give her a special wedding gift — a beautiful jade and pearl bracelet with a tiny gold tag that read, "Thank you, Doll."

We were married by the same judge, David Zenoff, who had joined Grant Tinker and Mary Tyler Moore the previous year. Grant Tinker was Allen's best friend — ever since the first *College Bowl* days. Grant was working at selling radio show ideas, and at his behest, Allen, who was living in Hartford, Connecticut, created the game. Pitting teams of four from colleges around the country, the show worked so well on national radio, the Luddens moved to New York to put *College Bowl* on national television. Early on, Allen had made a point of my meeting Mary and Grant, and I always said it was to make sure they approved. Our friendship has never faltered, through good times and bad. In spite of the fact that the judge tied a tighter knot for us than he did for them, Mary and Grant are each among my cherished ones today.

After an abbreviated honeymoon in Laguna Beach, the newlyweds took off for New York. This time there was no round-trip ticket.

Allen had stretched the long weekend as far as he possibly could — to the extent that, upon arriving, we had to go directly from the airport to the studio. The new bride was also booked to guest on the show. So that I would look halfway presentable on camera,

Mary.

Grant.

I rode all the way across country with my hair in pincurls, sneakily hidden under one of those stretch flower hats. With me, every day is a bad hair day.

My opponent on the other team was a special wedding present — Jack Paar. Jack didn't do game shows, so it was dear of him to make this exception, especially in light of his having played matchmaker with Phil.

In those days, they would tape the night show on Tuesday, two daytime shows on Wednesday, and the last three on Thursday. Not long after, they shortened the schedule to three on Tuesday and three on Wednesday, which cut the studio costs.

When some bright soul — was it Mark Goodson? — discovered that it was feasible to do all the week's shows in one day, it revolutionized the game show business. It took an enormous amount of preparation ahead of time; however, it was worth it. It was not only cheaper but much more convenient to do all the shows in one session, while the players were in makeup, into the swing of it, and the adrenaline was pumping, rather than have to rev them all up the next day. By bringing five changes of wardrobe, with ten minutes to dress between tapings, each show was a brand-new day. Dick Clark must hold the all-time record as durable host: on *Pyramid,* he once did twenty-five shows in two days. That's five weeks' worth of games! I can't help thinking of what the staff must have gone through to *set up* that many games.

That honeymoon evening it was the prime-time *Password,* which meant we only had one show to do. Whether Jack or I won that night I have no idea, but it was very festive. At the end of the show, instead of his usual password for the day, Allen wound things up with "Well, Mrs. Ludden, don't you think it's time for us to go home?"

When we did arrive home at last, the kids

were waiting with a warm giggly welcome. They had decorated the house with balloons and handmade paper banners of congratulations.

We were off to a good start.

Euphoria aside, with every new marriage there is the mandatory period of adjustment. In our case, there were five of us making the change from being friends to becoming a family. It was also a very busy summer for all of us, and everything was in a state of transition.

We had planned to do some remodeling on the house, until one Saturday morning shortly after the wedding. Audrey and Bob O'Brien, neighbors and dear friends of the Luddens, stopped by and insisted we come see a property in Chappaqua, another little Westchester village to the north. Before we knew it, we were in the car.

No denying — it was spectacular. Five and a half acres of old apple orchard and low dry stone walls. Previous owners had moved the little one-hundred-sixty-five-year-old farmhouse back from the road to where the old barn was — with its stone walls two feet thick — and proceeded to build a house that incorporated them both. There was a swimming pool that doubled as a skating rink in

The Luddens at home in Chappaqua, New York. Clockwise: Sarah, David, Allen, Martha, Mrs. Ludden, Emma, and Willie.

winter, and a pond that welcomed the same Canada geese each fall.

We didn't want to rush into anything, so we didn't actually buy it until that afternoon.

■ ■ ■ ■

On moving day, Allen supervised the loading of the furniture in Briarcliff; then he had to go to work in New York. My job in Chappaqua was to wait for the truck and supervise the *un*loading. When they arrived and the movers began carrying things into the new house, I soon realized I wasn't all that familiar with a lot of the furniture. I tried to sound confident when I told them where this or that went — all I could do was pray that I was at least close. Somehow, it all worked out.

When I suggested we refurbish a little paint here and there, I found out something about my new husband. Never one to go halfway about anything, Allen thought it would be best to do it all while we were on our feet. I soon learned that although Allen wasn't at all handy around the house (except for the garden), there wasn't anything he couldn't fix; he would simply pick up the phone. He knew *exactly* whom to call to do any job. As a result, our house was soon swarming with workmen — one day I counted forty-one — and I was running around with my swatches and wallpaper samples having the time of my life.

It all turned out beautifully, and I found

The King and I, *St. Louis Municipal Opera.* Top Row: Jean Sanders *(left of me) was a magnificent Lady Thiang and Charles Korvin an exciting King.* Wish *I could name the rest of this fine company.* (COURTESY PETER FERMAN)

I was ready to go back to work on TV — to get some rest.

Earlier in the year, I had signed to do *The King and I* for the St. Louis Municipal Opera, at their magnificent outdoor theater. I had played there once before with Jack Carson in *Take Me Along,* so I was more or less prepared for the fact that eleven thousand people filled the place for every performance; but the chance to be in a spectacular production of my favorite show, with that wonderful orchestra, and Charles Korvin as

258

the King, and my new husband coming to see it — well, that's as good as it gets.

Before the summer season ended, Allen and I did one more play together. It was something of a sentimental journey: once again, we all went back to the Cape Playhouse, then on up to Skowhegan, this time as a family. The play was *Janus,* which was unremarkable — light and airy summer fare — but we were impressed and totally charmed by the director and his wife, Gordon and Judy Davidson. We weren't wrong. Gordon Davidson went on to become the artistic director of the Center Theater Group in Los Angeles, and today he is the major mover and shaker in Los Angeles theater. Gordon and Judy haven't lost any of their warmth and charm along the way, and it's always a joy to see them at every new production at the Ahmandson and the Mark Taper theaters.

On this trip we were all living together — Willie and Emma, too — so the loons were a little harder to hear, but I knew they were there. I was beginning to catch on to something that was new to this only child: getting five people together to do something is rarely easy, and often impossible. So I tried to learn to roll with it. Most of the time.

■■■■

With the fall season, things settled into a more normal routine, although it's hard to use the word "normal" with all that gorgeous color happening around you. School started for the girls, and David was off to Andover to start prep school.

On Tuesday nights, Allen and I stayed in town at the New York Hilton, since *Password* taped just around the corner on Tuesdays and Wednesdays. The timing worked out so that I could sometimes guest on *To Tell the Truth* or *I've Got a Secret,* which often taped on similar schedules.

Every now and then we'd come in on Sunday evening, when Allen or I were invited to sit on the panel of *What's My Line*. He was the mystery guest one night when I was a panelist, and he answered all the questions in some weird voice he had dreamed up. I didn't have a clue, and it was Arlene who finally guessed him. On another occasion, turnabout was fair play. I was the mystery guest facing *him* on the panel, and I made my voice as deep as I could, answering in gruff monosyllables. You can imagine the audience response when blindfolded Allen asked me, "Are you a man?"

It would seem too obvious that they would

use us to attempt to fool each other. Didn't we know going in? Not by a long shot. Secrecy was a matter of pride on the show, and if anything was inadvertently tipped ahead of time, the spot was changed. Over a long period of time, with many shows in between, repeats worked. Under those blindfolds it was next to impossible to get a handle on a disguised voice, especially when the answers were so brief. The regular panelists would try to gain an edge by keeping posted on what showfolk were visiting in town or who was playing on Broadway, but it didn't always help. For that reason, even Mark Goodson was able to return and fool them every now and then, which he loved to do. The only thing Mark enjoyed more than creating games was playing them.

As well as being the Man in Charge, Mark was also a friend. In the beginning days of *Password,* when Allen was going through his desperate days after losing Margaret, he deeply appreciated Mark's personal concern and support. They would often have dinner together when Allen finished taping. Successful as Mark was, he was not the happiest of men in his personal life. He was always searching for something that continued to elude him — a lasting relationship. He was very social and hosted a lot of parties,

For darling An
incomparable Betty
White... with admiration
and much love —
MARK Goodson
1990

Mark Goodson — one of a kind, and a good friend. (Courtesy Mark Goodson)

both company gatherings and small private groups. Sooner or later during the evening, Mark would find me, to talk out his latest romantic derailment. Allen suggested I hang out a shingle.

Another Goodson-Todman show, *The Match Game,* was up and running, hosted by Gene Rayburn. It was great fun and turned out to be something of an annuity. The format of the original show consisted of two teams — one celebrity and two real people on a side — attempting to match answers for modest cash prizes. This tame version lasted for seven years on NBC before it was canceled in 1969.

The show resurfaced as *Match Game '73,* this time from California and on CBS. The format had changed but so had the audience, and this version had a somewhat racier flavor. This time, six celebrities tried to match the answers of two contestants. Gene would read the questions, everyone would write down their responses, then reveal them in turn. For example, "Cold *blank*" could be one of several things — cold water, cold shoulder, cold turkey; "*Blank* clock" could be time, alarm, grandfather's, et cetera. Harmless enough in theory; however, giving six flaky showfolk a stack of blank cards and marking pens is tantamount to handing fingerpaints to a troupe of chimpanzees. The endgame was an audience match — trying to match three answers collected from the studio audience in the warm-up before the show. There were three chances, each worth an increase in dollars. Somehow, the one that sticks in my mind was the day the question was "*Blank* willow." Maybe *you* can come up with something besides weeping, pussy, and tit.

The ingredient that made the show work was Gene Rayburn. Although supposedly the master of revels, in reality he was barely a cut above the outrageousness of anyone there. His quick mind and delicious sense of humor gave the panel something to shoot for.

The home audience must have enjoyed it, too, because they kept coming back for more, and *Match Game '73* advanced every year until *Match Game '79* was finally packed in.

Gene commuted to California from New York every two weeks to do the tapings; he flatly refused to move west. Does that sound like anyone else, only in reverse? Not too long ago, I was on the *Vicki!* show with Gene and was very surprised when he told me, off camera, that he came to regret that decision. Staying in New York had proved to be a bad career move, and he said he only wishes he had it to do over again. What a secure, sure-footed bunch we all are in this strange line of work we insist upon pursuing.

Around the first of November, my mother

and dad came back east for a visit, to meet the family and see our new home. (I had been out to see them whenever a job of *any* kind gave me an excuse in that direction. Secret intermittent waves of homesickness hadn't subsided entirely.) They both loved everything and everybody, and left for home very happy for their girl in her new life.

A few days later, I was participating in the usual nonsense on *The Match Game* when they called me into the control booth, between shows, to take a phone call. It was Mom's housekeeper, Claudie, from California. It seemed that Daddy had caught a cold on the trip home, and when it continued to get worse, the doctor insisted on hospitalizing him. They hadn't wanted to worry me, since he was doing okay — in fact, he was being released tomorrow. But now, my mother's doctor had put *her* in the same hospital because her blood count had dropped alarmingly low. Claudie was frantic and finally had to call me.

Somehow we finished the last show, and they got me on a plane that night.

First thing next morning, I went to the hospital and was considerably reassured. Mom was doing much better, and they would only be keeping her a few more days. Dad, as expected, was released that morning, and I brought him home.

We made it in time for him to watch the kickoff of the USC-UCLA football game, which was an annual must for him. Claudie and I got him all settled in the den, and I ran up to the store to get some favorite goodies for his lunch. I was back in less than forty-five minutes, but he was gone.

Right after I had left, his heart had stopped. Claudie called emergency, and they came immediately, but it was over before they arrived. They took him away. He just wasn't there anymore. I called Allen, who caught the next plane.

Then I had to go and tell my mother.

They couldn't release Mom in time for her to attend the funeral, but we were able to bring her home the following day. Allen had to go back to do the show, but he insisted I get her ready, and bring her home to us for a while.

It was on Friday morning that I called the *L.A. Times* to cancel her subscription. I can still hear the tearful voice telling me President Kennedy had just been shot.

We managed to make it back to Chappaqua. For that whole long, bleak weekend we all held each other very close as we watched the presidential funeral ceremonies

— and mourned with the rest of the country. For a couple of us, those ceremonies had a special double meaning.

It seems a strange context, but it was during that suspended weekend that it began to come clear to me what marriage is all about. An incredibly slow study, I came to realize that Allen and I weren't two separate entities; we were together, sharing this grief, trying to comfort others. It finally penetrated my thick skull that we were a unit. From that day forward, any problems we had — and there were some — came from the outside. At long last, he had taught me to stop running.

It had been quite a year.

Tess White's world had *totally* changed within those twelve months. Her family of three people and three dogs had evaporated. The three dogs had passed away within six months of each other; her daughter had moved far away; her husband of all those forty-two years had died.

Allen had gained what he sought. For better or for worse.

I had learned more than I'd ever thought I wanted to know.

Ultimately, we made it through.

14

David came home from Andover for the holidays, and it was good to have us all close as a family for our first Christmas under such different circumstances for everyone. It was snowy and beautiful.

Because I am such a devout Californian, people tend to assume my feelings are weather oriented. Not even slightly. I love the winter weather and actually do better when it's cold than when the sun is excessively hot. Some Californian! I do love to drive, but I learned to have great respect for ice and snow, and paid attention when Mother Nature said to stay out of the car. I can honestly say I enjoyed winter up in Chappaqua. In New York, it was another story — just walking down the street after a snowstorm could be a messy challenge. Didn't snow realize it belonged in the mountains and the country — *not* in the city?

Tess stayed with us over New Year's but

then opted to go home and pick up the pieces. I must say, she did a truly fine job of it. Between her hospital work and her involvement with the Motion Picture Mothers organization in support of the Motion Picture Country House, she worked hard, and she made a whole new circle of friends. She was soon off and running on her own two feet.

Allen's circle of friends was large and diverse. He had lost no time in having me meet some of the close ones. Mary and Grant Tinker were the first — and then I met Elaine and John Steinbeck. Allen and Elaine had been buddies since their early days at the University of Texas. That first evening, Allen took me to their apartment to meet them. Elaine's ease and warmth soon made me feel that I, too, had known her that long.

It was hard not to be a little in awe of John at first. It didn't help my state of nerves that at the moment we walked in, John was scratching out his acceptance speech for the Nobel Prize. After a brief introduction, John suddenly asked us to help him think of a synonym for a word he wanted to replace. *We* should help John Steinbeck think of a word? Don't ask me what the word was — at that moment I couldn't remember my name!

Later, after receiving his medal, John gave us that rough draft of his speech, to commemorate the night we met. It's hanging here as I write.

The Nobel medal itself is beautiful and round, about three inches in diameter, and heavily embossed on both sides. Elaine took it to an exclusive shop on the East Side to have it specially mounted so that both sides would show. When she went to give the man her charge, he stopped her, saying, "We know who you are, Mrs. Steinbeck. We don't do a lot of business with Nobel Prize winners."

John was a large bear of a man who tended to mumble, but you listened very closely, because you didn't want to miss a word. And he had a great laugh.

I was also thrilled to meet Charley, their most exceptional gray standard poodle. Before I ever laid eyes on him I was already in love with that wonderful dog, having read John's *Travels with Charley*. Old age finally claimed Charley. Eventually, John acquired a new friend, Angel — a white bull terrier, aptly named. Angel was never very far from John's feet, as he stood at his drafting table to write. Due to a chronic back problem, that was how John worked: standing up, writing in longhand. My computer and word-processing friends think of me as a Neanderthal, because I always have to write the first draft of anything in longhand. I simply tell them that if it was good enough for Emily Brontë and John Steinbeck, it's good enough for me.

On another occasion, we drove into New York one night to have dinner at Sardi's East (long since defunct) with an old army pal of Allen's, Charles Lowe, and his wife, Carol Channing. We had a marvelous time and found so much to talk about that everyone was fighting for words. That hasn't changed in almost thirty-five years — we are still talking up a storm whenever we are together, which is often. After World War II, Charles handled public relations for George Burns and Gracie Allen for all those years together, and has remained George's good friend. Carol Channing is unlike any other human on this planet. "Larger than life" is too easy and doesn't quite express how unique she is. A legendary performer, she is also one of the smartest people I know.

For years, Carol suffered from an allergy she developed to hair spray and had to maintain a specific diet of specially grown and prepared food. Wherever they went, Charlie would tote her bag of special dinner, put up in beautiful shining silver containers from

With George Burns and Carol Channing. That's Charles Lowe lurking in the background, keeping an eye on his wife. (COURTESY ALAN BERLINER)

Tiffany. This was universally known and accepted without a second glance. Waiters would automatically bring her a smile and a warm plate. Happily, the allergy has subsided somewhat in the past couple of years, and she has been able to broaden her menu a trifle. However, back when we first met, none of this allergic reaction had happened yet. When we'd go out to dinner together, I can remember Carol cleaning her plate, then polishing off whatever Charlie or Allen or I had left on ours. She was the only one I ever saw put butter on lamb chop bones and strip them clean. Hers and ours. And she remained reed slim. There ain't no justice.

At one point, Carol and I worked together on *The Love Boat*. We did the show five times, playing the same characters each time — two former showgirls with an ongoing love/hate relationship. We had such a good time that we thought it would be great fun to do a series together. We had an idea that we liked a lot for *The Pickle Sisters,* but we seemed to like it better than anyone else, because it never got off the ground.

When Carol opened in *Hello, Dolly!* it was the first Broadway opening night I had ever attended. I'm not saying this because she was our friend, but you could feel the electricity begin to build thirty seconds after the curtain went up. It was a spectacular evening. That was in 1964. As of this writing, Carol is on a brand-new tour of *Dolly* that will take her all around this country for a year, then on to Broadway, then London, Japan, and Singapore. Charles sends me the reviews from every city, and she is breaking attendance records wherever she goes and getting rave notices. If I didn't see the actual newspapers, I'd think Charlie wrote them himself. That kind of a grueling tour would drive anyone into the ground at whatever age, but it is life's blood to that one-of-a-kind lady.

Television games continued to grow in number and diversity.

Early on, back in 1949, when everything was new and no patterns had been set, Arlene Francis hosted — hostessed — a show called *Blind Date*. (This was pre–*What's My Line,* which didn't begin until the following year.) *Date's* format consisted of six college boys "telephoning" three girls, who were seated on the other side of a wall onstage, and trying to make a date. Each girl picked the one who most impressed her, sight unseen. The audience, of course, could see everyone involved. Familiar territory by today's standards, but a groundbreaker at the time. *Blind Date* was on and off the air several times between 1949 and 1953. Arlene left it in 1952; then it returned briefly in 1953 under the title *Your Big Moment,* with Melvyn Douglas, of all people, as host. Three weeks later he was replaced by Jan Murray and they went back to calling it *Blind Date;* then the whole thing faded to black in September of '53.

From that time on it was strictly the *master* of ceremonies where games were concerned. Ever on the cutting edge, by 1964 Mark Goodson figured it was time to shake things up and put a woman in the emcee position. It was more than flattering when he called and asked if I would be interested. Interested, yes. Eager — most assuredly.

The show in development at the time was called *Get the Message* and was somewhat indistinguishable from several others: two celebrities and a real person on each team, trying to figure out what phrase the contestant was trying to impart with one-word clues. Goodson-Todman's position as the number one game factory didn't happen by chance. "Developing" a new game to sell to a network meant endless office run-throughs, eliminating weak spots (hopefully) and making sure the game worked. From my standpoint, those practice sessions were invaluable, to get easy with the game. I soon discovered there was a major difference between *playing* a game and being the guy in the middle. I had the best tutor in the business, Mark himself.

Once he felt we were all sufficiently ready, the show was presented to the network — in this instance, ABC. They liked it. They bought it on the spot. Just one little hitch. They were convinced that the audience would not be comfortable with a woman driving the show — they must have a host. *Get the Message* went on the air in 1964

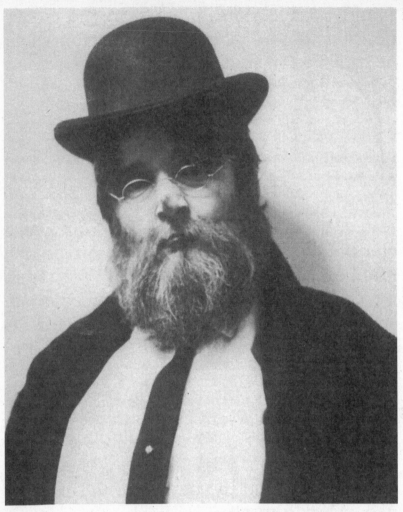

Betty as a guest on Masquerade Party. *After two hours in makeup, I came out and someone said, "Hi, Betty."*

with a man named Frank Buxton as master of ceremonies, soon to be replaced by Robert Q. Lewis. The show debuted in March and bit the dust the following Christmas Day. Whew! That was a close one! I would have taken the rap for the game's quick demise.

Perhaps justifiably.

(Incidentally, would you believe there actually *was* a game show called *Whew!* in 1979? Hosted by our own Tom Kennedy, it lasted one year. Whew!)

It was somewhere around this time, the mid-sixties, that Allen and I were invited to Columbus, Ohio, to help demonstrate a brand-new state-of-the-art television system — QUBE TV. It was a tremendous breakthrough and was touted as going to revolutionize the entire industry. It was designed to give the viewer a choice of *thirty-two* different channels to watch! It sounded sensational in theory, but it was a little overwhelming to see the actual presentation. The public was evidently not ready — QUBE only lasted a very short time and, to my knowledge, never went beyond Columbus. It wound up being just an early wide place in the road heading toward the Superhighway.

Sometime during our sojourn in New York, I was tapped to take over a radio show that Betty Furness had been doing for quite some time but now had chosen to leave. It was a little ironic in a sense, because people had often confused the two of us, which was understandable — both Bettys and both doing commercials. Every once in a while, even now, someone will smile smugly and say, "I remember when you used to open that refrigerator door and one time it stuck!" It was Betty Furness who handled the stubborn door so gracefully without missing a beat. The incident has been rerun many times as a classic blooper.

So, I took over the radio show, reading letters from listeners and answering their questions on a multitude of subjects. I couldn't get over how easy it was after television: all the information had been researched by the staff. The producer was very loyal to Betty Furness, and would barely speak to me at first. It finally got through to her that the change had not been any of my doing, but it took a few weeks for her to forgive me for being the wrong Betty.

Allen and I continued to do plays during the summer breaks. One of these, *Bell, Book and Candle,* brought us back once again to Cape Cod, and our favorite Cape Playhouse. (By now, the kids were all occupied with their own various summer activities.) This run turned out to be more important than we had any idea at the time.

After the show each night, Allen and I would head for a small restaurant near the theater, The Deacon's Perch, for something cold and a bite to eat — usually steamed clams. It wasn't so much the food and drink that brought us back each night; it was a young man at the piano, who soon got to know our favorite songs, and would launch into them when he heard we'd arrived. I say "heard," because this young Harvard student, Tom Sullivan, had been blind since birth. It certainly hadn't held him back as a musician, nor, I might add, with the girls who buzzed around him like humming-birds.

Tom Sullivan with the whole family. Season, Blythe, Nelson, Patty, Tom Jr., and Cay. (COURTESY OF SULLIVANS)

One especially pretty girl, Patty Stefan, stayed more in the background, but she was definitely always there. Allen, ever helpful, took it upon himself to make sure Tom was aware of what a gem she was — whether it was any of his business or not.

My husband was not one who could encounter genuine young talent and then just walk away without passing the word along. When we finished our play and returned home, Allen called Mike Douglas, who invited Tom to be on his show. As expected, Tom rose to the occasion; not only Mike but his whole audience were duly impressed, which made Allen very proud. Proud turned to smug when, before long, Tom had the great and good sense to marry Patty. They have been in our lives ever since.

More and more shows were moving to the West Coast; it began to take on the proportions of a general exodus. Classic dyed-in-the-wool New Yorkers — and no one fit that description more than Mark Goodson — found themselves having to go with the flow.

For quite some time, *Password* had been taping about three weeks a year in Los Angeles to be able to book some of the series people who were not readily available on the East Coast. Around 1967, the time spent in

California stretched to six weeks at a crack, and Mark was beginning to send out some quiet exploratory signals that a permanent move might not be out of the question.

I loved being out there, of course, but it seemed strange to be staying at the Beverly Hills Hotel, beautiful as it was, while in my own hometown. We had all been very pleased when Mom finally agreed to sell the house and move into a lovely, secure high-rise on Wilshire Boulevard; I'm sure that felt strange to her, too, although she handled the transition in good spirit. I kept my disorientation to myself, and it eventually diminished.

In light of my past record, I'm sure it's hard to believe that I wasn't pushing for the permanent move to California; however, I wasn't. Our family was settled, we loved our house, and another move was not a tempting prospect. The girls had had to change schools when we moved from Briarcliff Manor, and while the new school was just a short distance up the road, it still meant leaving friends and making new ones. As I knew from fairly recent experience, that could be a bummer.

The question of moving *Password* to the West Coast became academic before 1967 was over. In May, CBS had terminated the nighttime version of the show, and while we were sorry, of course, to see it go, it had enjoyed an excellent run in the highly competitive prime-time schedule. However, it came as a shock to all concerned — the audience included — when daytime *Password* was canceled in September.

Password still holds the record as the highest-rated game show *ever,* and the daytime show went off the air with ratings and share numbers that prime-time shows today would kill for. That is a real clue to how the world has turned and our business has fragmented. In 1967, Fred Silverman was the wunderkind who seemingly could do no wrong. He had brought CBS to the number one position. He later moved on and did the same thing for ABC. When he went for three and moved to NBC, his luck ran out. It took Grant Tinker to pull that network back from the brink of disaster.

Fred's reason for taking *Password* off the air was that he needed the time period to launch a soap opera he very much wanted to do — *Love Is a Many-Splendored Thing.* Giving birth to a new soap takes an inordinate amount of time, patience, and *money,* and even with Fred's magic touch, *Love Is a Many-Splendored Thing* just didn't make it.

On that last week of *Password,* Frank Gifford and I were the guests, and by now they were taping all five shows in one day. When we got to the fifth and final show, emotions were running a little high. Standing next to Allen as he gave his final password of the day, my smile was frozen, but tears were pouring down my cheeks, and Frank wasn't doing much better. Allen said his thanks and good-bye with his usual class, but I must have looked like Pat Nixon listening to her husband's concession speech when he lost the election to John Kennedy. We couldn't know at the time that *Password* would be back — in all its incarnations — for the next twenty years. Richard Nixon also came back, but then he got canceled.

Password was the first game show to use reruns of previously aired shows. Before someone came up with that gold-mine idea, old shows were simply erased, including a bunch of early *Passwords*. Nowadays, those repeats are not only money in the bank, but they also allow performers substantial time off without hiring a guest host. The home edition of *Password* was another record breaker, and over the years, the Milton Bradley company put out twenty-five different editions of the game. Today, we see Vanna White's picture on the home game of *Wheel of Fortune,* and after some on-air lobbying on his part, Alex

Trebek's on *Jeopardy!* Unfortunately, Allen was not identified on the *Password* box, so he did not participate in its success in the toy department.

From 1968 to 1970 reruns of the show appeared in syndication; then, with a few retouches, *Password* was back on the ABC network by 1971. In 1974, the game was changed to *Password All-Stars,* with a whole new format using only celebrities. By 1975, it reverted to *Password* and contestants once more.

Allen did other shows in between and sometimes simultaneously, but he always returned for each new version of "his" show. The program was revived yet again, in 1979, this time on NBC, using the title *Password Plus.* Illness was beginning to take its toll on Allen, and finally, in October of 1980, nineteen years to the month from the time he introduced the show, he had to step down. It was always a comfort to him — and to me — that the one to pick up the reins was almost like family, Tom Kennedy, né Jim Narz. By this time, Tom was one of the top game-show hosts in his own right. The show went off the air by 1982, but came back under still another name, *Super Password.* Another pal, Bert Convy, was now the master of revels, but it wouldn't be too long before Bert was cut down in his prime by a malignant brain tumor.

Password itself continues to have a life of its own and proves indestructible. Reruns of all the early shows are already appearing on the new Game Channel. So, once more Allen is back in the driver's seat, and "his" show has come full circle.

Back to where we left off: In 1968, it was Allen who made the definitive decision to move to California. There was really no choice if he was to continue to work in television, but *when* to move was a major consideration. Martha was starting college, and Sarah was finishing her second year in high school. Dave was already at Yale and was one of twelve students who had qualified for a five-year BA, enabling him to spend a year working in Madras, India. It became apparent that it would be best to make the move that summer, because Sarah would have two years of high school left. That would at least give her a year to settle into a new school before her very important senior year. After a family meeting, the die was cast. Allen and I would find a location in California as soon as possible. I was to come out a couple of days early to look at houses. Allen was working on a temporary project in New York, and my job was to weed out the losers in order to make the most of his limited time.

Having lived in California all my life, I was acutely aware of our potential for both fire and flood, which ruled out hillside or canyon property. There wasn't much I could do about the possibility of earthquakes, but, again, two out of three ain't bad. My folks had lived in Brentwood for many years, and I knew and loved the area, so the day I arrived I took a drive around just to reconnoiter — serious house-hunting would begin the next day. I drove by one place that rang a major bell, and it even had a for-sale sign in front of it! I drove around the block three times, then called the real estate lady I was meeting the next day, to see if we could look at it.

The "real estate lady" was none other than Elvia Allman, a character actress you would recognize in a minute. She had worked with us a couple of times back on *Life with Elizabeth,* in fact, but I had no idea she was in real estate. She had been recommended to us by Grant and Mary, since she had found their home for them. As luck would have it, the house that had caught my eye was on her list!

True to my job, I looked at twenty-six houses in the next three days, out of which there were five iffy possibles, plus the bell ringer, which I loved. I knew better than to give Allen a clue that I liked one above the others, or it would have been a done deal, and I wasn't up to that responsibility. Instead, on Sunday we went to look at all six houses. I stashed the favorite in the middle somewhere, then gave the performance of my life trying not to show partiality. My husband fell as hard for the house as I had, and in spite of his being the classic Libra of all time, he completely forgot about weighing his decisions. We were in business.

We moved west in August 1968, and right now — looking around some twenty-six years later — I must say I love this place even more now than I did then.

California, here we go again.

15

Allen became an instant Californian. No, I shouldn't exaggerate, it took him about twenty minutes. There is nothing more zealous than a convert, and he was soon extolling the virtues of living in California to anyone who would listen. Especially to New Yorkers — who didn't. For the girls, it wasn't quite that easy, and I could readily empathize.

Moving day was interesting. The former owner had delayed moving out twice, but finally promised faithfully she would leave by a certain day. That would make it just one day before our furniture, coming clear across the country, was due in. We had allowed a time cushion in case of any problems, but the delays had eaten that up and we were now down to the wire.

We arrived bright and early on truck day, expecting to find the house vacant, but guess who was still there? Her furniture was gone, but she was surrounded by a pile of odds and ends and personal belongings still to be dealt with, and she was not making any effort toward getting them into her car. I was busy trying to keep Allen's rather short fuse from igniting, but I almost lost it myself when she turned to us and said, quite seriously, "Perhaps I should have a garage sale."

Allen managed to get her stuff into her car at last, and we thought we had it made until she collapsed in my arms in a flood of tears.

"Oh, you don't know how I hate to leave this place. It has meant so much to me!"

Chicken heart that I am, I started to bawl with her, until she added nostalgically, "I've had two divorces in this house!"

That may have explained the smashed lock on the bedroom door.

The day after we moved in, I was busily unpacking boxes when the front doorbell rang. I opened the door to find Pat O'Brien, the wonderful Irish-American movie star, standing there, holding a cup of sugar.

"I thought I'd save you the trip next door to borrow this," he said.

Pat and I had worked together several times in New York on *The Match Game* and had enjoyed each other tremendously. It was a lovely surprise to find that, along with the house we loved, we had the bonus of Pat and his wife, Eloise, as next-door neighbors. There would be many a great over-the-back-fence conversation between Pat and Allen while they were both out gardening.

Pat didn't drink at all in the later years, but earlier on he liked to celebrate now and then. Our driveways were right next to each other, and one night, coming home from a party, he drove up the wrong one. Pat couldn't understand *why* his door key wouldn't open our front door.

Once we were in and more or less settled in our new home, Allen and I were invited to do a guest shot together on *The Odd Couple,* starring Tony Randall and Jack Klugman. Not only was it a good show and an extremely popular one (often it's one or the other), but both Jack and Tony were longtime buddies of whom we were very fond. The story line was fun. Allen and I were playing ourselves; Felix and Oscar had supposedly seen us at a restaurant, and wanted to be on *Password* in the worst way. (Exactly!) They finally finagle their way onto the show as contestants; Allen, of course, is the host, and I'm a celebrity guest. The game promptly goes to hell from there on, but I must say it was funny.

I have never seen an episode with a longer shelf life. It still turns up every now and then on some channel or other, to this day.

Sitcoms, for the most part, were taped on the West Coast, so it had been a long time since I had been on a situation-comedy set. I have to admit it felt good. I was like an old fire horse who smells smoke.

With so many game shows coming on and going off the air, it was a game in itself just trying to keep them straight. And the names of the hosts could be a bit confusing as well — Bill Cullen, Bill Leyden, Allen Ludden, Allan Funt (*Candid Camera*). My Allen got so used to being called Bill, he'd answer to it without batting an eye.

Allen had a passion for clothes, and would have no part of the practice of having his wardrobe provided in exchange for a clothes credit at the end of the show. He was usually on the leading edge of each new trend in men's clothing — open collars, turtlenecks, leisure suits. No, he never fell for a Nehru jacket. The two comments we heard most frequently regarding *Password* were, "Where do you get those great clothes, Allen?" and from waiters on the night shift, "Thank you, Mr. Ludden, for helping me learn English!"

During the summer following our move

west, Allen put together his all-time favorite show and sold it to Metromedia. He produced and starred in *Ludden Unlimited,* a combination talk and variety format where he put some interesting people together. One feature, "Ludden's Gallery," could have been a series in itself. Allen would invite two, sometimes three, well-known columnists to sit in together and compare notes on some particular star they had all interviewed. The different perceptions of the same person by professional writers made for a fascinating discussion. Now and then, one of the stars in question would put in an appearance on a subsequent show but never on the same program with the writers, because that would have served to inhibit the freewheeling conversation. That, of course, was 1969. Since then, the public appetite has been so jaded by tabloidism that I doubt if the same approach would work today.

H. B. Barnum headed up the music department on *Ludden Unlimited,* giving Allen the opportunity to sing occasionally, which he did surprisingly well and loved to do. (Allen recorded a lovely album in New York shortly after we were married — *Allen Ludden Sings His Favorite Songs.*) It also meant he could invite his guests to perform. I remember one show when a dance act billed as Hines,

Hines and Dad came on and blew everyone away. The youngest of the threesome, Gregory Hines, continued to dance his way up to Broadway and into films. Gregory and Mikhail Baryshnikov were a pair to draw to, dancing together on the screen in *White Nights*.

While Allen's show was syndicated, they taped at KTTV, a local television station. Around this time, I was invited to be a regular panel member on a new game show that was being put together at the same KTTV. I didn't even care what the game was about; once I heard that it would be hosted by none other than Rod Serling, I was theirs.

As it happened, the game, called *Liar's Club,* turned out to be tremendously enjoyable. The four of us on the panel were given weird but authentic objects, and it was up to us to explain their function. It was one more variation on the old classic parlor game of Dictionary — one of us would correctly explain whatever the object actually was, while the other three lied through their teeth. As an endgame, a fine abstract painting (borrowed from one of the local galleries) would be set up on an easel, and each of us would go up and "interpret" what the artist was trying to convey and the title of the work. Only one of us had the real story, but we all had somewhat outrageous imaginations. Good luck!

Pia Lindstrom was one of us; on her way to becoming a well-known television commentator, Ingrid Bergman's daughter was the class of the panel. Larry Hovis, Dick Gautier, and I filled in the rest of the seats. We all maintained a very serious educational demeanor, but in reality, given our collective lack of inhibition, we probably all should have been arrested. Individually we were good kids — we just got in with the wrong crowd.

Getting to know Rod Serling was a privilege not to be taken lightly. His magnificent writing for live anthology dramas during TV's Golden Age — *Patterns* and *Requiem for a Heavyweight* are two outstanding examples — are milestones in the television industry.

The Serlings maintained a place in the country in New York as an anchor to reality when Rod and Carol moved to California for his memorable series, *The Twilight Zone*. Rod's on-camera introductions each week not only set the mood for the program, but turned him into a star in his own right.

We didn't live far from each other, and every so often we would get together for dinner at our favorite neighborhood restaurant,

Johnny Sproatt's The Bat Rack. Those were great evenings, rich in conversation because all four of us were *interested* — in *everything*. I loved Rod's attitude concerning television. He believed in it. He felt that though much of it was admittedly dreck, some of it was good and occasionally fine. He was also convinced that it aimed at being better. It did — then.

Liar's Club, of course, had nothing whatsoever to do with the above. That local version of *Liar's* lasted a season. It would return in 1976 in syndication, hosted by Bill Armstrong for six months; then it continued until 1979 with, ironically, Allen Ludden as emcee. In truth, it was the most fun to *play* of all.

Rod was not a comfortable host, but oh, he was delightful to observe — especially when he fell apart. He was fine at running the game, where there were written words on cue cards, but if at any time he had to ad-lib, the ever-present deep tan would drain from his face and he would be struggling. Rod was a *writer,* not a glib on-camera *talker.*

At the close of any game show, it is standard operating procedure for the stage manager to inform the emcee how many seconds he has to wind things up and sign off. The dreaded stretch sign, indicating there is a bit of extra time to fill before the precise cutoff, is not a welcome one, even to seasoned glibsters, but for Rod it was quiet desperation time; with glazed eyes, he was like a cornered animal. It may only have been a matter of a mere fifteen or twenty seconds, but "television seconds" have a way of working in opposition — invariably, they are either too long or too short, according to the given situation.

Laughter was the surest and sometimes the only way to diffuse Rod's very real brand of panic. So all of us on the panel — altruists that we were — did our part to help him in his hour of need. First, we let the audience at home in on the fact that Rod had time to fill, then we all clammed up to watch him fight it out alone. Realizing what monsters we were would crack him up, and more often than not, the show ended with Rod laughing helplessly, shaking his head, and able only to wave good-bye. Hardly the in-control Rod Serling we may have envisioned. The audience was in on the joke, and everyone, including Rod, had a very good time.

What would Rod think of television today, I wonder? He would be saddened, I suspect, that big business has taken so much of it out of the hands of the creative community and the genuine broadcasters. He would probably be fascinated by the electronic magic — particularly in special effects — that has evolved since he moved on. Undoubtedly, he would assess the possibilities and then use them in his ongoing exploration of the worlds we live in.

Rod may not be with us in person, but that distinctive tight-lipped delivery of his is imitated, even on commercials, to this day. When and if the Superhighway becomes a reality, don't be surprised to find Rod Serling in a driver's seat.

If *Ludden Unlimited* was Allen's dream show, *The Pet Set* was mine.

Since before I was born, animals have been the one unwavering constant in my life. Whatever else was going on, my feeling for all animals never changed, and their influence has always been a positive one, even at sad times. I say *before* I was born because my mother and father were, if anything, even worse on the subject than I, so my interest may have started prior to my actual arrival on the scene. I love animals, certainly, but also find them endlessly fascinating and can never learn enough. I also have never passed up a chance to work them into whatever TV I might be doing. As early as my days at KLAC-TV, I tried to interest the station in a pet show called *The Bandit and Me,* but struck out (perhaps on grammar). Bandy took the matter into his own paws when he pushed his way onto the initial *Betty White Show.*

Knowing of my inordinate passion for the subject, Allen finally challenged me to put together the kind of show I would really want to do. In 1970, I took him up on it and outlined a celebrity-oriented animal show that would be as all-inclusive as I could make it. Allen sold it to the Carnation Company, and with him as producer, we were in business. And I was in hog heaven.

The basic premise was simple. I would invite a celebrity to bring his or her pet to the studio, and after a brief interview, we would excuse the pet, and the celebrity would stay with me as we moved through the various segments of the show.

For example: On one of our early programs, Jim Brolin joined us (he was doing *Marcus Welby, M.D.* at the time). He brought "Buck," his huge harlequin Great Dane. For the uninitiated, a harlequin Dane is white with black spots, which gave us an excuse to do a film piece from Jim's ranch house, to include his Appaloosa horses, also spotted. We had just been through an onslaught of torrential rains and flooding, so for segment

Jim Brolin and Buck on The Pet Set. (COURTESY PET SET FILES)

two, Martin Grangetto from the LASPCA sat in with Jim and me to describe the animal-rescue work during the recent disaster. Segment three was our production number, with beautiful examples of the five Great Dane colors: black, blue, brindle, fawn, and harlequin. As added starters we had a flock of six-week-old Dane puppies, and a couple of in-betweeners at the awkward teenage stage just for good measure.

Every show included a Wild Spot, for which Ralph Helfer would bring us an exotic animal from his Africa, USA, compound. The biggest thing we could find to go with Great Danes and big Jim Brolin for our finale was Margie, a veteran Asian elephant. She joined us on stage, responding to the subtlest of commands. Suffice it to say, it was a packed half hour. It was also another of the busier times in my career.

Once a celebrity guest was definitely scheduled, I would write the show tailored specifically for him or her, and then I would call around and book the animals I needed. I didn't want to go for just a bunch of cutesies — my aim was to sugarcoat authentic information so that the audience just might wind up learning something they hadn't known without feeling they were being taught. The dog fancy and the cat fancy were tremendously cooperative, and if the people I called didn't have what I needed, they would find it for me. As a result, when we were demonstrating a given breed, the dogs or cats we showed were as close to perfect examples as there were.

Sometimes potential *Pet Set* guests would

meet me at Allen's offices for a preinterview, and my poor husband never quite knew what to expect. For example, Kojak arrived in the backseat of a Lincoln town car, and we could hear his hooves ticking on the tile floor as he came down the long hall. Kojak was a miniature horse — a palomino Lilliputian stallion just twenty-six inches at the withers. That's *little*. Think how high a regular horse is at the shoulder, then measure twenty-six inches from the floor — that was Kojak. He had no pony conformation; he was a perfect little *horse*. We had his interview in the office, then he ticked back down the hall and was driven home.

Sultan was my favorite, if not Allen's. He

Sultan's interview at our office. He got the job!

was a full grown Bengal tiger. You didn't hear him padding down the hall, but as he got to our door, he put his paws up on the wall and touched the eight-foot ceiling with his nose. Ralph Helfer brought him into the office, where Sultan promptly jumped up on the desk for his interview. He got the job.

The show was on once a week, but we would tape two in one day for economic reasons. The pressure was always on just to stay even, let alone ahead; I was up to my derrière in work and in animals of every description; I was never happier. Interviewers invariably asked Allen if he had always been an animal lover. His answer was, "I just didn't know it until I met Betty."

To ensure the authenticity I spoke of, I would cross-check from several sources to preclude passing along misinformation. I kept running across the name Morris Animal Foundation as representing the definitive word on whatever it was I was looking for. So you can imagine my surprise to receive a call one day from the Denver headquarters of that very organization, requesting a meeting. Their executive director, Claude Ramsey, flew out, and we met for breakfast at the Beverly Hills Hotel. He said they had been following our show and were inviting me to join their board of directors. Flattering as it was, there was no room on my schedule at all, so naturally I heard myself saying, "Yes, I'd be honored to accept."

I have never regretted it and have served on that board for twenty-four years, three of them as president. I continue to be deeply proud of such a worthwhile organization. I am not into the animal rights issue; I am totally dedicated to improving the health and well-being of all animals, which is what Morris Animal Foundation is all about.

The Pet Set was syndicated in a hundred and ten cities around the country, and in the thirty-nine shows we did, we covered a wide variety of subjects and creatures. I felt like a kid in a candy store, because writing the show around each celebrity's specific interest gave me great latitude to use anything and everything that was available.

Lorne Greene (*Bonanza*) had German shepherds, so we did a whole thing on wolves, with two wolves on stage that we could handle. We also had a litter of German shepherd puppies and a litter of wolf cubs for comparison.

Mike Connors (*Mannix*) and his black Labrador retriever, Rufus, prompted us to do a show on guide dogs, and the 4-H kids who work as puppy raisers. For our Wild Spot we had Major, a big black-maned lion who al-

Of them all, Major was my favorite. Here he is onstage . . .

lowed a blind girl to "see" a lion for the first time by running her hands over his mane and tail and muzzle. But not his feet — he was ticklish!

Mary Tyler Moore came on with Diswilliam and Maude, her two poodles, so in her honor we had a poodle festival — all sizes, shapes, colors, ages, and flavors.

Gloria and Jimmy Stewart brought on their extremely enthusiastic golden retrievers, Simba and Beau. I introduced the Stewarts, and just as the camera cut to them, the dogs made a lunge, pulling their famous owners arse over teakettle — all we could see were flailing legs in the air. It was a whole new side of Jimmy Stewart.

Merv Griffin brought his Bouvier des Flandres, Keesh, and because Merv raised quarter horses, we brought in a prize quarterhorse stallion, as well as a mare with her ten-week-old colt. As a rule, you would never have that combination anywhere near

. . . and off. (COURTESY PET SET FILES)

Jimmy and Gloria Stewart with Simba and Beau. Jimmy wrote a beautiful tribute to Beau which he introduced on Johnny Carson's show.

each other, especially onstage, but they were very mellow.

Our crew was magnificent. Voices were kept low during breaks, cameras were moved slowly, mike booms were sneaked carefully in and out. It was thanks to their thoughtfulness and sensitivity that we never had one mishap. And, trust me, we had some animals that could have proven somewhat unpredictable: a water buffalo, a zebra, an ostrich, a full-grown "playful" black bear, five lions on stage at once, two and a half elephants — the list goes on. We had a representative

Mogul-to-be Merv Griffin with "Keesh," his Bouvier des Flandres.

from the American Humane Association off camera at all times, who used to laugh and say the animals were treated better than the guests.

Why not? They were the stars of the show.

The guests were treated well, too, I promise: Doris Day, Carol Burnett, Vincent Price, Burt Reynolds, Vikki Carr, Bob Crane, Johnny Mathis, Paul Lynde, Agnes Moorehead — again, the list goes on.

It just occurred to me — Rod Serling came to see us with his Irish setter, Mike, and had no trouble at all ad-libbing when he was talking about his dog.

After thirty-nine shows, we shut down for a short summer hiatus, fully expecting to be back in six weeks. In the interim, Carnation's advertising budget was reallocated, and they opted to put all their money into straight commercials rather than programming. It was more cost-effective for them, but not nearly as much fun. I was very grateful to those people and we parted good friends, but ever since that time I have been a little gun-shy about going on hiatus, for fear the candy store will be closed when I come back.

16

After *The Pet Set* bit the dust, I had to get back into the real world, so it was the game- and talk-show circuit once more, with an occasional guest stint on a dramatic series. One of the latter was *Ellery Queen,* starring Jim Hutton. It was a rare, for me, opportunity to play the heavy — ultimately revealed as the villainess who killed Eve Arden, no less. Even now I am often asked if I wouldn't like to play more dramatic roles, and I confess that killing Eve is about as dramatic as I want to get. To do in Our Miss Brooks is enough to get one drummed out of the industry!

Talk shows continued to come and go, but the *Merv Griffin Show* was the only one I actually enjoyed, as opposed to grinning and bearing. At this point, *The Tonight Show* wasn't in the mix for me. Back in 1961 Jack Paar had decided to leave the show, and Johnny Carson had been designated to succeed him. Through that summer after Jack left, NBC had a series of different guest hosts for a week at a time prior to Johnny taking over in the fall. Johnny took me to dinner one night during that summer, and I remember him saying, rather testily, "I wish they would stop bringing people in to audition for *my* show!" His show indeed — for the next thirty incomparable years.

It made perfect show-business sense for Johnny to avoid using people who were too closely associated with the Paar show, especially Jack's little coterie of irregulars. So, although we were old friends, I certainly understood not being invited to do the Carson show until several years had passed, which was into the seventies, post–*Pet Set*.

It was now 1973. The world had taken enough turns since the quiz-show scandals so that Jack Barry had finally made it back on camera the previous year, hosting a show called *The Joker's Wild*. He and Dan Enright were once again in the production business, after almost fifteen years following the *Twenty-One* debacle, and they were exceedingly successful.

One day, to my great surprise, I received a call from Jack to say that he was developing a new game show called *Hollywood's Talking,* and he had a sensational idea. How about using a *woman* as emcee?

I thanked him profusely for thinking of me, but I went on to explain what had transpired when Mark Goodson had had the same swell idea. Jack brushed that aside, saying that enough time had gone by that it was a whole new ball game (he should know), and the right moment had arrived — I *must* do the pilot for him.

After some network input following that first call, Jack agreed to compromise and do *two* pilots — one with me, and one with Al Lohman, of the comedy team Lohman and Barkley. In that way, the network could run some audience tests on both pilots and then make their decision. What was the result? The network was still dead set against a woman running a game, but they didn't want Al Lohman, either. *Hollywood's Talking* became Geoff Edwards's first network game show. Strike two.

Allen loved parties. He loved to go to them, and even better, he loved to give them. This was one of the few areas where we were not in complete accord. All my life, my idea of a party to love was four people — maybe stretch it to six — but with eight, for me it became a mob scene. However, Allen was so tolerant about my animal affliction that I really tried to cooperate in the party department with as good spirit as I could muster. Sometimes I even managed to have a good time for real. One of those more enjoyable occasions was a large cocktail party at Stu Erwin's home. Stu worked closely with Grant Tinker as Grant's lieutenant on each new project. (Back in 1950, Stu's father, a movie star, had done one of the very early television situation comedies, *The Stu Erwin Show,* with his real-life wife, June Collyer.)

On this particular late afternoon at Stu's, Allen and I found ourselves in conversation with an attractive young couple, Ava and Richard McKenzie. The more we talked, the more we seemed to have in common. We enjoyed each other so much that when the party broke up, we went on to dinner together. We learned that Richard was an artist, with his own gallery on La Cienega Boulevard, and that Ava was Fred Astaire's daughter. They were leaving soon to go live in London.

At some time during dinner, we also discovered that Richard was an Oz freak, as am I; I have a complete collection of the Oz books which I treasure. Nothing would do but they must come back to our house to see the books.

During all this time, the conversation

With Adele — who was one of the most dynamic individuals I have ever known.

never flagged for a moment. Inevitably, much to our surprise, dawn began to turn the windows pale, and we finally took the hint and called it a night — or day. It was the wonderful beginning of another of those special lifelong friendships.

We had thought it was polite party talk when Ava told us her father loved game shows in general but was a *Password* fanatic. Sure enough, it turned out to be true. A short time later, Ava invited us to a small dinner, prepared by the lady herself (to shame me, I'm sure), and we were overwhelmed to meet the legendary Fred Astaire. He in turn couldn't ask enough questions about *Password*. Fred's first dancing partner, his fabulous sister, Adele, was also there that night, and we were like kindred souls. It was the first of many happy times we would spend together.

Fred was such a consummate gentleman. Reticent and charming to the world; privately, when he felt comfortable with people, he was not above a little dishing. He wasn't as good at it as Adele, but when they were together, they could be devastating with just a few well-chosen — and funny — words.

Allen and I had been planning a very special vacation for quite some time. He was taking me on my first trip to Europe; we were going to Greece, Denmark, and England. We were scheduled to leave not too long after Ava and Richard were moving

to England, and we looked forward to seeing them in their new London digs. When
Adele learned of our plans, she issued a
very special invitation: we must all come
and stay a few days with her in Ireland,
where she spent the summer months every
year, and where she had once lived. Years
before, Adele had given up her highly successful career on Broadway, leaving her
partner-brother dancing alone, to marry
a British nobleman, Lord Cavendish, and
take up residence at Lismore Castle in
southern Ireland. Lismore Castle had been
the hunting lodge of the Duke of Devon-
shire, who was Dellie's father-in-law. When
her husband, Lord Charles, died, the castle
reverted to the Cavendish family, but Dellie
still returned to rent it every summer.

Small wonder. It was one of your better
fantasies. The property consisted of eighteen thousand acres of rolling emerald Irish
countryside, including the tiny picture post-
card town of Lismore. The castle itself had
two hundred rooms; the threshold leading
into the courtyard was laid down by King
John in "the 1100s." With all the castle's
Gothic grandeur, somehow Dellie made
those rooms she occupied seem warm and
cozy. Years earlier, when she was living there
as Lady Cavendish, it was Dellie who had

had modern bathrooms installed throughout.

After three days in London, Allen and I joined Ava and Richard to fly to Cork, then drive to Lismore, in County Waterford, for five perfect days.

One morning, we all came in from a walk

Wuthering Heights *starring Richard and Ava McKenzie with Betty and Allen Ludden.*

on the moors (!), to be given a message that Mr. Astaire had called from Beverly Hills. Dellie returned the call to find that Fred wasn't calling to talk to his sister or to his daughter; he wanted to speak to Allen to find out why a certain clue had been disallowed on *Password!*

The whole experience was like one of those dreams from which you awaken smiling and try desperately to recall next morning. Receiving the call from Fred Astaire simply added to the illusion. With anything as ideal as those five days, you should never press your luck by trying to repeat it. However, Adele is hard to refuse, and at her insistence, we went back the following year. Brigadoon was better than ever.

With all the wonderful memories I have of Fred Astaire, there is one moment I shall regret to my dying day. It occurred at a party at our house, and the evening was going exceedingly well. Fred was at his most debonair. I stepped out to the kitchen momentarily, to check on something, and I came back into the living room just in time to see Fred taking a few dance steps with comedienne Rose Marie. Ava was amazed: Fred never did that. I fully admit to being green with jealousy. Had I been there, *maybe* it could have been me he danced with — forget about being a generous hostess. No wonder I don't like the kitchen. As for Rosie, bless her heart, she will cherish that moment forever.

The Mary Tyler Moore Show had been on the air for three years and by this time was a full blown hit. It is hard to believe, in light of its all-time-classic status today, but during its first season there were some anxious moments.

From the beginning, Allen and I had been concerned observers on the sidelines as the show was being put together. We were emotionally involved because of our deep friendship with Mary and Grant. We sweated out revisions before it went on the air and ratings after. For the filming of the first show, Allen sent Mary a lovely flower arrangement built around the number "one." This became a tradition for the opening show each season, and it became more of a challenge every year to build the flowers around the appropriate number. That first season, it was thrilling to watch the show's initial shaky baby steps become steadier and see it gradually begin to run.

When we returned home from Ireland, it was time to send the "four" flowers. How could it be that three years had slipped by so quickly? The fourth season was about to get under way when I received a phone call one Saturday morning that quickly brought me to attention. It was from Allan Burns, cocreator with Jim Brooks of Mary's show and a lovely man. I assumed it was a social call until he asked if I would consider doing *The Mary Tyler Moore Show* the following week. There was a part they thought I would be right for. He went on to explain that they had written a script around the home economist at WJM (the fictional TV station in the show), and she was cloyingly sweet on the surface and something of a dragon underneath, with a tinge of nymphomania. I was born for the role!

Naturally, I told him I would be delighted. To do one of Mary's shows would be sheer pleasure, and the part sounded like we could have some fun.

When I hung up, I dialed Mary's number and said, "Guess who is coming on your show next week?" When I told her, she said, "Oh, no, you don't! I may not butt into the show often, but I *do* have veto power!" With that kind of response, I knew she was as tickled by the idea as I was.

Come Monday morning when I showed up for rehearsal, I received a warm welcome from the rest of the cast and the director, Jay Sandrich. I had met them all at parties with

Mary and Grant, but that was social; it was a trifle nervous-making seeing them under these circumstances.

We sat around the table for the first read-through, before we began to put the show on its feet. Sitting there with Ed Asner, Ted Knight, Valerie Harper, Gavin MacLeod, and Cloris Leachman may have been intimidating, but it was oh, so exciting. When we got up to start blocking the first scene in the set, it was all so familiar; after watching the show week in and week out, it felt like home. Talk about déjà vu.

The script was not only a funny premise, but it was written by the masters. It was "The Lars Affair" episode. Sue Ann Nivens, the Happy Homemaker, comes to one of Mary's customary dreary parties and proceeds to give Mary tips about *everything*. In the next scene, Phyllis returns to Mary's apartment at 4:30 A.M. to say that Lars had offered to take Sue Ann home, and he isn't home yet. Lars was always talked about but never seen on the series. Finally, a call comes through from Lars, explaining that in swerving to avoid a dog, they had run into a tree. *Fortunately,* they were able to find an all-night body shop where they had the car repaired. And Phyllis buys it! Before the show ends, Phyllis finally catches on that there is a bit

Sue Ann Nivens — the Happy Homemaker. (CBS/Landov)

of hanky-panky going on, and she comes to Sue Ann's TV kitchen set for a confrontation. Sue Ann has a fragile chocolate soufflé in the oven, which Phyllis manages to destroy by slamming a drawer.

During rehearsal, we realized that when Sue Ann desperately retrieves her precious but ruined soufflé, Cloris and Betty are stuck playing the rest of the scene with the gaping black hole of the open oven between them. There is no way of closing it — Phyllis wouldn't, she's too angry, and Sue Ann can't, she has her hands full with the hot soufflé dish. While we were trying to figure out what to do, as a gag I shut the oven by raising my knee. I was just horsing around, but Jay said, "That's it! No more problem!"

When Friday night came and we filmed the show in front of a live audience, the reaction to Sue Ann was wonderful — and very important. No matter how funny the part is, if a *guest* character is someone the *lead* character doesn't like, the audience can often get protective and not respond well to the newcomer. It might work in drama, but that syndrome can do you in when you're going for comedy. It was thanks to Mary's choice as an actress that Sue Ann worked. Rather than disliking her, Mary Richards found Sue Ann Nivens laughable, so the audience could relax and laugh with her.

It was almost too good to be true when, after the show, Allan Burns and Jim Brooks came up to say they were going to start on another Sue Ann script immediately — she would no longer be just a one-night stand, so to speak. Needless to say, I went home on cloud nine, and what made it all even better was that Allen was as thrilled as I was.

The next morning, Saturday, the doorbell rang around 11:00. When I opened the door, there were Mary and Grant, grinning and holding some beautiful flowers — *in the souffle dish from the night before!* They had come by to say how happy they were that rotten Sue Ann would be coming back. The four of us had a very impromptu — and *very* festive — brunch!

It was only three weeks before Sue Ann was back in another episode, and my career had been given a giant boost in the right direction, because she became a recurring character. That first year, I did twelve out of twenty-two shows, and then seven or eight for the remaining three seasons; but even when she wasn't there, Sue Ann was mentioned (not always flatteringly), which kept her alive. The same held true for Georgia Engel, who had joined the show the previous year as Ted Baxter's vague and lovely girlfriend, then wife. The company generously included both of us in any publicity or promotion as regular members of the ensemble. What a great club to belong to, and what a roster of members.

Mary herself set the tone for everyone without seeming to do so. She was *always* on time and never lost her warm good humor,

In the newsroom at WJM. (CBS/Landov)

but was very serious about being prepared. Even if they threw her a new monologue at the last minute, she didn't waste time or energy complaining; she simply learned it in record time, then nailed it in delivery.

Ed Asner is a curmudgeon by nature. His bark was always worse than his bite, but he loved to grumble. He was also someone who would not compromise on his convictions.

Ted, bless him, was such a talented actor. People had a tendency to confuse Ted Knight, the man, with Ted Baxter, the character, which did not please him. He often resented having to play the egocentric airhead we all enjoyed so much.

Valerie Harper was another mainstay. Unless Mary gave one of her bleak parties, Val and I never had many scenes together, but we have stayed friends and our paths often cross. Valerie, along with Dennis Weaver, established L.I.F.E. — Love Is Feeding Everyone — which continues to grow. Val left for her spinoff, *Rhoda,* late in the fourth season (my first). Today, she has a new series starting, called *The Office.* I wish her well.

Gavin MacLeod was solid gold support as Murray Slaughter, always upbeat and positive. I say that in spite of the fact that he sat me in a cake. After the show went off the air, I was delighted to see him be the first to hit it big as Captain Stubing of *The Love Boat.* He had paid his dues.

Cloris Leachman, as Phyllis Lindstrom, was no longer on every week by the time I got there. She was very busy both on TV and the big screen, but she came back for a guest shot every now and then. A *brilliant* actress, Cloris brings her own energy and tension with her and pours it out as she goes. Cloris may rehearse all week, then completely change her approach at the last minute on

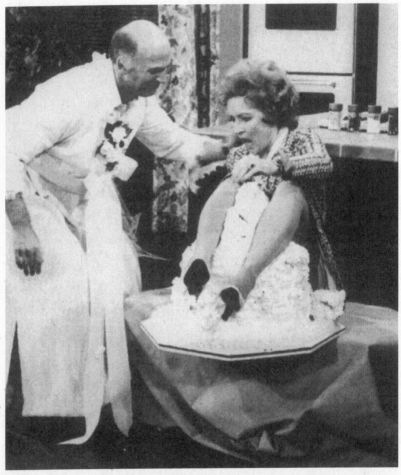

Murray gets even. Talk about being too icky sweet! (COURTESY CBS)

show night, which is disconcerting to those working with her but certainly keeps one's attention focused. There is no one quite like her.

On one occasion it was interesting to watch a small exchange between Cloris and Jay Sandrich, who as director tried to give her as much leash as he dared but now and then had to tighten his hold a bit. The premise of the show in question was that Phyllis Lindstrom decides she will go out and get a job. The scene is the employment office, where Phyllis, seated across the desk from the employment counselor (played by Doris Roberts), explains her own unusual and *sparse* qualifications. At rehearsal the first morning, when Cloris walked in and saw the set, she demanded it be reversed, as she preferred one side of her face to be photographed. Jay patiently explained that that was how the set was constructed and there was nothing they could do at this late date. The tug of war went on all week, and every time that scene came up for rehearsal, Cloris kept experimenting with new ways to keep her preferred side toward camera. Finally, Jay got very specific and told her to play the scene as blocked — he would make sure she was photographed well. Cloris did as she was told, but come showtime on Friday night, she suddenly played the entire scene with her back to Doris, facing out the other way. Doris was *livid,* and the cameras were scrambling. I honestly don't believe Cloris was even aware of making waves — she had simply found her way to solve her problem.

It wasn't until much later in the first season that I learned how my wondrous stroke of luck had come about. When "The Lars Affair" script came to be cast, Sue Ann Nivens was described as a sickeningly sweet Betty White type. Renée Valenti, the casting director, said, "Why don't we just get Betty White?"

Oh, no, no, no — they couldn't do that because Mary and Betty were friends, and if Betty read for the part and didn't get it, it might make it awkward for Mary. Well, of course it wouldn't have — you certainly don't get every part you're up for — but that was their decision. So the producers set out to read various actresses. It seems they went through about ten, but still couldn't find someone sickening enough for the part. Finally, it was Renée who said, "Just give the part to Betty. It's only a one-shot, and she's been around long enough that she won't hurt you."

Renée, I can never thank you enough.

■ ■ ■ ■

Mary is a diabetic and, as a result, watches her diet carefully. While the rest of us were chowing down, she used to use the lunch break to do what she liked best. A mirror would be rolled in onstage, along with a piano and piano player (he walked in). Soon, several of Mary's dance-class buddies would arrive, along with her dance teacher. They would have an hour dance class every day, which was a delight to watch. Then the dancers would scatter, and Mary would have a quick shower and something very light to eat as we went back to the afternoon's rehearsal.

This was all *very* noble, but once in a great while, Mary's halo would slip. She'd get a gleam in her eye around eleven o'clock in the morning, look at me, and say, "What are we doing for lunch?" That meant it was binge day.

When lunchtime rolled around, we would head for Art's Delicatessen. Sometimes one or two of the others would join us, but usually it was just the two of us sinners. We would indulge in humungous sandwiches and French fries. Mary would even start it off with a bowl of borscht — my chance to be noble. But wait — on the way back to the studio we would hit Baskin-Robbins for double-decker ice-cream cones!

"Mary, Betty — aren't you ashamed?"

"No!"

"Well — yes!" Let me hasten to add that this happened very rarely and long ago. Mary devotes so much of her time, energy, and money to the Juvenile Diabetes Foundation that the above was only an aberration; we knew it was wrong.

When Emmy time came around and I received a nomination for Best Supporting Actress for Sue Ann's first year, I was ecstatic. Everyone groans each time a nominee gushes, "It's such an honor just to be nominated — among all those wonderful people!" It makes me gag a little too, I'll admit, and yet I've caught myself saying those very words more than once. Do you know why it's such a tired cliché? Because, dammit, it's true!

Being at the awards ceremony when one is a nominee is undeniably exciting — even if you don't win, to which I can attest several times. It may be another flaw in my character, but when one *isn't* nominated, it's more fun to stay home and watch the proceedings on TV.

The whole MTM gang was there in 1975,

Ed presents Betty's Emmy.

with a goodly share of nominations among them. Best Supporting Actress is usually the first award to be announced, so I didn't have long to sweat it out. Ed Asner was the presenter and after naming the contenders, he smiled, then read my name. It had been twenty-two years since the first one, and now she had a friend. *That*'s what makes this business different — the highs seem so much higher!

Lightning does strike the same place twice, because the following year, amazingly, Sue Ann made the list again. I got all gussied up in a black-and-white chiffon gown they had given me on *The Carol Burnett Show,* and

Two happy people.

I was not only thrilled out of my mind to win for the second year in a row, but it gave me a chance to publicly thank Carol for the dress.

What made it absolutely perfect was that Allen had also won the Emmy as host of

Password. We flew to Hawaii the next day for a week's vacation. We could have made it without the plane.

Allen had maintained offices in Hollywood but moved Albets Enterprises, Inc., to the Valley when he found office space next door to the MTM lot. This was most convenient, for as well as his on-camera work, he had formed a partnership with Grant. EllTee Productions (for *Ludden-Tinker*) was to develop new daytime game shows.

During the summer hiatus of that first year of *Mary,* Allen and I vacationed in Bora Bora. Secure in the knowledge that we both had work we loved to return to, we could relax and enjoy some R and R.

Bora Bora is in the South Seas and certainly not on the beaten track, or at least it wasn't then. To get there was a fourteen-hour flight to Tahiti, then a change to a small plane for the hour-and-a-half flight to the island of Bora Bora. Here you boarded a motor launch and went by sea for forty-five minutes, then docked and got on a bus for the twenty-minute ride to the beautiful Hotel Bora Bora. We had expected it to be remote but were convinced when we found there was no phone service from the hotel.

It was a gorgeous setting. Our thatched-roof cottage was built on pilings over the lagoon. There was a window in the floor, where you could watch the incredible variety of fish swimming beneath you, and there was a large deck for sunset watching.

The second morning we were there, we went for a late breakfast and sat out on the beautiful terrace watching the new visitors arrive, just as we had come in the day before. By now, of course, after twenty-four hours, we were practically natives.

We talked about how relaxing it was to be so far from television. Much as we loved what we did, it was nice not to have to think of show business for a little while. The words were still hanging in the air as one of the new arrivals drew closer and was suddenly recognizable. It was Norman Lear!

He spotted us at about the same time and there was no escape for the poor guy: the path he was on led near our table. He greeted us warmly.

"What a surprise!" And then we all cracked up. Get away from it all, indeed! You can imagine what went through *his* head when he saw *us*.

He had been having some contractual problems with Carroll O'Connor, star of Norman's *All in the Family,* and, fed up, Norman had decided to take off for a few days to clear his head. "I brought a stack of books and plan just to fall down on the beach and read."

We assured him there was no need to panic, as we were there to do the same thing: "You go to your end of the beach, we'll stay at the other end, and you won't even know we're here."

After he moved on, I had a moment's concern. "What if he's here with someone secretly? What do we do then?"

Allen just stared at me. "Don't be ridiculous!"

It gives you a clue as to which of us was the nicer person.

As it happened, Norman *was* alone, and he and his books did stay up at their end of the beach — during the day. However, by cocktail time, he would be all cleaned up and waiting for us in the bar. There was a group of native musicians and dancers who performed every evening, and Norman and I took it upon ourselves to "translate" some of the Tahitian and Samoan songs for Allen, who didn't appreciate it at all! Norman also described the germ of an idea he was toying with for a nighttime soap opera, in which the grandfather was a flasher in a raincoat. It was not long after we returned to Los Angeles that *Mary Hartman, Mary Hartman* hit the air. I liked the way Norman told it better.

A couple of seasons later, Grant and Mary decided Bora Bora would be a great place to spend the Christmas hiatus, but they didn't want to go alone. Unlike the two of us, they usually preferred traveling with friends, and since Allen and I had been to Bora Bora, we were the logical contenders. Mary and Grant went over a couple of days ahead of us. We stayed to celebrate Christmas with the family, then left at midnight that night to catch up with the Tinkers.

Our cottages were next to each other but far enough apart so we had our privacy. Allen and I would snorkel all morning, while Mary and Grant went to play tennis or water ski or whatever. Every midday we would meet for an intense game of Scrabble while we ate lunch, then split off for our separate pursuits in the afternoon. Usually, after a short nap, Allen and I were back into the natural aquarium that was our front yard. We would meet for cocktails at sunset on one deck or the other before going to dinner. Damned if I know how she did it, but Mary would look her usual gorgeous self and I like a drowned prune. But we were *all* very tan.

Each night after dinner we'd return to our deck to see the manta rays come in, attracted by the light, and watch them perform their

Grant and Mary on our deck on Bora Bora.

breathtaking water ballet. These incredible creatures were right at our feet and looked like giant kites flying underwater. Black on top, white underneath, two or three of them were at least six feet across. We took countless pictures.

When we got home and returned to work, naturally Mary and I had to bring our pictures for show-and-tell. We spread them all out on the table, and I will admit there were a *lot* of manta rays. Finally, Ted, in his best Ted Baxter voice, said, "Boy, I don't know how you guys were able to keep up with all that excitement every single night!"

All the shared good times made the painful ones hurt even more. One weekend, Allen and I were devastated to receive a call from the Tinkers to say they had made the decision to go their separate ways. Grant moved out and rented a house in Benedict Canyon, in Beverly Hills. In their typically classy fashion, Mary and Grant didn't expect their friends to choose up sides. We continued to see them both — one at a time.

A few sad weeks went by. One night Allen and I had invited Grant to Chasen's for a quiet dinner. It was near his birthday, and that was as much as he would hold still for to mark the day. He called Allen late that afternoon to ask, "Can I bring someone?" It was the first time that had come up with either of them, and while it was to be expected, our hearts sank.

"Sure. Of course."

Grant went on to say he was picking his date up from work, so would we mind making the reservation a trifle late?

"Sure. Of course."

Allen and I were waiting at the table, determined to carry this off gracefully, when Grant arrived with his beautiful "date" — one Mary Tyler Moore Tinker.

To say we were four very happy people is belaboring the obvious. We touched glasses in a celebration toast. Grant loved to kid Allen about his habit of always touching my glass on the first drink. He would say, "Allen would leap over banquettes to click Betty's glass!" But on this particular evening, we all tipped.

I must also concede it may have been one of the shorter dinners we ever shared together. Grant's car was ahead of us as we pulled away from the restaurant and headed for home, but it didn't turn at Sunset Boulevard — it headed straight up Benedict Canyon.

17

Why did Mary choose to close *The Mary Tyler Moore Show* after seven successful years, when the show was still going strong? It was not a decision made lightly.

Mary wanted to dance. She loved it above all else and had worked very hard to become the beautiful dancer she was. If she was ever to realize her dream of doing a musical series in which she could dance regularly, she must make the move. So, Mary Richards was on notice.

Undoubtedly, the show could have gone longer, but by ending when it did, it went out on top. Instead of peaking and beginning to slide, as is often the case, it left the audience — and *us* — wanting more.

We were all aware, as we came in on Monday for the first read-through of the season, that this time it was different. It was Mary who put it into words:

"This is the first day of the first week of

the last year!"

We continued to taste each day of that last season, savoring it to the last drop.

Spin-offs were the name of the game. Ed Asner had a firm year's contract to do a weekly hour of *Lou Grant*. While he would play the same character we had known, he would move on to work for a newspaper, and the emphasis would be much more on the side of drama than comedy.

Valerie Harper, as we know, had already spun off with *Rhoda,* still playing Rhoda Morgenstern but now out on her own and eventually married.

Cloris Leachman's spin-off, *Phyllis,* was built around the same fluttery Phyllis Lindstrom, but after she was widowed. We never did get a look at Lars.

Later, Ted Knight would do a very successful syndicated series of his own, *Too Close for Comfort,* but that would not be done under the MTM banner.

Midway through the last season, it was a lovely surprise to be informed by the powers that be that they wanted to do a spin-off with me. As things developed, it became something of a good news/bad news situation. Because *Rhoda* was just holding her own and *Phyllis* was having a struggle in the ratings department, Grant and the produc-

341

ers felt it might be pressing their luck to send Sue Ann out alone. They thought she might be a little much to take every week, and if they knocked some of the edge off of her, they would destroy the character. So it was decided to build a whole new show. That's a tough assignment under any circumstances, made even tougher by the fact that the audience would be expecting something else.

The new format slowly began to materialize out of the vapor. I would play a character named Joyce Whitman, a television actress who lands a job starring in her own TV series. The fly in the ointment is that it is to be directed by her ex-husband.

I liked the show within a show idea; while certainly not a new concept (what is?), it had possibilities. We knew we wanted Georgia Engel with us, so she would play my best friend. The other characters would evolve from Joyce's work environment.

I had watched *Star Trek* from its inception — sometimes to my husband's mystification — and being a true Trekkie at heart, I wanted Joyce's series to be a space show of some sort. I thought this would give us some visual diversion in contrast to the home stuff. Everyone agreed and went off to write the first draft of the pilot script.

Meanwhile, *The Mary Tyler Moore Show*

was in the final countdown. When the last week arrived and we gathered as always on Monday morning, the atmosphere was so tangible you could almost see it in the air. We didn't really discuss it, we just all hung out together. There was no dance class at noon — we *all* went to lunch together, every day.

Vincent Gardenia was the guest that week, playing the new owner who was taking over WJM, and we included Vince in our lunch group each day. Long after the fact, I heard him say on an interview that he had never felt so out of place anywhere in his life — he didn't know where to look or what to say. And we were all so sure we were handling it beautifully.

We received our scripts, as usual, Monday morning, but they were minus the last scene. The writers didn't even try to face that one until rewrite night on Wednesday. We rehearsed all week, but the last scene we read through only once on Thursday, then blocked it Friday, just in time for dress and show. Do you know the feeling when you try and talk but the corners of your mouth keep pulling down, and you know you're losing it? By showtime, however, we had ourselves pretty well in hand, and actually it turned out to be a pretty funny show. We even made it into the final scene with flying colors. It was not until Ed, as Lou Grant, said, "I treasure you people!" that everything went to hell in a handbasket.

We weren't alone. The crew was crying; Jay, the writers, the audience — we cried through our bows, we cried through pick-ups. It was a night to remember.

We all had new projects to go to. We knew we would all still see each other. We knew no one had died. But something very precious would never *be* again.

Not long after, the exciting day arrived when the first draft of my pilot script came in, written by David Lloyd. David had done many of the Sue Ann scripts and was, perhaps, my favorite. I would never admit that within his hearing, of course, as we maintain the kind of funny put-down relationship that only people who love each other can afford. (We find odd ways of exchanging Christmas greetings to this day.)

No matter whose name is on a script, it usually winds up a collaborative effort, and I had the best: Ed Weinberger and Stan Daniels as executive producers, Bob Ellison as producer — killer writers, all.

It was a trifle disappointing that Joyce's space series was now a cop show called *Un-*

dercover Woman — a takeoff on the popular Angie Dickinson show, *Police Woman*. Ed Weinberger said they felt the space subject wasn't of enough interest and they weren't comfortable with it. All the *Star Trek* derivatives hadn't happened yet, so I could hardly argue with the best writing team in the business. Just because cop shows were not my favorites, I had to admit they were popular. They continue to breed like flies, even today. You win some, you lose some.

We couldn't keep referring to our project as "the show"; it had to have a title. *Sue Ann* was out; no one would know who *Joyce* was; so the working title stuck — *The Betty White Show. Quelle idée!* Perhaps the fourth time would be the charm.

Bill Persky was hired to direct. Another plus.

The producers remembered John Hillerman from when he had come in to read for the *Phyllis* show. He didn't get that part, but he had made an impression. John was cast as my somewhat superior and acerbic husband. You know John from his later work with Tom Selleck on *Magnum, P.I.*

Because the ensemble of players had worked like a charm on *The Mary Tyler Moore Show*, it was only natural to want to repeat. But that group had been polished over time and added to gradually. *Everyone* wasn't on *every* week. With our new show, all eight roles were cast and signed for thirteen out of thirteen episodes, meaning that each character had to be written into every show — a tall order for a short half hour. Except for the leads, there was barely time to bring the others in and out for a joke, let alone for the audience to get to know anybody.

Somehow the miracle-workers pulled together a good show for the pilot. They did their job so well, in fact, that the buzz started and we were touted as the hottest pilot on the market. Sure enough, we made the fall schedule on CBS!

Somewhere along the line I had missed the fact that the first team would only be there for the pilot. I have learned since that that is the norm for new projects from big companies, but it was something of a surprise at the time. Ed Weinberger and Stan Daniels were moving on to put *Taxi* together and David was going on his own busy way, so, with the exception of Bob Ellison, we had to put a whole new team together. One major saving grace: We still had Grant Tinker's steady hand on the company tiller.

The chemistry between John Hillerman and me was a little strange, to say the least. We could not possibly have been more different. I tend toward overexuberance, while John is like a still life. However, as we got to know each other we began to have good fun and used our differences to advantage.

Bill Persky had directed the pilot during the summer, but he, too, was committed to another series when the season started. As a result, we had a new director almost every week, looking for one to settle on. We were working three cameras on *film,* not tape, which has improved since then, but I still think it is cumbersome at best. As the weeks wore on, however, things began to fall into place, and the show began to grow.

Speaking of falling into place, we had one close call. On a particular show the script called for a body to jump from the second floor. We — and the audience — would just see it flash by outside the living-room window. Rather than use a dummy, they felt that a stunt man would make the bit more realistic.

It was afternoon dress rehearsal, which we did in front of an audience, and Georgia and I were playing the scene together as the big moment arrived. The audience gasped as the body fell, and then we almost fainted as the most bloodcurdling screams rang out from backstage. Everything stopped, obviously, and we rushed back to find that the stunt-man had missed the mattress and landed on the hard floor. Emergency came, and, thank God, the man wasn't badly injured — but painfully bruised nonetheless.

I was almost as concerned about Georgia. She didn't make a sound but turned whiter than milk and continued to shake violently. Georgia is a devout Christian Scientist, and we put a call in to her practitioner, who was able to help her. We somehow pulled it together for showtime that night, and, needless to say, a dummy was used. We should have used the one who thought of using a stuntman in the first place.

Time passed quickly. It hardly seemed possible that we had already done thirteen weeks; with the pilot, we had fourteen shows in the can. We took a two-week hiatus while they repainted the set and got us all freshened up. Our pickup was due sometime during our time off, and everyone was very optimistic. Even Grant and I, who were usually the two most apprehensive on such subjects, were fairly sanguine.

We had been off for about a week. One afternoon, it was getting near time for Allen to come home. I was upstairs freshening up when I heard his car in the driveway. I came tripping (not literally) down the stairs, and stopped short at the landing as he came in — accompanied by Grant Tinker.

We just stared at each other for a moment; then I got the words out.

"They didn't pick us up." It was a statement, not a question.

We went into the den, and Allen mixed us a drink as Grant told about the call from Bob Daly, president of CBS. Bob had given the usual preamble. He liked the show, the numbers were not bad and improving — about in keeping with *Lou Grant,* actually, but *Lou Grant* had a full season contract, of course — he was doing some juggling with the schedule, et cetera, et cetera, et cetera. Bottom line — they didn't pick us up.

Only Grant would have the sensitivity to come home with Allen to break the news. That shouldn't have surprised me, but it did. I deeply appreciated both of those special fellas that night.

I went upstairs and called each of the cast so they wouldn't have to hear it second-hand.

It is interesting how different people react in a given situation. Almost everyone I spoke to that night was as shocked and hurt as I was. Not that we hadn't all been through it before and would be again; but this had been our ship, and it had sunk. We all reached out to each other for comfort. One, however, and only one, out of eight, shook me by pouring salt in the wound.

"Well, I'm glad — I never did feel they were using me properly."

I could have forgiven that as a knee-jerk reaction, but it was repeated later in print. What really amazes me is to discover that that kind of self-centered attitude still rankles. It *is* interesting how different people react — even those of us old enough to know better.

The Betty White Show (IV) was not outstanding. I can't even say it was one of my all-time favorites, but we had given it our best shot, and one does get emotionally involved with the group of people, each time. John was devastated. He, perhaps, had had more fun than anyone, and we had grown to love each other dearly. He loved holding court in his dressing room after the show each week. It would have eased his disappointment a lot if he could have foreseen what good times lay ahead of him in Hawaii with *Magnum, P.I.*

One unintentionally funny evening did manage to take the curse off the sense of failure I was feeling. It was about a week after the cancellation. A very small group of us had been invited to dinner in one of the private rooms at Chasen's. There were nine of us — Grant and Mary Tinker, Bob and Ginny Newhart, Dick and Dolly Martin, Allen and Betty Ludden, and our host, Bob Daly.

At one point toward the end of dinner, Bob Daly casually mentioned that he felt he may have acted a little hastily in canceling our show — he still had some doubt in his mind but, of course, it was too late now.

Feeling as I did, those words were a sword through the heart, but to Bob Newhart and Dick Martin they sounded the charge. They proceeded to tell network president Bob what they thought of network judgment in general, and Bob Daly's in particular. They went on to defend our show in detail. Grant and Allen put in their two cents every now and then, but they weren't really needed — Martin and Newhart were on a roll. It was all done in a gentlemanly, conversational manner, but they got all their licks in. As champions of a cause, you will admit that was pretty good casting.

It was when Mary was filming *Ordinary People* that the Tinkers invited the Luddens to dinner at Dominick's. We had our usual drink at the bar before going to our table — there was a lot to catch up on. It was a few days before Christmas, and I remember we had a joke gift for them in the car — a silly floating Scrabble board so they could have a game in the pool. We'd give it to them later when we got our cars.

As our salad was served, Mary and Grant said they had something to tell us. It was said very calmly, but I suddenly was no longer hungry. They went on to say they were splitting up. This time for keeps.

Mary was nominated for an Oscar for *Ordinary People*.

Both Mary and Grant went on to happy, lasting relationships with other people. That's the good news. That night there was no good news.

I don't remember what happened to the damned Scrabble board.

Many, many months later, Allen and Mary and I were having dinner at Chasen's. As we sat down, our drinks came without being ordered. A small note came with them. All it said was "Banquette! Banquette!" We tipped to the echo.

That same Christmas, after our cancellation, I was still on the list for the annual CBS gift, which is always lovely. That year it happened to be a beautiful Lucite box with a hinged lid, upon which was etched the word NUTS.

Bob Daly got the last word in after all.

18

Musical variety shows were very much in vogue and all over the dial during this period. The best and certainly the most durable of these was *The Carol Burnett Show*. Allen and I had watched it every week for years, even before *The Mary Tyler Moore Show* became part of that incomparable Saturday lineup on CBS.

Carol and Allen and I were friends, dating back to the early days of *Password* in New York; she was one of the ace players of that and any other game that was ever invented. It was sometime during the second season Sue Ann Nivens was on Mary's show that I received a call from Carol, inviting me to guest on her show. I was thrilled beyond words. It had never occurred to me that I would ever get a chance to go over and play with those crazy, gifted people.

That show was not only a romp to do, but it opened a whole new door into the variety-show business. Of all the branches of television, musical variety is my favorite to work in. Between the sketches and the musical numbers, it is a constant challenge to attempt things you would never have dreamed of doing. Sometimes they work, sometimes they don't, but you have given it your best shot and had a marvelous time in the process. Today, the whole variety genre has practically disappeared from the scene. *Saturday Night Live* is about as close as we get these days, but it is another whole breed of cat. Production costs became prohibitive, which probably dealt the final death blow, but also, the audience appetite had become surfeited. It was the old "been there, seen it all" syndrome for which television is famous.

Doing a weekly variety show is comparable to putting on a one-time television special, except that it is produced each and every week, all season long — the challenge is mind-boggling. Carol and company managed to do it successfully for eleven years!

My first *Carol Burnett Show* was a marvelous experience, but not for the fainthearted, as everyone on the show was a multitalent. I tried not to think about that. What came as a complete surprise was how totally organized it was. It was a very complicated hour to put together each week, with the songs and dances and sketches, and costume and wig fittings, but somehow we were out on time every afternoon. Even on show day, the train was on schedule. Much of it was due to the professionalism of Carol and the rest of the cast, but full credit must also go to the very strong producer who kept everything on track — Carol's husband, Joe Hamilton.

The cast members were funny both on stage and off, and a more mixed bag of nuts would be hard to find:

Lyle Waggoner, who often wound up playing the witless hunk, was anything but witless. *Hunk,* yes! Offstage, Lyle was a very astute businessman, with a variety of profitable projects.

Vicki Lawrence had been discovered as a Carol Burnett look-alike when she was in high school and had grown up with the show. Over time, she had learned to take any challenge the writers threw at her and run with it.

Harvey Korman was the master when it came to variety sketches. He could play *any* character, regardless of age, weight, or gender. He had honed those native skills as Danny's foil on *The Danny Kaye Show*. The only thing Harvey couldn't handle was Tim Conway.

Tim Conway is a comic without peer, and you don't want to hear his answer to that one. He also has a wide diabolical streak. His specialty was coming up with something on the show that he hadn't used in rehearsal. Tim wouldn't actually change his performance, as Cloris had, but he might just save a tiny piece of business, or a bit of wardrobe that hadn't been seen prior to the actual taping, and it would get Harvey every time. Anyone who thinks those breakups were staged doesn't know the extent of Tim's deviousness or Harvey's susceptibility.

No wonder I enjoyed the show so much — it was back to the old game of kids playing dress-up, only this time it wasn't Western Costume Company, it was Bob Mackie. Once in a while, the show would generously give me something special that I had worn in one of the sketches, and I still have those things. Even after all these years, I can't part with them.

Of all the wonderful skits that were done, among Carol's favorites were the recurring "family" sketches in which she was Eunice, the downtrodden, unappreciated daughter of the irascible Mama, played by Vicki Lawrence. Ken Berry was Mama's flaky son and Dorothy Lyman his oversexed wife. From the first time I guested on the show, I was

Mama's Family. Top row: Carol Burnett, Harvey Korman, Rue McClanahan. Second row: Dorothy Lyman, Ken Berry, Mama herself (Vicki Lawrence), me, Eric Brown, and Karen Argoud. (COURTESY NBC)

tickled to be included in those sketches as Eunice's spoiled, rich, bitchy sister, Ellen. Mean as she was, Ellen was the apple of

Mama's eye and took credit for whatever poor Eunice had knocked herself out to do. Those family sketches ultimately took on a life of their own and became a series.

Carol's show had opened the gate to a whole new playground for me, and other variety shows followed. They served as a delightful change of pace, and, more importantly, later on they helped shore up my sagging morale following the early demise of *The Betty White Show*.

Each one of the musical-variety guest shots was enjoyable in its own way. For instance, I had a fine time on a John Davidson Christmas special, which was all done in an early Dickens yuletide setting. I got to sing with John and also do a number called "It's Turkey Lurkey Time," dancing on and off the tables in an English tavern. Now, aren't you sorry you missed that! Smirk if you will, but it was choreographed by Tony Charmoli, and you can't ask for much better than that. Later on, John had a daytime talk show and, like Merv, he let me bring on whatever animal friends I could borrow from the L.A. Zoo. We also worked together from time to time after John took over the hosting chores from Peter Marshall on *Hollywood Squares*, and even later, on *Pyramid*.

With Bob Hope and Howard Cosell on a Bob Hope Special.
(NBCU Photo Bank)

First *The Sonny and Cher Show,* then, after their marriage split up, the *Cher* show, were both extravagant, well-produced hours where the guests were made to feel very much at home. On one of them, and I can't remember which of the two shows it was, Cher and I did a musical sketch about the newly elected First Family of Southerners moving into the White House and trying to make their words understood by the staff, all to the tune of "Carolina in the Morning." That's a pretty good hint as to what year it was.

When the *Cher* ratings began to erode

a bit, the two performers reunited for one more season of *Sonny and Cher* but on a professional basis *only*.

Even then, Sonny was very much the businessman and always had many irons in the fire. Later, he campaigned for and went on to win the office of mayor of Palm Springs, California. He insisted, in spite of all those who chose to laugh at such a preposterous idea, that his goal was to win a seat in Congress. One week ago today, Sonny got the last laugh when he was elected to the United States House of Representatives.

Donny and Marie Osmond taped their variety shows from the Osmond Studios in Orem, Utah, not far from Salt Lake City. Paul Lynde was a regular, and that alone would have been reason enough to do the show, even if Donny and Marie hadn't been as nice to work with. Young as they were, they were — and are — such pros. Something else that made the experience so special each time, and like no other, was the incredibly gorgeous scenery.

You were given your choice of staying at a fine hotel in Salt Lake or in one of the chalets the company rented up in the mountains at Sundance. No contest. The chalet was a beautifully appointed log house, overlooking the world from every window. A driver picked me up every morning for the twenty-minute drive to the studio, during which the game was to see how many deer we could count.

At the end of the day's rehearsal, I was brought back up to the chalet, where a cook, furnished by the company, would have a delicious dinner waiting. After cleaning up the kitchen, she would leave. Oh, dear — it's not all beer and skittles in show business. I'll say it isn't — it's better.

I didn't see it in the spring, but Sundance was beautiful in the summer and spectacular in the fall. However, my favorite time was the winter week there. I landed in Salt Lake City in a cloud of skiers, just after there had been a good-sized snowstorm. The car met me for the drive to Sundance, and by now the weather was clear and lovely. When we arrived, however, the snow was so deep the only way to get up the last hill to the chalet was by snowmobile. Two of them, in fact — one for me to ride behind the driver, and one for the other bags. I tried to act as though I did this all the time, but it was a couple of days before I could make the trip without holding my breath.

The cabin was far from the madding crowd, which was wonderful, but this time, for some reason, they didn't want me to stay up there all alone, so they arranged for MacDuff to stay with me. MacDuff was the cook's wonderful shaggy terrier, and I was thrilled that she let him sleep over, then picked him up each morning. (Oh, how I wish I could remember that nice lady's name — I hate to keep saying "the cook." The same goes for "the driver" — they both took such good care of me.)

It didn't dawn on me until after she went home the first night that I would have to take Duffy out before bedtime. Armed with a flashlight, we went out into the pitch-black night. The snow was hip deep, but after falling down a couple of times we did fine. We didn't go far, as Duff caught on right away what he was out there for. He was a very willing guest and was perfectly content to sack out on the bed with me.

It was about 3:00 A.M. during that first night when I woke up suddenly to hear heavy pounding on the door downstairs and someone calling my name. I grabbed a robe and tiptoed down to investigate.

It was the driver, who had come all they way up to see if I was okay. It turned out that Allen had called to say good-night and found that the phone was dead. We had spoken earlier in the evening and everything had worked fine, but this time he kept trying and couldn't get through. Knowing Allen, he began to worry — a lot. He must have raised half the town of Orem before he could locate someone who could help, and by now he was getting a little frantic trying to find his wife. All this time I had been sleeping blissfully, with my guard dog on duty. Incidentally, with all that had gone on — the pounding and the calling of my name — there hadn't been a sound out of MacDuff. Now, just as the driver was pulling away to go back down and call Allen, there was a rather tentative bark from upstairs. When I got up there, Duff suddenly got very brave and told off the snowmobile as the sound of the engine faded in the distance.

Duffy stayed with me for the remaining nights, but we both understood that it was more of a social thing than protective.

One more dog story from that same week: One afternoon we got through rehearsal earlier than usual, and the driver, knowing my interest in animals, mentioned that a friend of his was the trainer up at Robert Redford's dog kennels.

"Bob is out of town, but my friend would be happy to show you the dogs if you'd like."

If I'd *like!*

Somewhere I had read that Bob raised

364

dogs, but I was totally unprepared for what we found. We drove up beside huge fenced runs, beyond which were heated kennels, all in impeccable condition. As we got out of the car, and before I could be introduced to the trainer, an army of Bernese mountain dogs came bounding toward us through the snow, all tails wagging. A Bernese is a Swiss mountain dog and one of the loveliest of canine creatures. Only sightly smaller than a Saint Bernard, all Bernese are marked virtually alike — long wavy black coat, with russet markings outlining white chests, and usually with white feet and tail tip. Their beautiful dispositions are just as uniform. I was completely buried in dogs and snow, and I can't say who among us was the happiest. Having lived with Stormy for eleven years, it was heaven to get my hands on all those gentle giants. We spoke the same language. Wouldn't you know, on top of everything else, Bob Redford would have dogs like that?

Let me square up here for a moment. My silly nonsense about the Redford crush is just that — fun and games for television interviews. What *is* true is my deep respect for what the man represents. Certainly I admire his fine work on both sides of the camera, but even more, his long-range view and his concern for the planet. I wish there were more like him.

There are some. One, I know, in the same genre: Clint Eastwood. When Clint was elected mayor of Carmel, California, it was not a celebrity gambit. He took the job for the express purpose of working for the community of which he has been a longtime resident.

There are just over three thousand eligible Carmel voters. On the day of Clint's inauguration, some sixty-seven hundred media folk showed up. It must have looked like a circus to the rest of the country. But the minute the dust settled, Clint got busy, and for the next two years he put his career on the back burner and was a working mayor. Quietly, he also did some beneficial things through his own personal finances. It is ironically typical of human nature that there were some who were put out when he refused to run for a second term. He had given two years, but, unable to do both, the time had come to get back to his real work. There were Oscars to be won for directing and producing *Unforgiven*.

It is heartening that these two tremendously talented men have the ability to see beyond themselves and give something back. I salute them.

But, of course, I will still indulge in my silly Redford nonsense.

Summer-stock musicals were a lovely stretch from those on television, because there was a chance to play the show more than one night, and there was also a live audience ready to have a good time. There was *not*, however, more time to rehearse — the whole show had to be put together in one week. But having the opportunity to do a *South Pacific*, for example, was worth all the cramming.

Allen and I usually did straight plays together because, as a rule, he could only get a couple of weeks off of *Password* at a time. With a play, we'd rehearse a week, then play a week. Allen always said he was one weak actor.

We did manage, however, to do four musicals together by rehearsing in New York. The first was Lerner and Loewe's lovely Scottish fantasy, *Brigadoon*. Newlyweds that we were, we enjoyed the romantic story to the hilt — or the kilt.

We played *Guys and Dolls* in Atlanta, at their big outdoor theater. It was interesting to watch the same thing happen every night: The show opened with a stage full of people, then Allen, playing Sky Masterson, made his entrance — not wearing his glasses. There was always a slight smattering of applause as he walked to a newsstand to buy a *Racing Form*. Opening the paper, he'd take the glasses from his pocket and slip them on, at which time the audience would explode. *There* was Allen Ludden! They hadn't recognized him without his glasses.

It was in Kansas City, at the Starlight Theater in Swope Park, that we did *Mr. President*. It was a spectacular production, and they really pulled out all the stops. The second act opened with me on a live elephant, and for the finale we had a full military band, umpteen American flags, and almost more servicemen than even that enormous stage could hold. Allen began to believe he had really been elected.

At one point in the show, when it was done in the theater on Broadway, a miniature plane was flown across the stage on a wire, representing the president's travels. We were outdoors and went them one better. Quite by accident, it timed out so that, just as we reached that moment in the show each night, the regularly scheduled 10:00 United flight came right over the theater. It was very effective. And free.

It was nice to go back to the St. Louis Muni Opera again to do *Bells Are Ringing,* and see some old friends — and one new one. That summer, a large skunk had taken up residence in the park and could be counted on to put in an appearance at the exit door near stage right once a night. We would hear a murmur at that side of the audience and, sure enough, there he'd be. An usher, on skunk duty, would usher him back out — very carefully. The big guy was so accommodating — he would lumber off, only to come back tomorrow. The reviewers could have had a ball with that, but thank God it never occurred to them.

Rain is an occupational hazard doing outdoor summer theater, and the audience is used to it, simply waiting out a light shower. One night during *Bells Are Ringing,* I was on stage alone and had just started singing "The Party's Over." Drip, drip. I could hear the ominous popping sound of opening umbrellas, but I kept on wheezing away. The general rule is to keep singing until the musicians stop playing, which they soon will to protect their instruments. On this particular night it wasn't raining hard, just sprinkling enough to get you pretty wet. The orchestra *finally* stopped and got out the plastic, but the sea of umbrellas out front never moved. Before I could make it off that huge stage, the rain stopped and the orchestra started the song from the beginning. The drizzle started and stopped through the whole damn number. What is a rather poignant moment in the show had somehow changed mood, and the lyrics took on a whole new meaning:

The party's over,
It's time to call it a day . . .

I also looked wonderful. I have bad hair to begin with — fine and thin — and what there was of it was, by now, straight and dripping.

From that day forward, whenever I looked particularly bedraggled, Allen would start to hum "The party's over . . ."

Lou Grant said it best. I treasure those times.

By a strange coincidence, the last stage musical I did was *Hello, Dolly!* for John Kenley. John, who had started it all by casting me in that first *The King and I,* put together a beautiful production of *Dolly,* and we played a week each in Dayton, Columbus, and Cleveland, Ohio.

Our dancers were members of the Cleveland Ballet Company, which made it very exciting. The famous waiter's ballet was just that, and stopped the show every night.

You can imagine what went on when I told my buddy Carol Channing that I was doing *her* show. To this day, whenever the subject comes up, I lie and tell her how *everyone* said we were *so* much better than the original Broadway company. Carol's response is always a flat "Your mother said what?"

The week in Columbus stands out for another reason. It was matinee day, and after the show, I had come back to the hotel for a bite to eat before the evening performance. The phone rang, and, out of the blue, it was Tommy Cochran. He explained that the Air Force Museum was celebrating an anniversary, and one of the functions was a large gathering going on at that moment in our hotel.

Tommy was his usual dear self. "Betty, Phil is here. He is one of the guests of honor. We are at the party downstairs, and I heard you were staying in the hotel. Would you consider stopping in for a minute to say hello to him?"

It was a strange feeling. I still had on my stage makeup — certainly not the way one would choose to look under those circumstances, and it was almost time to head back for the evening show. But there was no way I could walk away from this one.

Tommy came up and escorted me down

to the crowded ballroom. Phil was on the other side of the room when we came in, and he had his back to us. He turned and did a double take I won't forget, and headed straight for us. He came up, took me by the shoulders, and kissed me soundly.

"There!"

We said a few mundane things that I don't think either of us heard, and then I had to leave for the theater. The next day I received a beautiful bouquet of roses.

That was the last time I saw him. In August 1979, Tommy called to tell me his brother had died of a heart attack — while he was out riding his favorite horse.

19

Johnny Carson had been doing *The Tonight Show* for quite some time, and by now I was invited on as a guest every so often. Johnny also mentioned Allen and me in his opening monologue from time to time. He would give offbeat examples of what an egghead Allen was and how square our marriage must be. Things like:

"When Allen and Betty shower together, they play *Password*," or "Betty and Allen threw a wife-swapping party and nobody showed up."

We always got a big kick out of it and were very flattered, but each time we would hear from a few people who were upset because "Johnny Carson was saying those terrible things" about us.

Johnny and I would go on to do many of the Mighty Carson Art Players sketches together during the ensuing years. Those were the most ridiculous fun of all. For example, when Jerry Brown was governor of California, he was said to be going with popular singer Linda Ronstadt, who liked to roller-skate. That was too tempting for Johnny, so we did a scene based on the Governor and First Girlfriend. Naturally, I did the whole thing on roller skates.

Another was Tarzan and Jane "twenty years later," by which time Jane wanted a divorce. Tommy Newsom, from the band, was the divorce lawyer. Johnny and I were in brief leopard costumes, while Tommy, briefcase in hand, was in a business suit, tie, and boxer undershorts.

Our costumes for Adam and Eve, also "twenty years later," were even briefer, consisting of a few strategically placed fig leaves and a long blond wig.

Johnny finally went the whole way. One night, I played the first woman reporter allowed in the team locker room, and he was the reluctant ballplayer. So determined was she to get the story, she chased him right into the shower, where only a small towel kept us on the air.

When Johnny had an idea for a sketch, he'd call me to talk it down. I finally accused him of calling me whenever he wanted to take his clothes off. We did a lot of skits that were great fun, but the pièce de résistance was

Adam and Eve — twenty years later. (NBCU Photo Bank)

"dinner at the beach." California had been having its problems that year with record-breaking high tides, which had been doing some real damage.

The scene: a picturesque little restaurant, somewhere near Malibu. A violinist is playing his heart out as Johnny and I share wine by candlelight and gaze out at the sea. As a waiter serves our lobster, a small splash of water is seen outside the window. It isn't long before our romantic dialogue is interrupted by a much larger splash — this one reaches the table. The third time, of course, is the killer. Through the window comes five

A romantic dinner by the sea with Johnny Carson. (NBCU Photo Bank)

hundred and fifty gallons (literally) of water, completely wiping us out.

There was no way of rehearsing the water part, so we had just talked it through. The director had told us, "Now, when the water hits you, pretend to be washed off your chairs."

Neither Johnny nor I had expected quite the impact there was, and trust me, friends, it didn't take any pretending. When that much water hits you, you are totally washed away — if there hadn't been a wall to stop me, I would have been in downtown Burbank. I lay there for a moment, facedown, during the applause, and Johnny said later he thought I had drowned. The hardest part of the whole thing was getting changed and pulled together in time to get back out to the desk and couch when they came back after a two-minute commercial. You can guess what my hair looked like.

"The party's over . . . !"

Dinah Shore did as much for television as anyone you could mention, and she was not only deeply loved, but universally *liked* in the process.

As well as being a star in prime time, Dinah set a standard for daytime talk-variety shows that no one has been able to touch. *Dinah's Place, Dinah!* — there were several variations,

Dinah's Valentine Show: Jimmy and Gloria Stewart, Dinah, Betty and Allen, Hal and Fran Linden.

but all guaranteed entertainment. What's more, she somehow managed it without including abuse, rape, or incestuous siblings.

Allen and I both enjoyed doing her show, either together or separately. You could count on interesting people with something to say rather than freaks and weirdos (except for us), and there was always lots of music. Allen was her official garden person and building hanging baskets was his specialty. When our garden couldn't hold anymore, he built hanging baskets for all of our friends — whether they wanted them or not. I was allowed to bring animals on the show with one proviso — *no snakes!* But Dinah much preferred giving me cooking lessons, which I could have done without. She swore she would turn me into a real chef one day and make me love it. She never did either one, bless her, either on or off the screen, but not for lack of trying.

Dinah Shore knew *everybody* — not as the presidents or top athletes or writers or superstars that they were — but as down-to-earth friends. How lucky we were to be included.

One time when she was in the hospital, recuperating from having been hit in the eye with a tennis ball, Dinah happened to watch *The Pet Set* one afternoon and saw Burt Reynolds guesting with his basset hound, Bertha. She liked what she saw, not necessarily the basset, and wrote Burt a funny fan letter. Burt wrote a funnier one back, and Dinah answered in kind. Burt's response was, "We have to stop meeting like this. How about dinner?"

Burt had been a friend of ours for some time, growing out of his appearances on *Password* when he was doing his first series, *Dan August*. He also did the pilot of a game show for Allen, *Look Who's Talking,* which unfortunately didn't sell.

We had a small group for a barbecue party

one Sunday afternoon — Allen did the cooking, I was busperson — and when Burt was invited he said he'd be bringing a date. We knew that he and Dinah had been quietly seeing each other, but this was their first "public" appearance together. It turned out to be a great surprise party for our guests.

Burt's wise-cracking, smart-ass public persona was in direct contrast to the warm private Burt we all knew, and the love he and Dinah shared was very special. It went so deep that it later managed to survive as a true friendship, weathering all the troubled years that lay ahead for Burt.

Painting in oils was more than a hobby with Dinah; she was excellent. One Christmas her gift to her friends was a favorite of her beautiful seascapes, printed in limited edition. Personally inscribed "To Betty and Allen with love, Dinah," it is a long shot of a wide beach, empty except for two tiny figures in the distance taking a sunset walk, hand-in-hand. It wasn't hard to guess who those figures represented.

There are always the chronic hipsters who insist on being terminally cool. For those, Dinah's upbeat attitude and perpetual smile was something to put down. "She's so sweet she'll rot your teeth," they would say and get their laugh, even from the lady herself. What they didn't know was how very hip Dinah was, and how often her smile covered pain. Being positive was her *choice*.

Allen and I loved our vacation time together. We made several trips to Hawaii — Napili Kai, on Maui, was our favorite — but more and more, we found ourselves heading north to Carmel, California. I had been going up there ever since I was a kid, and Allen had grown to love the area as much as I. Even in the beginning, when he was trying to talk me into getting married, he would say, "I'll build you a house in Carmel."

Boy, did he ever.

We usually rented the same Carmel cottage each time, and we had just about decided to buy it and remodel when we drove by a piece of property one day that wouldn't take no for an answer. We knew we would never find anything ever again that could compare. After a long night of soul-searching, rather than risk losing it, we bought it. Just to have it safe, mind you; we wouldn't build on it right away.

No, of course we wouldn't. Well, we couldn't get to an architect fast enough! We found Edward Hicks, a Carmel resident himself, and, along with his wife, Mary

Ellen, and our young poodle puppy, Timothy, we began to plan our dream house. The serendipity was that in the process we developed a permanent friendship with Ed and Mary Ellen.

It's a classic cliché that a couple must *never* build a house together — it is instant divorce.

Allen building his garden at Carmel.

Something must have been wrong with us, because we had a wonderful time. Whenever we could steal a couple of days, we would head north to spend the whole time running around making the countless decisions and choices that go with the building process. The stone, the wood, the tile, the roof — all that before you could get to the really important stuff, like lighting fixtures and drawer pulls. Sometimes we wondered what it had been like to go up there and just relax, but visualizing the finished product was our carrot on a stick.

So preoccupied were we that, before we knew it, Christmas had come and gone and we were heading for another new year.

Henny and Jim Backus had a lovely tradition. Every year since 1961, they had thrown a black-tie starter party early in the evening on New Year's Eve. You'd touch base with so many old friends (and new); then by ten, everyone would head out for their various commitments.

That year, 1979–1980, however, was special. We were not only seeing in a new year, but a brand-new decade. New Year's Eve parties can often be less than festive affairs, but Henny Backus and Ann Ellsworth decided to do something extra in honor of the occasion, and they threw a beauty. This time it was at Ann's house. Jimmy, who was suffering from Parkinson's disease, was not well enough to be host, but he came in to say "Happy New Year" to all his buddies.

So many of the fun and famous were there. Morty Jacobs was at the piano, and all evening everyone took turns doing numbers. George Burns did several — why not? Morty was *his* piano man who had been with him for years. Steve Lawrence and Eydie Gorme were most generous. Allen even got to sing his favorite, "A Foggy Day," which he would do on the slightest excuse. Midnight was ushered in with a flourish, as a troupe of Highlanders in full Scottish regalia, bagpipes wailing, marched through the rooms.

No one could ask for a better welcome to a fresh new decade, and we were looking forward to so much good stuff.

It wasn't too far into January when Allen began to have days when he just didn't feel at the peak of his form. He'd run a slight temperature and lose his energy, but then he would bounce back and feel fine.

Allen was never one to be reluctant about going to the doctor. When something seemed wrong, he didn't waste time — he always wanted to get it fixed right away. These low days began happening too often to ignore, and he went to check it out. The doctor, however, could find nothing wrong. Nor could a second opinion. He went through not one, but two CAT scans, neither of which showed any problem. But his temperature continued to spike.

Finally, in May, the doctors wanted to do a gallium scan — that was a new one on us. We waited a day and a half until the Good Samaritan Hospital could bring in the element needed for the procedure. The results showed a hot spot, and surgery was indicated.

Prior to the operation, Allen had made the doctor and me solemnly promise to give him the straight story as soon as he woke up. I'm sure neither of us had foreseen how tough that promise would be to keep. Immediately following the surgery, it was my beloved longtime family doctor, Dr. José de los Reyes, who had to tell me, "Bad news, darling." They had removed as much of the cancer as they could, but had not been able to get it all.

When Allen woke up in the recovery room, his first word was, "What?" When the doctor told him, he just stared at me and tried to squeeze my hand. . . .

It was at that very moment that a nurse came to the other side of the bed and, leaning across Allen, pointed at me. Full voice, she said, "Are you who I think you are?" As the doctor took her away, she called over her shoulder, "Aren't you Betty White?" There were several other beds in the room, also filled with people in trouble. I couldn't believe it had happened.

But that was nothing compared to the rage I felt when I finally had to leave after Allen, at last, fell back to sleep. At the desk on the way out, this same nurse had the guts to shove a piece of paper at me, saying, "Can I have your autograph?" I hope I never again come that close to striking another human being.

To this day, I can't watch hospital-based television shows, no matter how well done. Our little scene would probably be used as comic relief. The memory makes me sick even now, after all this time.

We were told that Allen's future would be measured in months. He made a relatively fast recovery from the operation, and it wasn't too long before he was back doing *Password Plus*. While he was off the show, *Password* had been in the very capable hands of a good buddy — Tom Kennedy.

It was determined that with Allen's cancer of the stomach, neither radiation nor chemotherapy offered hope, and after much consultation, we — the doctor included — opted against either one. No doubt, this many years later the choices might be more promising.

We didn't kid ourselves that everything was peachy, but Allen felt so good — for which we were most grateful — that we decided to move on and make the most of every day for whatever time we had.

Tess was aware; we told David, Martha, and Sarah where things stood and how we were going to handle it. Grant, of course, knew; and when Mary came to the house to visit prior to Allen's going back to work, we told her what the situation was, knowing it would go no further.

Beyond that, we kept it to ourselves. Allen was adamant on the subject:

"Once people know you're terminal they start killing you off. I don't want people looking at me to see if they can notice any changes. To hell with that!"

It was a lovely summer and a busy one. Allen and I even did a *Love Boat* together, in which he had to ride a horse! The house in Carmel was progressing, and whenever we went up for a couple of days to check, we could see it taking shape. In October we were able to clear a whole week.

At dawn one morning, on our third day

up there, Allen got out of bed, and we both knew there was something very wrong when he couldn't get oriented. Ed and Mary Ellen Hicks came in no time after my call, and we managed to get him to the Monterey Community Hospital. Allen had suffered a massive stroke and the prognosis was that he wouldn't make it to nightfall.

I called Mom, then David, who called the girls, and they all caught the first planes available. By now, the media had picked up the news at the hospital, and our secret was no more.

Allen did make it through that nightmare, but it took a while. He was in a coma for two weeks. We kept talking to him and he gradually began to respond. Perhaps out of self-defense, bless his heart. By the time the kids had to return to work, they were able to take some hope with them.

During this same time, Mary had her own tragedy to deal with, when her son, Richie, died. That night, around midnight, I was called to the phone at the nurses' desk. It was Mary. For ten minutes we tried to comfort each other, but that night we both truly believed it was the end of the world. The Tinkers were divorced but Grant was a pillar of strength for both of us during those black days.

■ ■ ■ ■

After three weeks, it was Grant Tinker who chartered an ambulance plane and brought Allen back to Good Samaritan Hospital and his own doctors in L.A. Eventually, he was able to come home, where he continued to improve. In addition to the cards and notes and flowers from friends, the unbelievable outpouring from people who knew him only through television helped his recovery more than I can say. He kept saying, "I can't *believe* it!"

Tom Kennedy continued to take good care of *Password*.

The house construction still demanded attention, but somehow it was completed in February 1981. We furnished one of the bedrooms, and by March, Allen was well enough for us to fly north to see it. He slept there two nights, which made it *our* house for all time.

Every afternoon during Allen's last stay in the hospital, Grant would just drop in. The hospital is in the heart of downtown Los Angeles, and Grant's office was clear out in Burbank. When Allen asked, "What are *you* doing here?" Grant's answer was, "I was in the neighborhood."

Very early on the morning of June 9, Allen lost the battle — five days short of our eighteenth wedding anniversary.

Allen.

20

Grant and his lady, Melanie Burke, came to
the house in the afternoon of the day Allen
died, and we had a warm unhurried time
together. I didn't learn until weeks later that
Grant had come directly from a lunch meeting with Thornton Bradshaw, where he had
been offered — and had accepted — the
job of chairman of the National Broadcasting Company. I was unaware that he had to
go back into a meeting after they left me;
he gave no inkling that he was under any
pressure. They were there to talk about his
friend and comfort his friend's wife.

When I asked if he would say a few words
at the service, he said, "Why don't you not
worry about that. I'll take care of it." And
he did. Instead of a funeral, he put together
a celebration of Allen's life and the fact that
his troubles were over. Special friends came
to add their voices in the beautiful chapel
at Forest Lawn: Tom Kennedy, Burt Reyn-

olds, Bert Convy — some from across the country, like Mark Goodson and Gene Rayburn — and, of course Grant. Then, as he had requested, Allen went back to the small town of Mineral Point, Wisconsin, where he was born. There, with the children, we had the funeral.

An added postscript. At the L.A. Zoo, there is a large area next to the koala house designated as Ludden Plaza. So many memorial gifts came in from people who were aware of our interest in the zoo, including one very large anonymous gift, that they chose to honor Allen in that wonderful way. It wasn't difficult to realize who that anonymous donor was — he was a true best, best friend.

Grant had done all that while he was involved in turning his own life upside down. The chairmanship meant either move to New York or commute, to run a company that at the time was in deep-dire straits. When I finally did learn the news and realized when it had all happened, I tried to tell him how much it meant and say thank you. Grant stopped me with "Hey, if I can't figure out my own priorities, I shouldn't take the job."

There were times, I'm sure, when Grant wondered if the job could be done at all, but he gave it his best. He managed to turn the arrows from down to up, and NBC was once more flying high — at a cost of five of the toughest years for Grant Tinker.

The quality time that Allen and I had together, even after we became aware of what was in store, is something for which I will be eternally grateful. My mother had been given no such cushion — many women aren't — and how she made it through with no warning I will never understand. Tess and I were always inordinately close, and now, without talking about it, she seemed to have an uncanny sense of when to move in to comfort and when to stay back and just let me put one foot in front of the other.

Back to work, the salvation. Once again, I thank God for the business I'm in; you spend your work hours pretending to be someone else, which literally forces you out of yourself.

Carol Burnett had brought her variety show to a close in 1979. Now, after doing some dramatic roles, she had decided to do a special based on the family sketches. She included mean Ellen in the plan, which was a pleasant surprise. I was glad to get busy, and especially with Carol and company.

There was only one irony. The plot of the show concerned Mama's death, the funeral, and the way her various offspring reacted. It doesn't sound like too many laughs, but the writers had put a marvelous spin on the subject, and it was truly funny. Privately, the timing was just a little too close to my own situation for comfort.

The audience loved the show. They responded so positively that a new series, *Mama's Family,* brought Mama back to life.

Vicki Lawrence, of course, and Ken Berry and Dorothy Lyman were on every week, but Carol made only occasional guest appearances. I signed for seven out of thirteen episodes, which was a legal breakpoint. Appearing in seven shows or fewer, I was considered a guest and could do other things as well; more than seven shows in thirteen would make me a regular, and therefore exclusive. It was a fine arrangement, and I enjoyed it.

The show had a very successful run and I think it might still be going, but Vicki finally opted to get out from under the gray wig and all the padding and the rolled stockings. You can't blame her, but she was so great in the part it was hard to let her go.

The game shows were still on my agenda

whenever I could work out the schedule. *Hollywood Squares* was one of the very popular ones, and I did it every once in a while. Peter Marshall was the emcee. Cliff Arquette, as Charlie Weaver, and Paul Lynde were two of the stable of regulars, and along with the guests, there were nine celebrities on each show. Pete had his hands full.

I had met the producer, Rick Rosner, but didn't know him well, so I was surprised to receive a call from him in 1983, asking me to come into the office and look at a new game he was putting together. He thought it would be an interesting switch to have a female emcee.

Well, all I could do was laugh, and then I had to explain why. Rick insisted that enough time had gone by (I'd heard that argument before), and would I just come in and see a trial run-through — he was sure I'd fall in love with the game. He outlined the general idea, and, I must say, it didn't really grab me, but I didn't want to be rude and agreed to come in and see the run-through.

Knowing how hard it is for me to say no when someone is that enthusiastic, I asked my friendly agent, Tony Fantozzi, to come with me. He could be the bad guy and tell Rick he didn't want me to do the show. That turned out to be no help at all, because Tony liked the show a lot and proceeded to urge me to do it.

So much for my support system. But it didn't really matter, because the network still had to approve a woman hosting a game, and we all knew the chances of that happening.

We met a couple of times to rehearse my emceeing the game, and, I have to admit, the more I played it, the more fun it seemed. God, I'm easy!

Rick scheduled a presentation run-through for Brandon Tartikoff of NBC. Brace yourself. He not only bought the show, he thought it was a brilliant idea to have a woman emcee! The world does turn.

The only thing Brandon objected to was the name. Rick Rosner wanted to call it *Studs*, but had to compromise with *Just Men*. (At the time a stud was equivalent to a hunk. A few years later the definition became a bit racier, and a salacious late-night show hit the air called *S.T.U.D.S.*) *Just Men* was just fine with me.

The format, such as it was: seven celebrity men — actors, sports figures, musicians, whoever — would write down their answers to a silly given question (e.g., "Do you have a quick temper?"). Two competing female contestants would try to predict those answers. Each girl would choose one of the men and would have sixty seconds to ask him yes-or-no questions. Based on what she had learned about him, she would try to guess his response to the original question. If she was right, she got a set of car keys. Whichever girl wound up with the most keys won and had the chance to pick one of the keys and try to start the new car onstage. If it started, it was hers; if not, she returned on the next show.

As games go, it was almost as absurd as it sounds, but the fun was in the ad-lib responses and the way the men reacted to each other. The same seven men would play all week, then a new group of seven would come in. It was a mixed bag, with people like Tommy Lasorda, John Ritter, George Brett, Mr. T, Garry Marshall, David Hasselhoff, and the like. As per usual, we did the week's five shows in one day, and on the Monday show the guys tended to be a little stiff and on their dignity. By the second day they had relaxed, and by Wednesday they had sorted out the white hats from the black. By Friday's show, I needed a whip and a chair.

For me, it was great fun, since I wasn't stuck behind a podium but was free to move around with a microphone to catch their remarks and responses.

The viewers were enthusiastic, but we lasted only thirteen weeks. The reason we were canceled is funnier, I think, than the show ever dreamed of being. Grounded at home for a couple of days with a bad cold, the chairman of NBC had a chance to watch the show — and absolutely hated it. That chairman, you will remember, was one Grant Tinker. The thing that really turned him off was what made it so much fun for me — my not being anchored, but able to move around.

At any rate, we were off the air by the time I got nominated for an Emmy. The awards for daytime were held in New York, so I didn't attend. Can you possibly imagine my shock that night when they called to tell me I'd won? I'm sure it was gender-oriented, but I was tickled nevertheless. It gets even sillier. Because our thirteen weeks on the air over-lapped into the next Emmy year, I received another nomination the following year! *Just Men* was a short but interesting little adventure.

Keeping busy *was* the answer, so I packed the schedule tight. The problem with that gambit is that it is hard to *un*pack later, especially when some of the commitments are long term. With Allen gone, I took on some added responsibilities with Morris Animal Foundation. I did the same in my work with the L.A. Zoo, where I have been a trustee since 1974. I am still up to my neck in both organizations, and no way could I walk away from either one.

So, in 1982, when I was approached to write a book on animals, I was in a frame of mind to think, sure, I'll squeeze it in somewhere. I was new at the game and didn't realize quite how much was involved.

The publisher was William Morrow and Company. There was a nice young man to work with me named Tom Watson, which almost scared me off at first, because the last thing in the world I wanted to do was a "celebrity" book "as told to." But, not to worry, Tom didn't want that either; we worked together and grew to be great buddies in the process.

The book was about animals used in therapy — guide dogs, hearing dogs, therapeutic riding, hospice cats. We explored various programs that were just beginning to take shape where animals themselves were the therapists, working with the physically disabled, the elderly, autistic children, prisoners, and more. The medical community was also beginning to evaluate and validate the physical benefits that average pet owners

With coauthor Tom Watson and canine TV star "Boomer" at book signing for first book.

derive just by hanging out with their four-legged friends. The term "human-animal bond" was relatively new at the time, and it is heartening to find both the term and those programs commonplace today. The book was titled *Betty White's Pet Love* (their title, not mine, I assure you) and subtitled "How Pets Take Care of Us."

Tom and I both wrote, sometimes separately and sometimes together at my house. We were kindred spirits, not only in regard to our love for animals, but in our appreciation of hot dogs and peanut butter and jelly sandwiches. At first we would have one or the other whenever we worked together, but the decision making soon became more than we could handle, so we wound up having both every time — with sweet pickles. We lived through it, and *Pet Love* was published in 1983.

Getting used to being one person instead of two is a major bummer, and there is no easy way around it. No shortcut. Just about the time you begin to think you are getting it together, something unexpected trips you up and sends you back to square one. Like the day I was in Robinson's in Beverly Hills. I had finished whatever I was there for, and on my way out of the store I walked by the television department. I heard the voice first. I turned to look, and there was Allen in a full-head close-up on every set in the place.

I can't ever remember a sensation quite

like that — before or since. I was frozen. It was evidently a rerun of a *Love Boat* that we had done together. Now, that was an hour show, with *many* other people in the cast. It wasn't even a shot of us together — just a single headshot of Allen, laughing and making some kind of speech. What kind of weird timing brought me to that spot at that precise moment? I have no idea how long I stood there. Maybe ten seconds — maybe an hour. Thinking of it still turns me cold this minute.

In the beginning, there is a whole year of those terrible "firsts" — his birthday, your birthday, your anniversary, all the holidays. Each time one came and went, however, it was a small victory, achieved with the help of those around me. My mother and my dogs formed the inner circle (and, believe me, she would totally understand my bracketing them). Then there were the friends who set about putting the pieces back together, each in his or her own way. They know who they are, and I'm deeply grateful.

Lucille Ball was convinced that the sure cure for *anything* was backgammon. She was passionate about the game and was a champion player. I'd arrive at her house, the board would already be set up, a sandwich would be on the side, and we would get right down to the business at hand. By now, certainly, you know how much I love all games, so you can appreciate what a painful frustration it was for me to flunk backgammon. In self-defense, I have to say that, as a comedienne, Lucy was the best; as a teacher, she was the worst. The problem was, she loved the game so much and was so damned good at it, she would play it almost like solitaire, while I had never been near the game before. Lucy would tell me to shake out the dice. Well, that much I could do, but before I had a chance to even look, she would push my piece to its spot on the board and in her bass-baritone say, "See, that means you move here." Then she would take *her* turn. She'd shake out the dice, then with fingers flying, make her move. I would beg her to hold on a second and explain what she had just done, but she would simply bat those long eyelashes at me and growl, "Your turn!" I would have been totally intimidated had it not struck me so funny. After about three lessons I retired from the field, but the lady had accomplished what I'm sure she had set out to do: she had given me a challenge, and made me laugh in spite of myself.

Allen and I had the best of all worlds in our two secretaries. Allen's gal, Gail Clark, and mine, Pat Schrott, had been best friends for years while their kids were growing. This meant they could take over for each other seamlessly when one or the other was away. Coincidentally, about the time Allen stopped working, Pat got remarried. Gail didn't miss a beat; she picked up my life and made sense of the jumble I was in at the time, and has been doing so ever since. Above and beyond that, she has become the kind of supportive friend that comes by rarely in a lifetime. I

With my right arm — my secretary Gail Clark. (© AMERICAN BROAD-CASTING COMPANIES, INC.)

love her down-to-earthness. Many of today's women have decided the term "secretary" is demeaning and insist on being called a "personal assistant." The first time I introduced Gail as my personal assistant she laughed, saying, "Betty, secretary is just fine. That's what I wanted to be and I worked hard at school to learn to be a good one. I'm proud of it." That's my kind of girl.

My mother, who had been my strength all through Allen's illness, began having some days that were not as good as others. Much as she tried to bluff it out, it got to the point where she had to go in for some extensive tests to see what was going on. Several years before, Mom had been through a bout of hepatitis, resulting from a series of blood transfusions, and it had left some residual problems. She would be all right, the doctor said, just not as strong anymore.

It was perhaps the biggest selling job I'd ever had to do in my life, but I finally talked her into coming to stay with me for a while. Leaving her apartment in Century City was a tough call because it meant her independence, but since it was "only for a while," she agreed to come. It was good to have her near.

The book was published. That was the

good news. The bad news was that it meant a book tour of fourteen cities. It goes with the territory, and they warn you up front that if you aren't prepared to promote it, save yourself the trouble of writing the book. I was doubly glad that my Tess had made the move in with me. She and the dogs were able to keep each other from getting lonesome for the two weeks I was gone, and there was a housekeeper to keep the house going.

That fall was a good time. We were able to make a couple of visits to Carmel together, and between the daily walks and the sea air, Carmel couldn't help but make someone feel better.

Pet Love had been out a few months when my literary agents at the time, Bart Andrews and Sherry Robb, said there was interest at Doubleday in my doing a second book. They suggested a collection of short pieces regarding my feelings on a variety of subjects: on love, on fear, on anger, on whatever I wanted to address.

My friends, and even my mom, took a rather dim view of my taking on such a time-consuming effort again so soon, but it did sound doable, and it would keep me home — at least until I finished it. Besides, it wouldn't be due for almost a year. I couldn't resist the temptation, and this time I would try to solo.

At the start of a project, deadlines are always touched upon lightly and referred to in vague terms:

"We would expect a manuscript by — oh, sometime in March."

No pressure. However, once under way, somehow it becomes a firm "February fifteenth." Always earlier, never later. That is not a complaint; without that due date, I'm sure I would always be *writing* a book, never finishing one.

Lucille Ball and Carol Channing were my "sponsors" at the book signing for book number two.

The best thing about the Doubleday experience was getting to know my editor, Loretta Barrett. I liked her immediately and had great faith in her opinions. What I didn't know then was that Loretta would lead me into a whole second career.

Doubleday, too, wanted my name in the title, for whatever celebrity value there might be, so, since the essays in the book were all "on this" and "on that," plus my longevity, I thought a good name for the book would be *Betty White: On and On.* It was Loretta who pointed out that could easily tempt a critic to use it against me. "She certainly does go on and on!" The title they came up with was fine with me. *Betty White: In Person.*

Allen had been gone three years. It was hard to believe. The ache was still there — always will be — but the searing pain had subsided, and I felt I was moving along on a busy but even keel.

Silly me.

21

1984 was no longer a figment in George Orwell's future; it had actually arrived, and with it came a shot of adrenaline for prime-time television. As mentioned before, early in that year CBS had pronounced situation comedy officially dead and expected the other networks to follow suit. NBC, however, refused to lie down and introduced a brand-new sitcom on their fall schedule called *The Cosby Show,* which proceeded to take off like a bird.

Poor NBC, that is, which had been practically on life support in 1981 when Grant Tinker came aboard, had come back stronger than anyone, including Grant, had anticipated. With the advent of *The Cosby Show,* the recovery was complete: the ratings went through the roof and continued to climb. There were instances where comparative ratings were figured "exclusive of *Cosby*" as the numbers were so out of line. Situation comedy was back in business, if indeed it had ever been out.

I was still working on *Mama's Family,* plus assorted guest shots. One day a letter arrived that caught my attention, saying that the production company Witt-Thomas-Harris was putting a new show together and would like me to keep it in mind. Paul Witt, Tony Thomas (Danny's son), and Susan Harris (Paul's wife), all three dynamite writers, had formed a partnership and already had a couple of strong shows in their stable, *Soap* and *It's a Living.* Jay Sandrich would be directing the pilot of this new show, and they were very excited about the concept.

The letter was a new one on me, and I wasn't quite sure what to make of it. It was almost like a Save the Date card. The part I did like was Jay Sandrich. He had directed almost all of *The Mary Tyler Moore Show*s, and he was brilliant. All Tony Fantozzi was able to find out was that they were working on a concept that would include Bea Arthur.

Ultimately, a script did arrive, and now I really started to sit up and pay attention. So many scripts come in, and you read them all, each time hoping for the best. The majority are less than good, some bad enough so that mediocre is a compliment. Now and then it's a delight to find one that shows promise. But this script, entitled *The Golden Girls,* knocked my socks off. The premise — four older women living together in Miami — hadn't sounded particularly attractive, but the script came alive with some of the best writing I'd seen since MTM.

There were the usual meetings, interspersed with waiting periods that seemed to go on forever. I learned that Bea Arthur would be playing Dorothy, and an actress from New York, Estelle Getty, had been signed to play Dorothy's mother, Sophia.

It was assumed that I would be Blanche, the well-to-do Southern woman to whom men were the breath of life. The fourth character was Rose, and they had settled on Rue McClanahan. Rue had worked with Bea for five and a half years on *Maude,* and she and I had worked together for a couple of years on *Mama's Family,* where she played mousey Aunt Fran. We hadn't met Estelle as yet, but she had come from a highly successful run on Broadway in *Torch Song Trilogy.*

The next report I heard was a call saying a decision had been made to switch parts. I would be playing Rose, and Rue would do Blanche.

I was heartsick. From the script we had

read, we knew the strong character of Dorothy, and her brutally frank mother, Sophia. We understood the lustful Blanche, but I hadn't a clue who Rose was. Then I heard that Jay Sandrich was the one who had suggested the switch, pointing out that if Betty played another man-hungry character, it wouldn't matter how differently she approached it, the audience would think it was Sue Ann Nivens revisited.

It suddenly made perfect sense — not just because I loved Jay, but because he was absolutely right. And he should know, after spending four seasons with Sue Ann. It was also Jay who gave me the definitive clue to Rose Nylund.

"She is not dumb — just totally naive," he said. "She believes everything she is told and in her innocence, always takes the first meaning of every word."

What a great measuring stick to give an actress. It not only helped me find Rose, but love her and keep her on course through the next few years. She didn't understand sarcasm, so the others could say terrible things, but the words all sounded fine to her. She was so literal in her thinking that if someone said they could eat a horse, she would call the S.P.C.A. But Rose was not weak. She had her own set of rules that made perfect sense, if only to her, and she also had a fierce Nordic temper on occasion.

Rue, on the other hand, took Blanche and ran with her — farther than I would ever have dared to go. She was wonderfully outrageous and outrageously wonderful. The result was, we were all happy as clams with our roles. Once again, thank you, Jay.

We did the pilot in April 1985, and it was a real treat to work with such pros. When you threw out a line, you had to brace yourself, because you knew it would be coming right back at you over the net and you'd better be ready. That's when it gets exciting. Jay paid us a compliment that I treasure to this day. He said he was working with four comedy black belts.

The night of the taping was nerve-racking because all the NBC brass was there, plus the whole Witt-Thomas-Harris contingent. It was hardly your ordinary happy-go-lucky audience, ready to be entertained. These folks had a lot riding on what they saw, and often that kind of group forgets to laugh. But not this time; the show couldn't have played better, and everyone was thrilled. Hurdle number one.

Following any pilot, there is the inevitable wait while decisions are being made, or

413

worse, while other pilots are being considered. There is nothing to do but get on with your life, because no hints or updates will be forthcoming until "the call," saying thumbs-up or thumbs-down. None of that has changed much through the years. Didn't it start with the lions and the Christians? (No matter what you've heard, that *was* before my time.)

Fortunately, for me, the timing had worked out so that I could get the book almost done during that period, which made the wait seem short. When "the call" did come in, it was terrific news. *The Golden Girls* were in business and would start taping in July to go on the air in September. We had made the NBC fall schedule! *Big* hurdle number two.

The pilot, which would be our first on-air episode, was being touted around town as the one to watch. Oops. From the last *Betty White Show* experience, I knew that could be the kiss of death.

The next very important hurdle was the meeting of the affiliates, where the show was presented to the station managers who would be carrying it. The buzz at the big party that night was very positive, not only among the affiliates, but among their wives as well, which sometimes can mean a lot. So far, so good, but the advertisers had yet to be heard

414

from, and there had been some apathy about how marketable four old broads in Miami would be. Their big meeting was held back in New York. It was at their morning session that the new shows were presented.

With the three-hour time difference, it was about nine in the morning, California time, when my phone rang. I picked it up to hear Grant Tinker say, "Well, Betty, I wouldn't make any big plans for the next couple of years — you'll be busy." He said the advertisers had loved it and thought the *Girls* would be fun to spend a half hour with every week. For laid-back Grant, it was a rave.

By now, the word "hit" was being bruited about. I am usually the incurable optimist, but I was still leery. I'd been to that point before, and once burned . . . I wouldn't be able to relax completely until the audience vote was in. But in the meantime, it was a lovely feeling to take to work when we started taping in July.

There were a few adjustments at the start, but it felt good. We would read through the script on Monday, rehearse all week, then tape the show twice on Friday, before two different audiences. I loved it because it was our old MTM schedule. Friday taping gave you the weekend to clear your head before starting a new show again on Monday. It also gave the writers just an inch more of breathing room. Bea and Rue had always taped on Tuesday with *Maude,* which they loved because it gave them two more days to work on lines and interpretation. Coming from a long run on stage, Estelle had to get used to doing a new show every week. Whatever schedule each of us had become accustomed to was the one we liked best. The writers made the final call and opted for Friday taping.

We had known that Jay Sandrich could direct only the pilot — he was the director of *The Cosby Show* from New York during the regular season. Paul Bogart, a good director, was hired to do our series.

Paul's approach was totally different. Any comments or suggestions from the writers or producers must be filtered through him, and he referred to us as "my actors." It was almost as though "they" — the producers, the guys putting up the money — were the enemy, and Paul our protector. This was the absolute antithesis of the way the MTM gang had worked, where everyone had spoken freely.

Part of the daily schedule was to do a run-through for the writers and producers after rehearsal every day. It was a lot easier to understand what they were going for and to discuss suggestions when they could communicate directly, rather than through a rather defensive interpreter.

This didn't seem to bother Bea and Rue and Estelle as much as it did me, but it evidently bothered Paul Witt and Tony Thomas a *lot,* because Paul Bogart was replaced after the first three shows.

Tony and Paul brought a director in for us to meet before he was hired — one Terry Hughes, who was from England. They thought a good way for us to get acquainted would be to have lunch together, so a catered luncheon was brought in and set up in a very small room down the hall that barely accommodated the table and five chairs. Yes, just five. After Paul and Tony got us situated, they went out and closed the door, leaving poor Terry Hughes alone with the four dragons.

By the time we emerged from that little dining room, we had all fallen in love with this charming Britisher. The vote was unanimous that he *was* our director, which I'm sure came as no surprise to Paul and Tony.

Terry is tremendously talented, with a stack of awards to bear witness, unfairly handsome, and has a delicious sense of humor, or in Terry's case, humour. He also didn't seem to feel that actors were some anointed creatures who must be "protected" from the outside world.

The love affair between us all lasted for the next five years. By the sixth season, Terry was offered the chance to direct a major motion picture, and there was no way we could expect him to pass up the opportunity. But, oh, it was a tough parting.

In the first episode, which had been our pilot, there was one more character, the gay housekeeper, played by Charles Levin. When the script was originally written, no one could foresee how well the four women would mesh together, nor how strong Estelle's character, Sophia, would become. Also, with a housekeeper there, the girls wouldn't have had as much access to the kitchen, where so many of our close four-way scenes took place. We used to solve most of our problems around the kitchen table — over cheesecake. So, after the initial show, the part of the housekeeper was written out. The reasons were all valid, but it was a heartbreaker for Chuck Levin. Can you imagine the disappointment of seeing the show picked up, then finding you were no longer a part of it? He took it in good spirit, bless him, and came by the set to say hello from time to time. As for us, we

The Girls: Estelle Getty, Bea Arthur, Betty, Rue McClanahan.
(NBCU Photo Bank)

spent the first year explaining that he had
not been written out because he was gay.
Which, just for the record, and who cares,
Chuck wasn't.

NBC gave us some great promotion, so
that when we went on the air in September,
The Golden Girls nudged *Cosby* aside, and for
our debut that first week we were number
one. Cos stepped right back in, of course,
but we managed to hang on to a spot in the
top ten every week for the first five years of
the show. With audience approval like that,
we had cleared the last hurdle. We were a

genuine hit.

What came as a big surprise to all concerned was the way *Golden Girls* cut across all the demographic lines. Over half of our mail came from kids, but the twenty-, thirty-, and forty-something and beyond were well represented. It tickled me whenever some very small person, tugging at mother's sleeve, would point and say, "There's Wose!" Too young to pronounce it, they still knew the character — all the characters. Ruesy always said that the ones who approached her were *much* taller, and their voices were deeper.

How was our show able to reach all the age groups? Perhaps because we weren't specifically aiming at any one of them, but mainly, I think, because we were truly funny.

Professionally, things couldn't have been better. But for the first time in her life, after being in the studio audience for virtually every show I ever did, my Tess was not up to coming to the tapings. By this time, either a nurse or our good friend Lee Moorer would come in every day until I got home from work. Mom and I would have a catch-up session over a glass of wine, then play Trivial Pursuit until dinner. She couldn't sit up at the board, but we would read the questions to each other. We were both fierce contenders, and I was really trying my best, but she usually won. On Saturday nights we would watch *Golden Girls* together and tape it so that she could see it again, if she wished, during the week.

Oddly enough, Bea Arthur's mother was going through a similar challenge at that same time and had come home to stay with her daughter, too. By a strange coincidence, but only that, we seemed to have a plethora of mother-daughter scripts that first season, and in our situations, some of them cut close to the edge for Bea and me.

Mom's body was falling apart, but that mind of hers stayed razor sharp. For two nights before she was taken to the hospital in November, she really creamed me at our game, in spite of my best efforts. That has always been a great source of comfort to me. The lady couldn't keep her body from letting her down, but my mother — the same bright, funny, loving Tess I had always known — was with me to the very last. After just two days in the hospital, she slipped away.

Three weeks later, we were rehearsing one afternoon when Bea was called to the phone. She came back to say her mother had just died. She went home then but came back to work the next day, just as I had done. We were a family, too, and somehow it just seemed the only place to be.

When the Emmy nominations were announced after our first season, the show itself, each of the four of us, Terry Hughes, several of our writers, and a number of our technical people were all nominated. I couldn't believe having backed into another show of that caliber — *twice* in one lifetime.

On the night of the awards, it was a strange feeling when they got to the Best Actress in a Leading Role category. Each of our performances was so tied to the other three, it was impossible to separate them. Choosing any one of us was choosing us all. When my name was called and I got up to the microphone, I tried to make that point, but my mouth was so dry and my breath was so short I'm sure I must have sounded inane. I was backstage in the press lineup when I heard the roar — *The Golden Girls* had just won for Outstanding Comedy Series.

The next day on the set was an odd one. Things were somehow quieter than usual. Estelle gave me a big hug and kiss — but she did it outside, before we got into the studio. The crew couldn't have been warmer or sweeter, but the congratulations were all whispered. Even the *big* win — for the show itself — was just not mentioned.

It was a relief to get that day over and go back to business as usual. The reaction had come as a real surprise, and I had learned something — I'm just not sure what the hell it was.

For the first five years of the show, we *all* were nominated every year, which was something of a record in itself. By the first three years into the show, *everyone,* producers, writers, director, actresses, had his or her own Emmy, and we could all relax and enjoy. I'll guaran-certain-tee one thing — that first year's coolness was never allowed again. We celebrated!

We could relax — everybody had an Emmy. (NBCU Photo Bank)

At the start of our second season, when we came back in July from hiatus, Terry Hughes had some exciting news for us. Our show had been running in England for several months and was very popular. As a result, *The Golden Girls* had been invited to London to take part in the annual Royal Variety Show for the Queen Mother, at the Palladium Theatre. We were to go for a week in late November — what a way to start the holiday season.

We were all beside ourselves, and it was tough keeping our minds on the job at hand. We finally had to simmer down long enough to figure out what we would actually *do* in the Royal Variety Show before the Queen Mum.

The writers, plus Tony, Paul, and Susan, put their talented heads together and chose three of our best around-the-table kitchen scenes. By blending them together, they came up with a very funny piece of material.

November finally arrived, and the trip lived up to all our anticipation. London itself was like fairyland, with all the elaborate Christmas decorations already up. It even snowed a tiny bit on our drive in from the airport. The press greeted us warmly, and we discovered that other American friends

— Mickey Rooney, Ann Miller, Michael Feinstein — were in the lineup for the show as well. There was also a line of Rockettes from Radio City Music Hall.

It was quite a feeling when we arrived at the theater for rehearsal, and I realized I was actually standing on the famous stage where so many great performers had appeared. Having heard about the Palladium all my life, I had come to picture it as a huge auditorium, so it was a surprise to find that it was a nice, but not extraordinary, regular-sized theater.

We were briefed on protocol for both our onstage and offstage encounters with the Queen Mother. She would be seated in the Royal Box at stage left, and we were instructed to bow to her, and then to the audience, but not to stare. At the end of the show, the entire cast was to line up for a final curtain bow, then remain on stage, where the Queen Mum would arrive and greet each of us as she moved down the line. We were to respond to whatever she said to us, but we were not to initiate any conversation. The ladies were to drop a small curtsy. If I hadn't been nervous before, I was now.

It was an exceedingly long show with a huge cast. Bea, Rue, Estelle, and I were all in one big dressing room, where we were instructed to stay until we were called on-stage. Our turn was scheduled about half-way through the lengthy program, so we had plenty of time to tense up. The fact that we could neither see nor hear anything that was happening onstage made it even more nerve-racking. There was talk of making a break for it, but we chickened out.

The call finally came. The audience greeted us like old friends, and after we made it through without anyone falling down, they gave us a lovely send-off. We even remembered both bows.

After the final curtain, with the whole cast assembled, the stage was extremely crowded. We were in a double line, the Rockettes behind us.

Soon, the Queen Mother arrived, accompanied by Princess Anne. The latter was in a deep green velvet gown with a portrait neckline that set off her truly exquisite complexion. Her grandmother was all in gold, with a diamond tiara that was enough to cool off the entire stage. Not to stare, indeed!

As the Queen Mum moved down the line, she made some gracious remark to each one; the ladies all dropped a small curtsy as she approached. I happened to be the last one in our foursome, and after she greeted Bea and Rue and Estelle, as she got to me, she indicated the scantily clad Rockettes behind us and said to me, "Aren't they beautiful girls?" I curtsied, and replied, "Yes, and such lovely bodies." She lit up with a radiant smile which belied her eighty-six years and added, "Oh, yes! *Lovely* bawdies!"

The next day, the reviewers were particularly kind to *The Golden Girls,* which served as frosting on the cake before we headed back home to the real world.

Come to think of it — our special showbiz world wasn't all that real either.

22

The fringe benefits that accompany being in a successful show are noteworthy. The day following the Emmy Awards that first year, after I'd won, Barbara Walters called from New York to invite me to do a one-on-one interview for her next special. It was to be done from my home, something I usually try to avoid, but Barbara Walters was something else again.

I had met Barbara years before in New York, when she and Allen had broadcast a couple of theater openings together, and even on the phone, she picked right up from where we'd left off as if we had seen each other yesterday.

The morning of the interview, a truck arrived around seven, soon followed by another, and an army began taking over my house. It was October, but Barbara wanted a Christmas show, and my living room was the target. They installed stone logs in the fireplace so we could have a gas fire without the noise of a real one (they are still there, incidentally); they completely rearranged my furniture; they brought in enough lights to shoot a feature film; then, as a finishing touch, they distributed a truckload (literally) of blooming poinsettias. I didn't recognize my room. It was gorgeous.

Altogether, there must have been fifty people working together quietly, cheerfully, and carefully. There was a food truck that served breakfast for the whole crew. By lunchtime, tables were set up on the lawn, and they had a hot lunch.

Early that morning I had panicked when I saw them moving in, but soon realized all I had to do was stay out of the way and try to explain the whole thing to the dogs.

Barbara arrived around eleven. No fanfare, no entourage; she just showed up, like a warm friend arriving for a visit. After the makeup and hair people worked their magic, we settled in for the interview itself, and I was able to see, firsthand, what makes this woman stand alone in her field. Without losing her focus or her warmth, she takes the interview exactly where she wants it to go, and her mental editor is in action as she goes. When something works well, she doesn't belabor it. She leaves it alone and moves on.

Before we were through, she led me into talking about losing Allen, something I certainly hadn't intended to do. But with the firelight and the flowers, sitting in the same room where he and I had spent so many Christmases, it all seemed perfectly natural. Then, before it got too heavy, she eased us on to something else. She continued until she recognized a good tie-off for the interview, at which point she thanked me and stopped. A lesser talent would have dribbled on and on, then sorted it out later in the editing room.

The efficiency of that whole operation was mind-boggling, but no more so than the know-how of Barbara herself. A class act.

The crew then proceeded to put everything back the way they'd found it, and by the time the last truck pulled away around seven o'clock that night, you would never have known they'd been there — except, of course, for my new stone logs and the carload of poinsettias, which continued to bloom through the real Christmas.

Another serendipity: *The Tonight Show* called and invited me to host one night when Johnny Carson was off. I had done it once before and found it to be much scarier than doing the Paar show or Merv Griffin. Don't ask me why you knowingly agree to put yourself through that torture again, but, of course, I said okay. I say don't ask, but we *know* the answer. Let's face it, it's an ego trip of the first order. But then, the Barbara Walters interview was not exactly an exercise in self-effacement. It's a syndrome that bears watching.

After all the early conditioning on *Hollywood on Television,* I think I would get the bends without a commercial to do every now and then. At any given time through the years, there usually have been a couple of continuing national accounts and one or two regional ones, seen only in local areas. However, during the MTM years on CBS, I could finish out preexisting contracts already in place before signing with the show, but could not take on any new commercial, because it was strictly against that network's policy for their series people.

Later, at NBC during *The Golden Girls,* it was a little different. I was not encouraged to add any extras, but when an existing account ran out, I was permitted to replace it in kind, that is, a national for a national or a regional for a regional. The only ironclad rule was that they could not run on opposing stations on the night *The Girls* aired, which was Saturday. That was a remarkably tolerant attitude for any network, and it was much appreciated.

Commercials are lucrative, certainly, but I also enjoy doing them because you can be yourself for a change. (The jury is out as to whether that's good or bad!) My one prerequisite, however, has always been that the product be one I believe in and use. Maybe it's a reaction to hearing all those schlock pitches in the early days. In today's climate it may sound archaic, but I still have a thing about integrity. Call me crazy.

It was through a series of commercials we did together for the Southern California Edison Company that George Burns and I became friends. We had met several times at Henny and Jim Backus's New Year's Eve preparties, but that was always in passing — working together was different.

The commercials were well-written and fun to do. They were about heating and cooling your house without wasting energy, and who was a more perfect authority on saving energy than George? I was his foil. Every year, Southern California Edison would renew our contracts in the spring, then spend the summer preparing the commercials for us to shoot in the fall. George was ninety when we did the first spots, but each year we would have to arrange the shooting days around George's busy schedule of personal appearances.

This went on for four years. Finally, the following spring, the sponsor regretfully notified us that they would not be continuing the campaign. They confided to my agent that, because of the lead time involved, they could no longer take the risk of George not being up to working in the fall. That was four years ago, and George has been working almost steadily ever since. As of this moment, George will turn ninety-nine in less than a month!

George and I share something else — we have each been special friends of Charlie Lowe and Carol Channing for more years than anyone can count. Charles has remained very close to George, even though not working with him, and, as for Carol, whenever she feels the need of comedy advice on whatever she is doing, she calls her mentor, George. The four of us have dinner often, which is always delightful, but I remember one evening that was even more special.

Among other friends we share with the Lowes are movie producers Ross Hunter and Jacque Mapes. They had included Allen and me in their "family" ever since I had done a television movie for them a few years back (*The Best Place to Be* with Donna Reed), and it was through them that we got to know another legend — Helen Hayes. Even after we lost Allen, Ross and Jacque continued to include me. One evening in the course of conversation it came out that Helen Hayes and George Burns had never met. Well, that was a clarion call to action for Hunter and Mapes. They called Carol and Charles and the four of them set out to arrange a blind date for George and Helen.

There were nine of us that night, in a small private dining room at Chasen's. Charles and Carol and I picked up George, and we got there ahead of Helen, who arrived last. This delicious first lady of the theater knew exactly what she was doing. Looking absolutely *beautiful,* the ninety-year-old legend made her entrance and, with a giant twinkle in her eye, walked straight up to George. They were both about the same height, and wound up standing nose-to-nose. Before anyone could introduce them, Helen simply said, "Well, hello there!" George responded with, "Hi there, kid, it's about time." That set the tone for the entire evening.

It was my privilege to sit between Helen and George, both of whom were at the peak

With Helen and George on their first date.

of their form. George would tell a vaudeville story, Helen would top it with a theater
anecdote, and the ball would be back in
George's court.

Ross had told me earlier in the evening
that Helen was out from New York for only
three days this trip, to see friends, and
was staying with Jacque and him; with the
number of friends Helen had, it had been
a constant merry-go-round ever since she
arrived.

"Frankly, Bets, I don't know how she does
it. Jacque and I are exhausted."

Sure enough, it was almost eleven-thirty when everyone finally began to take their leave, for Chasen's sake, if not our own, yet the nonagenarians were still going strong.

I wouldn't take anything for that evening.

Ever since we met them in those early days on Cape Cod, Tom and Patty Sullivan had stayed in touch. Months, or even longer, would go by without our actually getting together, but we were always aware of what was going on with each other. We shared the same service for trips to the airport, and the drivers would carry messages back and forth between us. I was always especially interested in updates on Tom's wonderful guide dog, Dinah.

Tom had spent three years as special correspondent on *Good Morning America,* traveling all over the country to track down his stories, much of the time accompanied only by Dinah. She would get him through airports and into hotels; she served not only as his eyes, but as his road manager and boon companion. She also just happened to be one of the most beautiful golden retrievers ever.

As inevitably happens with everyone — even gorgeous redheads — age caught up with Dinah and she finally had to be retired as a working dog. Tom and Patty assumed that the lady would enjoy a well-deserved rest at home with their German shepherd, Cay, for company. So, Tom went through the process and got a new guide, a two-year-old black Labrador retriever, named Nelson.

No one had consulted Dinah, but she soon made it abundantly clear that she didn't like this new game plan at all. As far as she was concerned, this obstreperous interloper had taken over her job, and her master, and she wasn't needed or wanted anymore. She would have no part of Tom or Patty; she wouldn't eat; she crawled under the bed in another room, refusing to budge except when she had to go outside. She simply didn't want to live anymore — not under the new circumstances.

We had been on for a couple of seasons with *Golden Girls* when all this had occurred. Tom and Patty came over for dinner one night and told me the whole story. They were heartsick and had tried everything they could think of, with no result. Tom was desperate. Did I know anyone who would be able to give her the kind of complete attention that would get her through this?

I certainly couldn't do it. I had a full schedule and, with two small dogs and a cat, a full house. So, of course, I opened my big mouth. "Would you like me to try her, Tom?"

Perhaps I didn't know it at the moment, but that was one of the best ideas I ever had.

So, Dinah came to my house to see if a change of scene might help her. *Help* her! She had a new job! She may have been eleven, but she was suddenly acting more like a five-year-old. There was so much to do. She had to help my housekeeper, Edna, run the house; she had to keep my dogs and the cat in line; she had the gardener, and the poolman, and the mailman, and the UPS man to keep an eye on. She was back in business — and, oh, what joy she brought to us all.

One day I was talking to my friend Jerry Martin about Dinah's life on the road with Tom, when it suddenly struck me that her story should be told. When I called Tom, he jumped at the idea, and another book was under way.

This time it wasn't hard work but more like a labor of love. Tom and I didn't write together. He wrote about his life with the young Dinah on the road and what she had brought to him in the way of interdependence. I wrote about what I learned through Dinah — about adjusting to change and to age; about my friend Tom; about blindness itself.

Tom Sullivan and Betty — coparents of the beautiful Dinah, at a book signing. (COURTESY TAD MOTOYAMA)

When we each had a couple of chapters, I called Loretta Barrett, who had been my editor at Doubleday on the last book. I asked her as a friend to give me her honest opinion as to whether the project had merit, since it was impossible for me to be objective with this big red dog following me around.

Loretta loved the material. And, as we keep saying, timing is everything. It so happened that Loretta was in the process of leaving Doubleday to take the big step of opening her own literary agency, Barrett

Books. While Tom and I continued to write, Loretta went out and sold the book — to Bantam.

Tom and I would talk on the phone a lot, and we'd send our pages to each other to keep caught up, but we each wrote our own chapters and then alternated them in the book.

When *The Leading Lady: Dinah's Story* was published, we had to work the book tour around Tom's speaking engagements and my *Golden Girls* taping schedule. It wasn't easy, but it was worth it to go on record for this remarkable dog.

Dinah made fifteen years by three days. She couldn't quite make it to the day the book came out.

It hardly seemed possible, but we found ourselves in our fifth season, and *Golden Girls* was still such a joy to do. There was a major celebration when we completed our hundredth episode. Paul and Susan and Tony presented us with beautiful gold watches, engraved with 100 GOLDEN GIRLS A MILLION THANKS — LOVE, PAUL, TONY, AND SUSAN.

Our ratings were consistently high; the nominations continued at Emmy time; in the sitcom business, it was the best of all possible worlds. "If it ain't broke, don't fix it," but as we all know, that's often a rule to be broken.

Being scheduled on Saturday night was considered a liability back in 1985 when *Golden Girls* opened. But, Saturday be damned, we took the nine o'clock slot and made it our own for five years. After all that time, it came as something of a jolt — to us, and to the audience — when NBC suddenly announced it was moving us up an hour, to eight o'clock. An hour can make a tremendous difference in a long-established habit pattern — and it did. One week, at nine o'clock, we were in the top ten — number six, to be exact. At *eight* o'clock the following week, we dropped to number sixty-three. Grant Tinker had left NBC by that time; the network must have had its own valid reasons which we weren't privy to, but happy campers we were not.

Over time, we managed to make the climb back up, but never to our old position. We comforted ourselves with the fact that we still had a delightful show to do each week.

One morning, before we started rehearsing, Terry Hughes called Bea, Rue, Estelle, and me down to the other end of the studio and sat us down. I think we all had a premonition of what was coming.

He explained that he had received a major offer to direct a big-screen comedy, *The Butcher's Wife,* and at that point Meg Ryan was to be the star. He wanted us to know how much he loved our show, but offers like that don't come around often. We realized, certainly, that opportunity must be invited in when it comes knocking, so what could we do but wish him well, and try to enjoy the weeks remaining before he left? When hiatus time came in March, we had to bid our British buddy a fond and reluctant farewell.

For decades, any interviewer worth his or her salt has sooner or later asked me, "Is there anything in television you haven't done that you have always wanted to do?" And for those same decades, my stock answer has been, "I would really like to do a romantic love story."

At long last, someone heard me and set out to write one for me. Lynn Roth not only wrote a nice love story, but she sold it to NBC and produced it. It was called *Chance of a Lifetime,* about a widow who, in carrying on her husband's business, becomes an uptight career person. When, to her shock, she is diagnosed as terminally ill, she opts to keep the news to herself and sets off on one last adventure. She goes to

Mexico for a final fling, in the course of which she meets and falls in love with a very attractive man. When the diagnosis turns out to be a mistake, she desperately tries to backpedal, but the man pursues her to a happy ending.

From the beginning, my first choice for leading man had been Leslie Nielsen. Leslie, however, had long since turned from playing romantic parts to become wildly successful with his outrageous *Naked Gun* comedies, so I didn't think there was a snowball's chance of getting him. Nothing ventured . . . I wrote him a note asking if he would possibly consider doing our movie. He said, "Yes!" No hassle, no drawn-out negotiating games — just a simple "Yes."

That attitude makes life not only easier, but a lot more fun, and it prevailed throughout the picture. Another very funny pal, Ed Begley, Jr., played my son, and we all had a marvelous time.

In her desperate attempt to live it up, the widow had even signed on for bungee jumping, and our hero has no choice but to follow. Well, that reads all right in the script and there were doubles to do the big jump, but Leslie and I still had to make it look believable. They strapped us into harnesses and put us on trapezes suspended beneath hot

With Leslie Nielsen in Chance of a Lifetime. *Tough duty.*

air balloons (we had his and her balloons), and all we had to do was let go, to land, we hoped, on mattresses below. Granted, it was only fifteen feet in the air, but to a devout acrophobe it might as well have been fifty. We made it, you'll be surprised to learn.

When we finished the scene, Leslie murmured, "I don't recall your mentioning this in your note."

So, I got my love story. Now, when an interviewer asks if there is something I haven't done that I have always wanted to do, I can just say, "Nope."

By now, *Golden Girls* had been in syndication for several years through Buena Vista Television, a Disney subsidiary. We were in forty-seven countries and doing very well. It's fun to get fan mail from all over the world, and while the language may be different, the word "photograph" is usually recognizable, and the message is clear. It knocks me out to send a picture to Sri Lanka, for instance, of all places.

When we began our seventh season of *Girls,* we were pretty much aware that it would be our last. Bea had begun to get restless the season before, and our last year was no fun for her at all. She wanted out, and she made no bones about it. She wanted to go to England; she wanted to do a musical; she wanted to do a lot of things. Our show just didn't happen to be one of them. Well, we had enjoyed a good long run and were reconciled to the fact that the time had come to move on.

None of us even considered doing *Girls* without Bea. It would be like taking one leg off of a table and expecting it to balance. So we had no idea what to expect when Paul Witt and Tony Thomas called Rue and Estelle and me up to their offices for a meeting.

After the usual amenities, Paul and Tony began to spell out their appreciation for their good fortune — they now had *eight* shows up and running. Great as that was, it was a very full plate, and they were tired. The last thing in the world they had in mind was to face putting together another show. *However . . .*

They then went on to say that Susan Harris Witt had come up with an idea they couldn't resist, and they proceeded to describe it.

Dorothy, Bea Arthur's character, would get married, but not to her ex-husband, Stan, with whom she had had an on-again, off-again relationship for seven years. No, this would be someone completely new, and the whole thing would take place, develop, and resolve in a one-hour *Golden Girls* episode that would close the season — and the series.

Then, the following season could begin with a new series, using our same characters but in a new environment. With Dorothy moved out, Blanche, Sophia, and Rose would sell the house and buy a small hotel in one of the reclaimed and currently popular sections of Miami.

For seven years the *Girls* had been living together, as much as a hedge against loneliness as for economic reasons. But they had always faced life from the shelter and security of their home. Now, by leaving that familiar setting, these characters, whom the audience knew so well, would be forced to do what so many women these days were having to do in real life — meet the world as it comes through the front door and deal with it.

As well as being good writers and producers, Paul and Tony were also no slouches in the selling department. They didn't ask for an immediate reaction. They wanted us to think it over, sleep on it, discuss it among ourselves, and then we would have another meeting.

There was a lot to think about. There were some pros and there were some cons, but the idea of bringing the women out into the real world was an intriguing one. After much discussion and soul-searching, several meetings later we all agreed to have a go at *The Golden Palace* — which was the name of our new hotel.

■ ■ ■ ■

When it came time to do the final one-hour *Golden Girls,* it was a very strange week. It wasn't quite as emotionally draining as the last *Mary Tyler Moore Show* had been — at least not openly. Bea was happy to tie off the series, and the rest of us were looking forward to the new adventure, but none of us was immune to the fact that it was the end of a very important seven years in our lives.

It was a delight to find who had been cast as the man to sweep Dorothy off her feet — Leslie Nielsen, if you please. It was great getting to work with him again so soon. I accused him of being a first-class two-timer, after our big romance in *Chance of a Lifetime,* and wanted to know who was the better kisser. He said, "I don't know — I haven't kissed Sophia yet!"

By the time Friday arrived, the audiences for both shows were really charged up. They, too, were very much aware that it was the closing performance. When we were taking our bows at the end of the second — and last — show that night, Paul and Tony and Susan joined us onstage. They handed each of us a slim jewelry box, containing an exquisite heavy gold bracelet. Engraved on the clasp is "GG." When you open it, on the back of the clasp is a tiny "7."

Witt-Thomas-Harris. Class is such an overly used word, but sometimes it's the only one that fits.

23

Over that summer, power meetings (as opposed to just meetings) had been going on between Witt-Thomas-Harris, NBC, CBS, and Buena Vista. When all the dust finally settled, *The Golden Palace* was leaving the Peacock and set to air on CBS.

The new show took a little getting used to, which was to be expected. When *Golden Palace* started shooting for the following season, the series opened with Blanche, Sophia, and Rose moving out of the house and into the hotel. It actually *felt* like we were leaving home.

There were some new cast members: the chef, who dominated the kitchen, so consequently was on a collision course with Sophia; the young black manager of the hotel; a little boy who just showed up and wouldn't leave. Also, each week there would be a guest celebrity written into the script, which was fun because we never knew who would show up for read-through on Monday morning. You can imagine how tickled I was the morning Eddie Albert walked in.

The action took place primarily moving between the big kitchen, the dining room, and the huge lobby which were all adjoining. We did log a lot of time behind the front desk. I was right back where I started with *Tom, Dick and Harry*. No feather duster this time. Once in a while we would go outside for a scene or two, or to one or another of the hotel rooms upstairs (it was the same room, redressed).

We shot the first two episodes before the fall season started, with a highly rated comedian from England playing the role of the chef. Unfortunately, he was used to doing stand-up and couldn't get the hang of ensemble playing at all. Paul and Tony nipped the potential problem in the bud with some instant and inspired recasting. We reshot all the kitchen scenes from the first two shows with Cheech Marin (of Cheech and Chong) now playing the part, and by the time we went on the air, it was as though Cheech had been born in the part. Don Cheadle played the young manager, and Billy Sullivan was the little boy. Billy was such a nice kid and a great little actor. However, it became more and more difficult to find ways of working him into the story line each week, so after a few weeks, he was written out of the show. It was a tough pill to swallow, but Billy took it like a trouper and still visited us often. He also came to all our subsequent cast get-togethers.

The show was enjoyable, the reviewers were kind, and the ratings were satisfactory. In other words, *Golden Palace* was a moderately pleasing show — not a grabber.

With the number of other shows they had going, it was physically impossible for Paul and Tony to keep hands on, as they had with *The Golden Girls*, although one or the other usually attended Monday read-through and dress rehearsal.

Rose Nylund's longtime love, Miles, played by the wonderful Harold Gould, came along for a couple of shows. Being an actor in great demand, Harold had another commitment he had to fulfill, so the writers had Miles marry Nanette Fabray. The cad.

Dorothy's character was kept alive by us referring to her now and then, and Bea made one guest appearance for a two-parter.

The season continued; it didn't progress. Soon a pattern began to emerge. There had been many rewrites during the week on *Golden Girls*, and as a rule they were improvements — just minor fixes here and there.

With *Palace,* far too often we would start out with one script Monday, with major changes on Tuesday, and several times we received a whole new, unrelated script on Wednesday. What had caught our interest originally — the idea that these three women were trying to compete in and cope with today's world, as it was happening just outside the lobby doors — somehow got lost in the shuffle. In desperation, one or another of us would be given a funny run of dialogue, not necessarily connected to the story line, and it would be like doing *Golden Girls in the Lobby.* There were some good shows mixed in, but not enough.

There was one show that went very well. It dealt with the rescue of racing greyhounds. In the course of the comedy we were all able to get across the very serious message of how many of these fine dogs are destroyed each year when they don't win races, and to celebrate the people who work at finding good homes for them. Naturally, I would like that one, but I wasn't alone — we received more mail on that episode, by far, than on any of the rest. Marco Pennette, whose idea it was, did a good job making his point in the script.

Once the basic problems with the show were identified, things began to improve.

By the end of the season, while CBS had not given us a firm pickup yet, they were most reassuring. They told Paul and Tony they were something like 96 percent sure of renewing but had to give themselves a little leeway until all the new pilots had been seen. Not the most sanguine way to sign off for the summer, but Witt-Thomas-Harris were very optimistic.

By the end of May, the long-awaited new fall schedule was announced — and we weren't on it. Tony said he had been told, for what it was worth, that we were listed on the schedule until the night before the announcement, but in countering some move by one of the other networks, we didn't make the cut. *C'est la* cotton-pickin' *vie!*

It was disappointing not to be picked up, but it was by no means the heart-wrenching loss it had been at other times. I think what I missed more than the actual show itself, aside from the people involved, of course, was the structure it afforded. Working for three weeks, then getting a week off to give the writers a chance to catch up, is, to me, the best schedule in the world. And it's a different show each week, so the routine doesn't settle into a rut. However, any habit pattern wears off quickly, and there is always plenty to do — all those things there was no time for when the days were "structured." Such as beginning to make notes for a new book, for instance. I'll never learn.

In between whatever else may be going on, the animal work continues. Knowing my commitment to Morris Animal Foundation, Tom Sullivan had expressed interest in finding out more about it. He should have known better than to do that in my hearing. I asked him to accompany me to one of the board meetings in Denver, and he and the organization fell in love with one another. He accepted their invitation to become a member of the board (Tom's guide dog, Nelson, was included, of course). To cut to the chase, Tom Sullivan is now serving his second term as Morris Animal Foundation president! Some new threads to be woven into the Sullivan part of my tapestry.

In September of 1993, an invitation came from the Chicago Museum of Broadcasting that sounded intriguing. They were putting on a series of six two-day seminars for women in broadcasting, entitled "From *My Little Margie* to *Murphy Brown*." The first one would deal with early television, and they were inviting three contemporaries from that era to participate: Gale Storm *(My Little*

Margie), Jane Wyatt *(Father Knows Best),* and Betty White *(Date with the Angels).*

We all accepted, if for no other reason than it would be a chance for three old friends to get together. However, typical of the Chicago Museum of Broadcasting, they had put together a fascinating two days.

We did countless interviews on both radio and television, and they covered a wide range — from polite nostalgia to stimulating conversation to challenging confrontation, depending on the interviewer.

The two days wound up with a big luncheon, after which clips of our old programs were shown, and then Gale, Jane, and I went up to the stage to field questions from the five or six hundred women present.

There are a couple of basic questions that have been asked through the years, and, sure enough, they showed up in most of the Chicago interviews.

"Did you have a struggle getting started in the business because you were a woman?"

"Was it difficult dealing with the men in power on a day-to-day basis?"

The word "power" was an added starter, and I was surprised at how often I heard it during those two days.

It was fascinating how many interviewers overlaid the early shows with *today's* interpretation. One journalist took *My Little Margie* to task by saying that Margie only lived through her father. When we cited the number of shows in the fifties that were built around women, her response was, "But look at the titles! My *Little Margie,* I *Married Joan,* I *Love Lucy, My Favorite* Husband, Father *Knows Best!*"

I tried to make the point that all of these shows were about women, with women in the starring roles. *My Favorite Husband,* for instance, started on radio with Lucille Ball before Joan Caulfield brought it to TV. Nor were they all husband-and-wife sitcoms — some were about unmarried working women: *Private Secretary* (oops, I should have known I'd strike out with that one), *Our Miss Brooks.* But it didn't faze the woman, so all I could do was add to her laundry list of shows with some strictly female gender titles: *My Friend Irma, Meet Millie, Beulah, I Remember Mama, A Date with Judy, Life with Elizabeth, The Donna Reed Show* . . . on ad infinitum.

She conceded a reluctant shrug.

The closest I came to losing my cool was the day a particularly determined magazine writer, with more opinion than research, said, "Did it ever occur to you what *harm* you women were doing, portraying these female stereotypes?"

Turning to me, she said, "In *your* case, allowing this authoritative voice to dismiss you? 'I shall leave you, Elizabeth!' "

My back teeth may have been clenched, but I kept "sniling." "Oh, come on, let's not lose our sense of humor altogether. Alvin would walk out simply because he didn't have an answer and was trying to salvage his dignity. And when Elizabeth shook her head at the 'Aren't you ashamed?' she made it abundantly clear that she couldn't wait to do it again the next time. I'll grant you there have been inequities, but let's not paint everything — then and now — with the same brush."

That woman was the only one who raised my temperature. I minded my manners at the luncheon, even though many of the questions from the floor were along the same line.

Gale Storm made the point that back at that moment in time, it was generally expected that a girl would grow up with the avowed intention of finding a mate, getting married, and having a baby. In that order, I might add.

One question was well meant, but revealed some shortsightedness. "How is it that, in those days, we had successful programs that didn't have violence or overt sexuality — but strong family values?"

Jane Wyatt addressed that one. "Look around you at what is going on today. Art imitates life, not the other way 'round. On *Father Knows Best* we always espoused 'the right way.' Mr. A [Mr. Anderson, played by Robert Young] would handle all the decisions and the difficult undertakings. Subliminally, of course, *she* had put him up to it. Except for those in abusive situations, in the fifties most of us were not aware that we were put upon. We thought of ourselves as behind-the-scenes motivators and were often portrayed that way."

After hearing so many questions regarding "contending" with men over the foregoing two days, I had to say that, in our day, *The Battle of the Sexes* was a tongue-in-cheek name for a game show, not the all-out war it has become.

For four separate series of shows, I had worked, not only as a performer, but as a producing partner with two strong men, and if I was treated as a second-class citizen, I admitted I was too dumb to know it. I also had to make the point that we had a woman director at the time, which was rather unusual. However, Betty Turbiville had not been hired because she was a woman, but simply because she was such a damned good director.

Without treading on any feminist toes, I tried to indicate that that was another time and place, and it is specious to overlay today's values on where the world was over forty years ago. I couldn't help wondering out loud how our contemporary television shows and lifestyles and attitudes would be perceived by some future group of young women, say about forty years in the future.

In answering the question "Was sexual harassment a problem?" I had to come clean and shamefacedly admit to never having been chased around a casting couch.

All in all, the Chicago experience was most worthwhile and thought provoking. Jane, Gale, and I were happy to have been a part of the exchange of ideas. We were also grateful for the chance to defend ourselves.

The clips that were shown that day of our early shows were fun to see in that situation. Jane Wyatt and I had spent many of our earlier years being mistaken for one another. Time and again, a cab driver or a waitress or a salesperson would greet me as Miss Wyatt, or send their regards to Mr. Young. Jane had had the same experiences. She tells the story of being on a fishing trip with her husband up in the wilds of New England, and when they stopped in at a tiny place for coffee, the man behind the counter said, "Hello, Miss White — aren't you ashamed?"

Jane and I had never been able to see the resemblance ourselves. However, that day in Chicago, seeing the scenes from *Father Knows Best* and *Date with the Angels* so close together, there it was on the screen. We weren't sitting at the same table, but we kept turning and nodding at each other. Afterward, Jane said, "When I saw you in those clips, I saw me!" I agreed wholeheartedly, so we finally have that settled.

A serendipity of the trip was being able to have a little visit with Sarah. She is happily settled in Chicago, and is codirector of a very successful business, offering self-defense instruction and spa facilities to women and children. She and Nancy Lanoue, her partner in Thousand Waves, attended the luncheon, as well. It was good to have a couple of self-defense experts on my side.

Martha Ludden passed her bar examination a couple of years ago, and is now working in Washington, D.C. David is a tenured professor at the University of Pennsylvania in Philadelphia. He is teaching Far Eastern studies and returns to India from time to time. Allen can be very proud of his progeny.

■■■■

When I returned from Chicago, I found a couple of little blurbs Tony Fantozzi had sent me — one from *People* magazine — saying that Betty White would be joining the cast of Bob Newhart's show, *Bob,* about to start its second season. This was news to both Tony and me, as we hadn't heard anything from anybody. We just chalked it up to a slow news day.

The original *Bob Newhart Show* from the old MTM stable, followed by *Newhart,* had been long-running smash hits on CBS, spanning several years. This past season, Bob had gone on the air with a new series entitled *Bob,* wherein he played a cartoonist who had left his job with a greeting-card company to go to work for a comics magazine specializing in monsters. The series had not taken off as expected, possibly because Bob's character was given a slightly harder edge this time around — not what his loyal fans expected to see.

After a season of less than satisfactory ratings, the decision was made to deep-six the monsters and have Bob return to the greeting-card company for the second season. The entire cast was changed, with the exception of Bob's wife, played by Carlene

Watkins, and daughter, played by Cynthia Stevenson. It was decided that the card company would now be in the hands of the old boss's wife, the boss having absconded to Tahiti with his dental hygienist. The wife is somewhat testy as a result and could be a good balance for nice guy Bob.

When they called Tony to invite me aboard (the squibs in the paper had been slightly premature), Tony felt it would be unwise to jump right into a full-time series so close to the demise of *Golden Palace,* so he made one of his six-out-of-thirteen non-exclusive deals. We both felt that playing Sylvia would be interesting, since she was nothing like either Sue Ann Nivens or Rose Nylund — a whole new ball game. Most of all, I was delighted at the chance to work with Bob at last, after knowing him for so many years.

The first time I ever saw Bob Newhart was when I was lucky enough to be on the Jack Paar show the night Jack introduced "this really funny kid I saw in Chicago." He proceeded to give the newcomer a tremendous buildup, which can sometimes be tough to live up to, but not for young Bob. He came out and fractured the audience with his low-key delivery and hysterical material.

Going to work on the new series was like old home week for me. Bob Ellison, who had produced *The Betty White Show* (IV) at MTM, was one of the writers, while two other young men, Don Siegel and Jerry Parseghian, had written for *Golden Girls*. The whole crew was studded with people with whom I had worked so many times.

To distinguish the revised format from the previous year's *Bob* took quite a bit of explaining in the first episode of the new season. It was important to have as many see it as possible to know what was going on and who the new people were. Jere Burns, the devious flake of *Dear John* fame, had been added as my son, trying to weasel his way up in the company, which was a real plus.

Good promotion was vital for the kickoff, so Bob and I did a zillion interviews, sometimes individually, often together. I don't think we missed anybody. It was not our favorite thing to do, but we both really wanted this to work.

And now, boys and girls, guess what happened?

In what must be the most baffling network move of all time, *at the very last minute,* CBS decided to flip-flop our show with the one preceding us. As a result, instead of premiering at 9:30, as we had been promoting all over the dial, the show went on at 9:00. It was not only too late to correct the listing in *TV Guide,* but every major newspaper across the country had us scheduled for 9:30! There were a few published explanations after the fact, but by then the boat had sailed. Missing the opener was confusing to the latecomers. Bob was bitterly disappointed and rightfully so. So was I.

The shows were enjoyable to do because the cast and crew were such a good group of people. We were shooting on film, which is not my favorite thing. Film cameras are so much bigger than those used for tape that they made things a little unwieldy and crowded on blocking and show days. There are two definite schools of thought on film versus tape. Many feel that the look of a filmed show is so superior to tape that it is worth the inconvenience and the added cost. Perhaps that is true with a dramatic show, but, in my opinion, tape is much crisper. Besides, you can play it back immediately to see whether or not something worked. I'm sure I'm outnumbered, but hey — it's my book.

Bob's trademark, of course, is his stammer, and he cracked me up one day when we were talking about his first *Bob Newhart Show,* with Suzanne Pleshette. On one of the early shows they were running long, and the director said, "Bob, if you could just pull your speeches together a little, we could save some time." Bob's answer was, "This stutter built me a house in Bel-Air. Don't mess with it."

He also told about being on a plane not too long ago and listening to the comedy channel on the headset. Suddenly, on came his first album, *The Buttoned-Down Mind of Bob Newhart*. Somebody had reedited it and taken out all the pauses, for whatever reason — perhaps to fit it into their program. You can imagine what that did to Bob's comedy timing. "Well, it was just awful," he said. "I looked around to see if anybody else might be listening to the same show — I wanted to apologize to them. It got so bad, I wanted to go up to the front of the plane and say, 'No — listen, folks — *this* is how that routine should go!' "

Bob Newhart is a joy, and for many years was a mainstay of the whole CBS network. For that reason I think they treated him very shoddily on this last go-round. They shot eight episodes, and after screwing up the launch of the show, they wound up airing only six shows — they ate the other two. And they didn't even give him a clean cancellation. They took him off the air and left him dangling, with a lot of vague talk about possibly coming back later in the season. Shame on them. They could have handled Bob Newhart better than that. He had earned it.

24

During all the time I have been wheezing away with this opus, what has been happening with the construction of the Information Superhighway? Which by now, incidentally, has even acquired a nickname — Infopike.

Early on, I compared the advent of television and its impact on the world to today's Superhighway and its potential outreach. I hasten to concede that the comparison really doesn't hold up at all, in light of the Highway's complexities. I think it was an effort on my part to understand something I never will. (I may not be alone.)

Television as we knew it then was a single new development that opened many windows. You either accepted it and bought a TV set, or you opted to wait until they got the bugs out. This new entity is a tad more complicated.

Come to think of it, I don't think we opted in those days — we just decided.

The Infopike, if you will, is coming on apace, ready or not, and is enveloping us even as the arguments continue about how to handle it. The Interactive Highway is already here and represents the coming together of video, computer, telephone, and cable technologies. Once the battles over turf rights are resolved — or legislated — it is only a matter of getting access to enough homes to start making a difference in how we entertain, educate, and clothe ourselves. Or buy stamps. Or get our news on demand. Or order tickets. Or choose dinner from menus on request. Or whatever we can dream up. Not just us — the race to hook up audiences to interactive TV is global. In Europe, Japan, the United Kingdom, tests of systems are already under way.

The initial logjam was the long fight within the telephone industry between the long distance companies and the Baby Bells, the bone of contention being the legal barriers keeping them separate. The cable industry, too, joined the fray.

The courts have been gradually dismantling those barriers. Congress, however, failed to enact Information Superhighway legislation in 1994. Come last November's elections, the balance of power changed radically, so we will have what amounts to a whole new highway patrol. No matter how the legal problems are finally solved, their resolution is inevitable. So where do we go from here?

One of the first considerations of broadcasters is how to draw up long-term contracts with talent. To survive on the Highway, they *must* protect exclusivity. Consequently, when renegotiation time comes, news talent, for instance — let's say Mike Wallace or Barbara Walters — will certainly want to be compensated if their shows are being offered on services other than their own networks. The various guilds and unions must wrestle with similar problems.

Interactive television is not that new. It has been around for some time, and there is a plethora of electronic games to prove it. Youngsters have no problem with these, and for the most part, they are looked upon as a good way for children to learn computer skills early. However, the whole genre is in a constant state of change — being upgraded or simplified — so that computer-literate children are faced with learning whole new systems on an ongoing basis. While we're at it, let's hear it for the grown-ups who are trying to stay current — at whatever cost.

Speaking of interactive, sex is already

firmly ensconced in the back alleys of the Superhighway. Cyberporn is thriving. Cyberswingers communicate with each other through bulletin-board networks with provocative names — KinkNet and ThrobNet, for example — and furnish a wide choice of X-rated movies and interactive adult games. Participants claim it is the ultimate in safe sex. We must remember that even cavemen were known to draw dirty pictures with charcoal. That, too, was before my time.

So, what about us computer illiterates? Take heart, they promise we'll still manage to get along. That is, if we don't mind voice mail — where you have to fight your way through strings of numbers and choices before finding a real human to speak to. If then.

Sometimes I feel a small chill when I hear the words "The computer is down." What if one day they *all* went down? Now cut that out, Rod Serling! But I'll tell you when I feel a *big* chill — it's when I'm in a department store or a checkout line at the market, and the computer fails. Often, the young person behind the counter simply cannot add the numbers — at all.

We can survive, they say, without computer literacy, if we are aware of what computers can provide and analyze how to make the most of it for ourselves. Okay.

As James Branch Cabell said, "The optimist proclaims that we live in the best of all possible worlds; and the pessimist fears this is true."

The latest progress report on the Infopike is from December 1994. In Orlando, Florida, eight months late, a handful of homes were connected when FSN, the Full Service Network from Time Warner, clicked on. What I find interesting is that it was Warner Cable who took the first disastrous step into interactive television with QUBE — some twenty-five years ago. It failed miserably then, but it was a harbinger of things to come. Guess it wasn't just a wide place in the road after all.

If you are still with me, many thanks for your perseverance. This would be a good spot to tidy up the loose ends and draw this epic to a close. I *will* stop, but some of the ends will have to stay loose, as they are still pending. By the time you read this, you will know more about what I'll be doing than I do myself at this moment.

The television business has changed over the years, but never so much as in the last four or five. Magazine and talk-show formats

My William Morris agent and great friend, Tony Fantozzi — The Mustache! (Courtesy Ralph Edwards Productions)

are having their moment in the sun, and as usual when something seems to be working, the clones appear. Remember Mickey Mouse as "The Sorcerer's Apprentice" in *Fantasia* when he dreamed that all the brooms and buckets were multiplying? Well, talk shows are today's brooms and buckets.

After *The Golden Girls* shut down, I had been approached several times to do a talker of my own. Even Tony Fantozzi — or The Mustache, as we lovingly call him — had touted the idea, since the new batch of series outlines coming across his desk were getting worse.

Thanks, but no thanks. No way would I inflict one more talk show on the American public. There were seventeen of them on the air at the moment. The number went up to thirty-three a few months later. As of this present writing there are just twenty-two, but it's only 11:00 A.M. Few make it, but for every one that fails, three new ones spring up. Buckets and brooms!

Recently, Rich Frank, chairman of Disney's telecommunications arm, called and asked for a meeting. That was a meeting I couldn't sidestep — not just because of his position, but because he has been a very good and supportive friend all along the way.

Rich had invited a couple of Disney people to the meeting, and Tony had brought two other men from William Morris. We all sat around a large and rather intimidating table in one of the conference rooms.

Rich opened the conversation by saying, "Betty, you talk first and then we will."

Betty: "This is your meeting. I have nothing to sell."

Rich: "We are aware that you don't want to do a talk show, but we want you to do an hour strip. You can do anything you want."

For the uninitiated, a strip is an hour show

across the board, Monday through Friday. Admittedly, the term is a thought thrower.

After the laugh, we got back to business. When Disney says, "You can do anything you want," there is no way to stop your mind from beginning to churn.

The only thing I had ever even idly toyed with was perhaps to do a show from a real house using the appropriate rooms to suit the subject matter. I proceeded to ad-lib a vague outline, without having a clue where I was going. I was shooting from the hip, but

With Disney chairman, Rich Frank. (COURTESY DISNEY)

as I warmed to the subject, the idea began to sound pretty fair, even to me.

The Disneys immediately sparked to the concept, saying they had wanted to do a home shopping show from a real house, but they couldn't find a way to accommodate the studio audience.

Betty: "Oh, didn't I mention — no studio audience!" We would play to just the one or two people watching at each set at home. There should be an intimate flavor to the show, as opposed to a performance atmosphere. I am interested in a whole lot of things that I always intend to find out more about and I'll bet I'm not alone. I have a sneaking suspicion that curiosity is alive and kicking inside many of us. Rather than a typical talk show, I envisioned more of an exploration in company with the home viewer.

I have never been to a meeting quite like that one. Usually, it is you who are the one trying to sell something you want desperately, and nerves are playing havoc with your presentation — sweaty palms, shortness of breath. If you don't get an immediate turndown, you are faced with the waiting period while they mull; more often than not, two weeks later you receive a diplomatic but firm "Pass." On this occasion, however, it all seemed so unreal that I felt completely relaxed. We *were* in the Magic Kingdom, don't forget.

Demographics have become the name of the game in our industry. For a long time, ratings were judged on household (how many sets in use?) and share (what percentage of sets in use were tuned to a given program?). Of late, the third rating has become possibly the most important: demographics (percentage of men and of women in each age group). The ideal target audience was considered to be 18 to 49 years old; recently the age group dropped to 18 to 39; as of now the ideal is 18 to 34 and counting. In light of all this, it was time in our conversation to address an important consideration, and since no one else brought it up, I did: why in the world were they talking to someone like me who is, shall we say, no spring chicken?

Rich responded with their reasoning: he explained that in testing I had an approval rating that spanned a lot of time, which gives me a frame of reference. I was familiar to people; a couple of generations had grown up with me; they trusted me. I closed my big mouth. If that was Rich Frank's considered opinion, I was not about to try and talk him out of it. However, I felt better that the potentially delicate subject had been brought out into the open.

It was a great meeting, and best of all, at the head of the table was the man to say no or go — there was no higher authority who had to be consulted before a decision was made. So — we walked out with a handshake and a deal.

Tony took me to brunch at the Hotel Bel-Air to celebrate. A major commitment had just been made. I should say Tony was celebrating; I was in shock — a combination of excitement, amazement, and alarm. What had I done?

In the ensuing weeks, everybody and his brother, with the exception of Rich Frank and Suzy Polse (one of the Disneys present at the original meeting; a great gal who was now in charge of expediting the project), tried to talk me out of the house idea. Finding an appropriate house that was also big enough to handle an entire television crew was a major challenge. "Couldn't we build you a nice set and then invite a studio audience?" I stuck by my guns.

What to call this effort? Kiddingly, I had suggested *Yet Another Betty White Show,* but they didn't buy my sarcasm. They did go for the title I really wanted: *The Betty White House.*

Ultimately, the perfect house was found and we taped a twenty-five-minute pilot presentation. I had won the battle for the house but lost several other skirmishes regarding the kinds of subjects I wanted to explore. The Hubble Space Telescope, for instance. I was fascinated by the fact that we had been able to put an eye in the sky, only to find we had blown it with a defective lens. What really got me was that we had then sent up a repair crew and *fixed* it, in time to let us have a good look at the comet impact on Jupiter. I wanted to talk to the fella who did that, and to include some youngster in the discussion who had his or her heart set on becoming an astronaut.

That idea was shot down. "Nope. Can't do that — the audience wouldn't be interested. But what we *do* want is a couple of 'hunks' who will grab the women tuning in." I hoped not literally, but who knows?

My shiny little premise took some major hits until it was finally hammered into just one more talk show. It looks great, but doesn't challenge the imagination an iota. The pilot presentation is out in the marketplace as we speak, but don't hold your breath.

A few weeks ago, Disney called to set up yet another meeting, on a different subject which meant a different department. In the course of these pages I have put you through enough meetings to last you a lifetime, so I will spare you the step-by-step and cut to the chase:

Another branch of the Disney television tree produces their situation comedies. They had a series idea they were very high on and thought would be good for Marie Osmond and me. We would play mother and daughter. (I would be the mother.)

They outlined the premise, which did sound interesting, but what had caught my ear was the mention of Marie Osmond. Having worked with Marie, even as young as she had been at the time, and seeing her great success in her present nationwide tour of *The Sound of Music,* I know what a dynamic trouper this girl is. How can you turn your back on an idea like that?

When I explained that I was committed (I really *should* be committed) to *The Betty White House,* they knew all about it and said there was no conflict. No conflict from their side of the desk maybe, because both were Disney projects, but does anyone have a clue these days how to do a five-day-a-week hour-show *plus* a series? It's no longer 1951 when things were simple.

Rich Frank sent a message: "I hear you're

doing business across the hall." I braced myself for the objection, but he said "I think it's great. The best news would be if they both sold, but one or the other would be fine."

The pilot has been completed for the ABC network. Marie was as delightful to work with as I had expected her to be. We had the added bonus of little eleven-year-old Ashley Johnson playing Marie's daughter, my granddaughter; Ashley is a terrific little actress and a real sweetheart. It would be fine if this project worked out. Can you tell where my rooting interest lies? All we can do, however, is wait until the ABC fall schedule is announced to see if we made the cut. By the time you read this you will know a lot more about what I'll be doing than I do from here.

And now, here is a shocker.

I was literally closing this opus when the news broke this week that Rich Frank has suddenly resigned his post at Disney!

Personally, I am devastated. To me, working for Disney has always been synonymous with working for Rich Frank, my friend.

Professionally, it's a whole new ball game, and just what effect it will have remains to be seen. Of course, *you* already know. Just between us — how did it all come out?

The only thing I can say for sure at this point is — here we go again!

P.S. Just got word we made the cut, so we'll see each other in the fall. As I was saying — here we go again!

CONCLUSION

Well, that's my story, and I thank you for sticking with me.

It has been a wonderful ride and it isn't over yet. As I write this, I'm due to appear on *The Tonight Show with Jay Leno* and a few days later on *Craig Ferguson*. Soon I'll be going to Atlanta to shoot a Hallmark Hall of Fame movie, *The Lost Valentine,* that will finish in time for me to start the second season of my latest series, *Hot in Cleveland.* And I was floored to learn that my *Saturday Night Live* gig has earned an Emmy nomination.

This all sounds like such an ego trip, but please don't take it that way. I'm simply sharing my delight and amazement that I'm still being dealt in, and my gratitude for your support through the years that has made it possible. As long as this ride keeps going, I'll be on it. I hope you will too.

Now I will let you up and here's a prom-

ise: I will not write *Here We Go Again* —
again.

Many thanks,
Betty White
August 2010

INSERT PHOTOGRAPH CREDITS

Page 1, top: Hulton Archive/Getty
Page 1, bottom: © American Broadcasting Companies, Inc.
Page 2, top: © American Broadcasting Companies, Inc.
Page 2, bottom: © American Broadcasting Companies, Inc.
Page 3, top: CBS/Landov
Page 3, bottom: CBS/Landov
Page 4: NBCU Photo Bank
Page 5, top: Carlo Allegri/Getty
Page 5, bottom: JPI Studios
Page 6, top: © Ron Tom/American Broadcasting Companies, Inc.
Page 6, bottom: Jim Humphries
Page 7, top: © Dean Handler/American Broadcasting Companies, Inc.
Page 7, bottom: Matthew Imaging/Getty
Page 8, top: NBCU Photo Bank
Page 8, bottom: Michael Caulfield/Getty

ABOUT THE AUTHOR

Betty White is has been on television for over sixty years, beginning in 1949. She has starred in many successful series, made numerous guest appearances on game and talk shows, and narrated the Tournament of Roses Parade for twenty years and the Macy's Thanksgiving Day Parade for ten.

White has received 6 Emmy awards and 18 Emmy nominations. In 2010 she was presented with the Screen Actors Guild Life Achievement Award.. She is also the recipient of three American Comedy Awards (including a Lifetime Achievement Award in 1990), and two Viewers for Quality Television Awards. She was inducted into the Television Hall of Fame in 1995 and has a star on the Hollywood Walk of Fame.

She is the author of three previous books and lives in Los Angeles.